# TOP ARCHITECTS of the WORLD

TADAO ANDO
**DOMINIQUE PERRAULT**
**ZAHA HADID** RAFAEL MONEO
**CÉSAR PELLI** SHIGERU BAN
**JEAN NOUVEL** BEN VAN BERKEL
STEVEN HOLL EDUARDO SOUTO DE MOURA

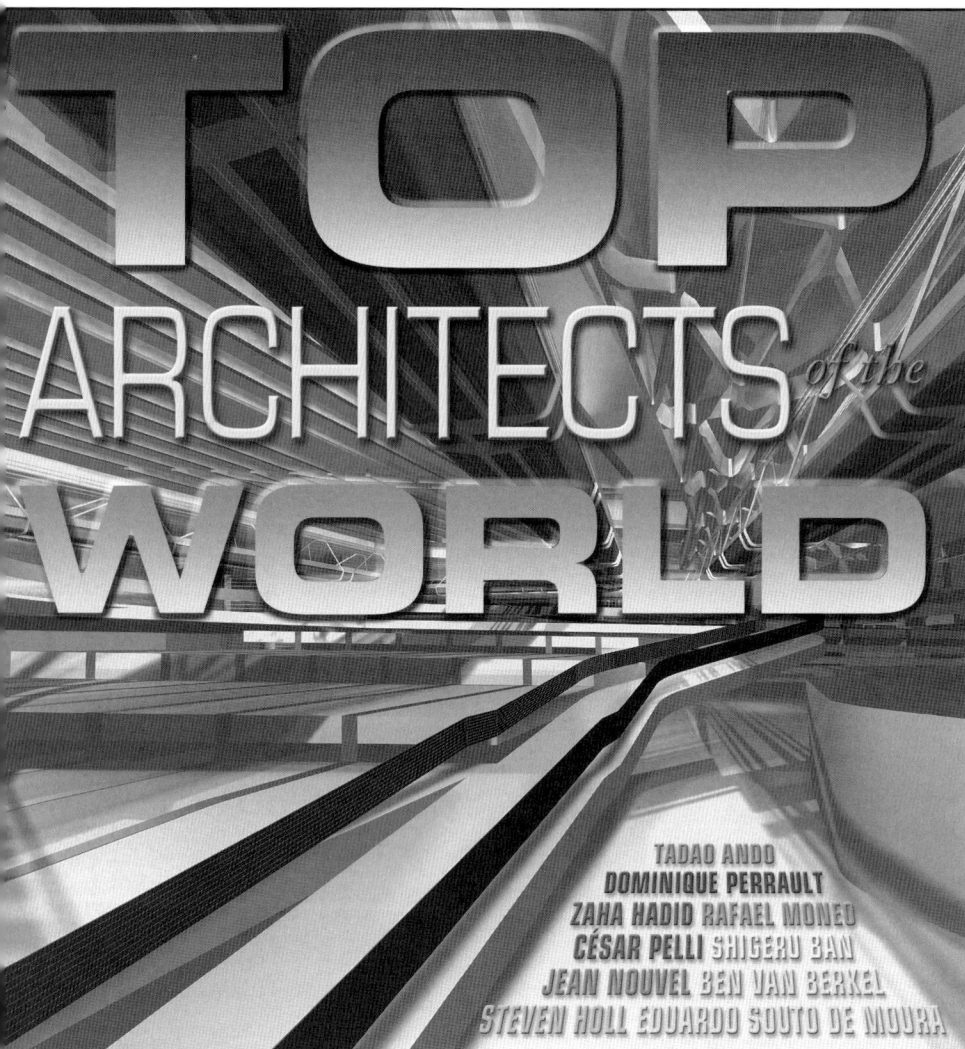

RAFAEL MONEO

Hotel Sea Hawk

Diputación 2002

Bank of America

**130**

SHIGERU BAN

Main Street-River
Hotel Brooklin

Torre Agbar

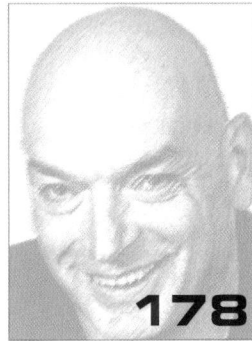

**178**

BEN VAN BERKEL

Loisium Visitors'
Center

Simmons Hall

Musee des
confluences

**212**

EDUARDO SOUTO DE MOURA

**118**

L'Illa Diagonal

Museum of Modern
Art of Stockholm

CÉSAR PELLI

**148**

Atsushi Imai
Gymnasium

PAM-Paper
Art Museum

Japanese Pavilion
for Expo 2000

JEAN NOUVEL

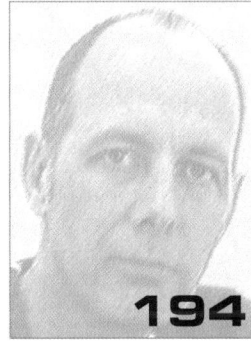

**194**

Interview

Mercedes Benz
Museum

National Museum
of Twenthe

STEVEN HOLL

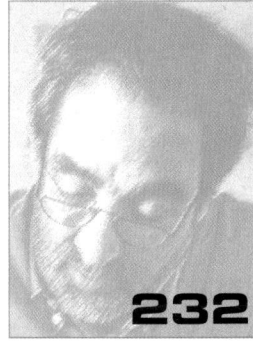

**232**

Interview

Casa do Cinema

Residential Building
in Oporto

**Copyright © 2004 Atrium Group**
**Published by:**

Atrium Group de ediciones y publicaciones S.L.
Ganduxer, 112
08022 Barcelona
Tel. +34 932 540 099
Fax: +34 932 118 139
e-mail: atrium@atriumgroup.org
www.atriumbooks.com

**ISBN:** 84-95692-41-4
Dep. Legal: B-39224-2004

Printed in Spain
Ferré Olsina S.A.

**Author**
Mary Cambert

**Artistic Editor**
Alejandro Asensio

**Editorial Staff**
Mireia Vergés
Marc Grau
Roberta Vellini
Xavier Roselló
Marc Grau
Carlos Rivero

**Photo Documentation**
Sean Rovira
Astrid Marteen

**Special Colaboration**
Pepa Folk
Bettina Ferrer
Javier Fernández
Conrad Vilaplana

**Production**
Juanjo Rodríguez

**Design and Layout**
Manel Peret
Jordi Calleja

**Image Production**
Ignacio Martinez

**Translation**
Mark Holloway
Eva Marín

## Photographs

Komyo-Ji Temple [14]: © S. Ogawa / © M. Matsuoka.

Modern Art Museum of Forth Worth [22]: © M. Matsuoka / © Tadao Ando.

Pulitxer Foundation for the Arts [28]: © R. Pettus / © M. Matsuoka.

4x4 House [32]: © Mitsuo Matsuoka.

Multifunctional Sports Complex [44]: © Dominique Perrault Architects.

Central Media Library of Vénissieux [54]: © G. Féssy / © A. Morin.

Masterplan Donau-City [60]: © Dominique Perrault Architectes.

Opera House Mariinsky II [64]: © Dominique Perrault Architectes.

Rosenthal Center of Contemporary Art [70]: © Ronald Holbe.

Multimodal Stop at the North Terminus, Hoenheim [88]: © Helene Binet.

MAXXI: National Center of Contemporary Art [96]: © Zaha Hadid Architects.

Phaeno Science Center Wolfsburg [102]: © Helene Binet.

Central Building – BMW Plant [114]: © Zaha Hadid Architects.

L'Illa Diagonal [120]: © Ramón Camprubí / © David Cardelús / © Iván Bercedo.

Museum of Modern Art of Stockholm [126]: © Wenzel.

Hotel Sea Hawk [132]: © Taizo Kurukawa / © Osamu Murai / © César Pelli Associates / © Yukio Yoshimura.

Diputación 2002 [136]: © Timothy Hursley / © César Pelli Associates.

Bank of America [142]: © Timothy Hursley / © César Pelli Associates.

Atsushi Imai Gymnasium [150], PAM-Paper Art Museum [160], Pavilion for Expo 2000 [172]: © Hiroyuki Hi.

Main Street-River Hotel Brooklin [182], Torre Agbar [188]: © Jean Nouvel Architectes.

Mercedes Benz Museum [200]: © UN STUDIO.

National Museum of Twenthe [204]: © Christian Richters.

Loisium Visitors' Center [216]: © Lucas Wassman.

Simmons Hall [220]: © Ronald Holbe.

Musee des confluences [226]: © Steven Holl Architects.

Casa do Cinema [238], Residential Building in Oporto [244]: © Luis Ferreira Alves.

# TOP ARCHITECTS

At the beginning of this century, contemporary architecture seems to be as marked by diversity and fragmentation as all other cultural areas. As in art and fashion design, where there is presently no prevailing tendency imposing itself over others, there is no dominating trend in architecture.

What we can actually call architecture is a very small percentage of what is constructed. While newly constructed landscapes are marked with repetition and the vulgar reuse of old solutions, it seems that singularity in architecture is becoming appreciated more and more every day. This can be seen in the existing desire to create buildings that are 'unique' and that possess the power of becoming symbols of the cities they are built in. A certain cult of the individualism of the so-called 'star architects' has also been developed. Globalization and growing cultural interconnection have favored the appearance of these international figures that build all over the world. As ironically commented by the architect Oscar Tusquets, "The starlets of architecture travel around in a twelve-seater bus. Before somebody gets

# OF THE WORLD

on, somebody else has to get off." There is no a doubt that not all architects get the same amount of attention from the media or the publicity. This attention often seems to lead to new opportunities as Jacques Herzog provocatively stated: "As 'star architects', we often receive incredible projects that allow us to explore areas unknown to the majority of architects." Those who receive commissions do not only seek quality in their buildings, but fame and fortune as well. For many politicians, the architects in the 'star system' provide a form of guarantee. It is similar to someone who does not know much about fashion and

therefore selects an expensive handbag from a known name. Even though architecture as a representation of power has always existed (what is a monument or a church if otherwise?), we are now in a time of growing media coverage. Never before has an international competition had the public repercussions of those responding to the competition for the New World Trade Center on Ground Zero in New York.

The topography of contemporary architecture has been marked by a diversity of languages and attitudes. Along with the persist-

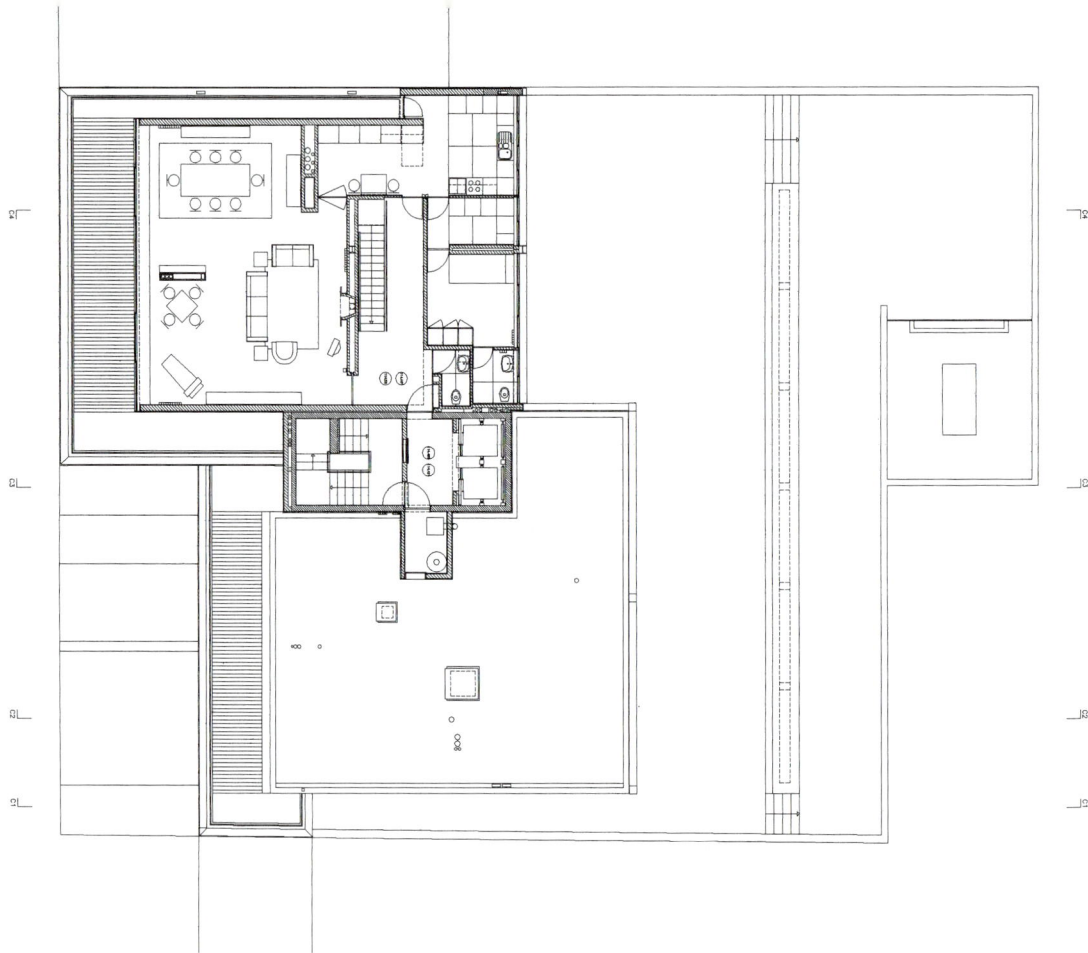

ent visibility of the 'star architects' there are also many other architects working. It is, without a doubt, somewhat adventurous to seek communal characteristics in this confused landscape. I will limit myself to point out some of the themes that have cropped up most frequently throughout this study.

## Urban Buildings

The concept of 'urban buildings', those that integrate and redirect pedestrian flows in the city, is presently in the limelight. These are not new ideas, although they have rarely been ex-

pressed with the strength possessed by projects developed by **Zaha Hadid** or **Ben van Berkel**. Presently, the function of museums, auditoriums or sports centers is as much to reactivate or requalify urban areas as it is to display art or house sports. The desire for the general public to include these buildings in their everyday lives is evident.

According to **Ben van Berkel**: "The architect should act as a public scientist" and develop the capacity to foresee future relationships between the building and its visitors.

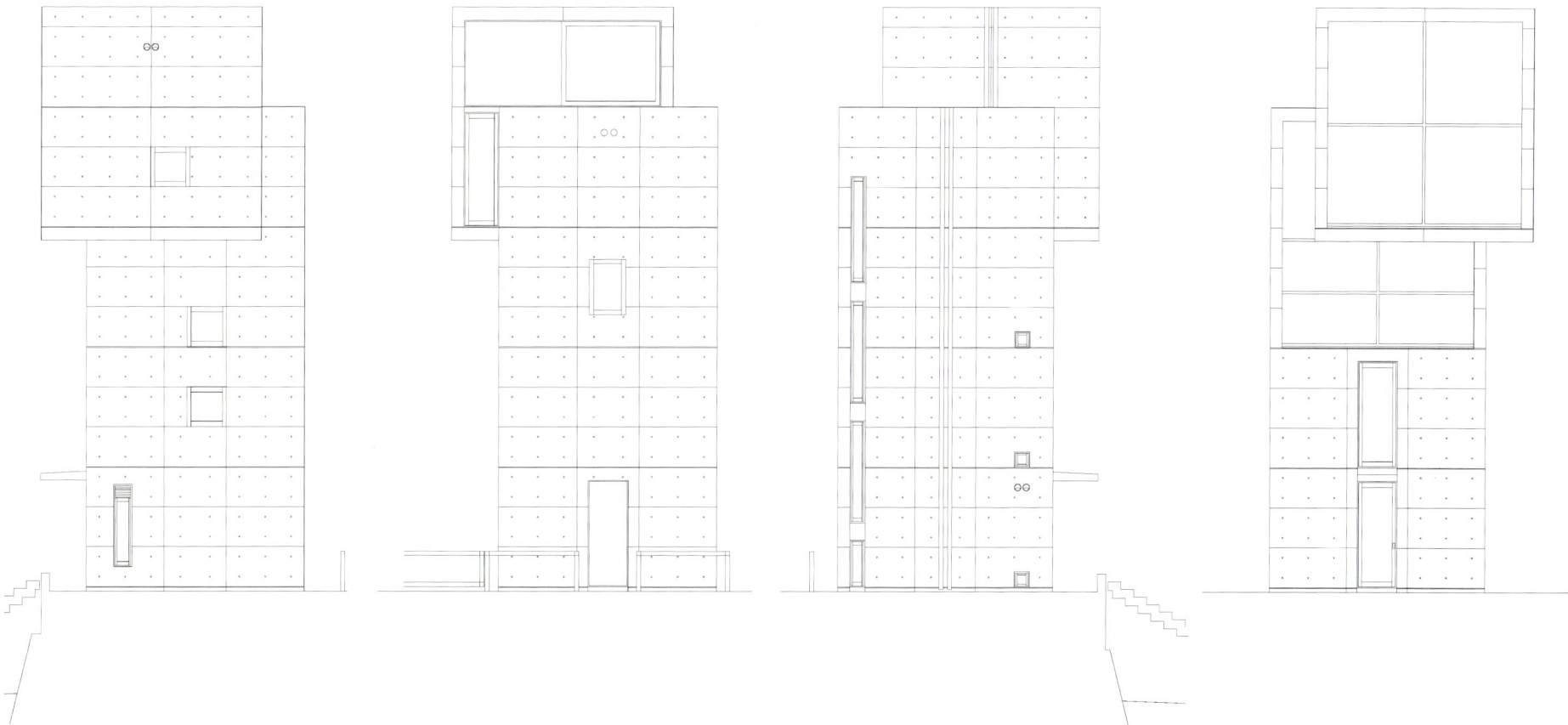

## Specific Project

The specificity of each and every project is an aspect that tends to be insisted upon. The context of a project understood in its greater sense (place, history, clients, future users… etc.) determines that no two projects can be exactly alike.

As stated by Dominique Perrault: "Every project is a prototype." This is to say that each project not only requires its own solutions, but also consideration of what technologies are most suitable for its construction.

## Collaboration

Architecture has always been an activity developed in collaboration. The client, the promoters, the constructing industries, technical collaborators along with the architect's own office should work in a coordinated way to ensure that the common objective, the construction of the building, is a success. Nowadays, these collaborations are becoming more and more complex: the agents implicated in the works are multiplying. Now, we rarely find a lone client, a constructor who does not subcontract, or an architect who works on his own. The architect is becoming more and more a coordinator.

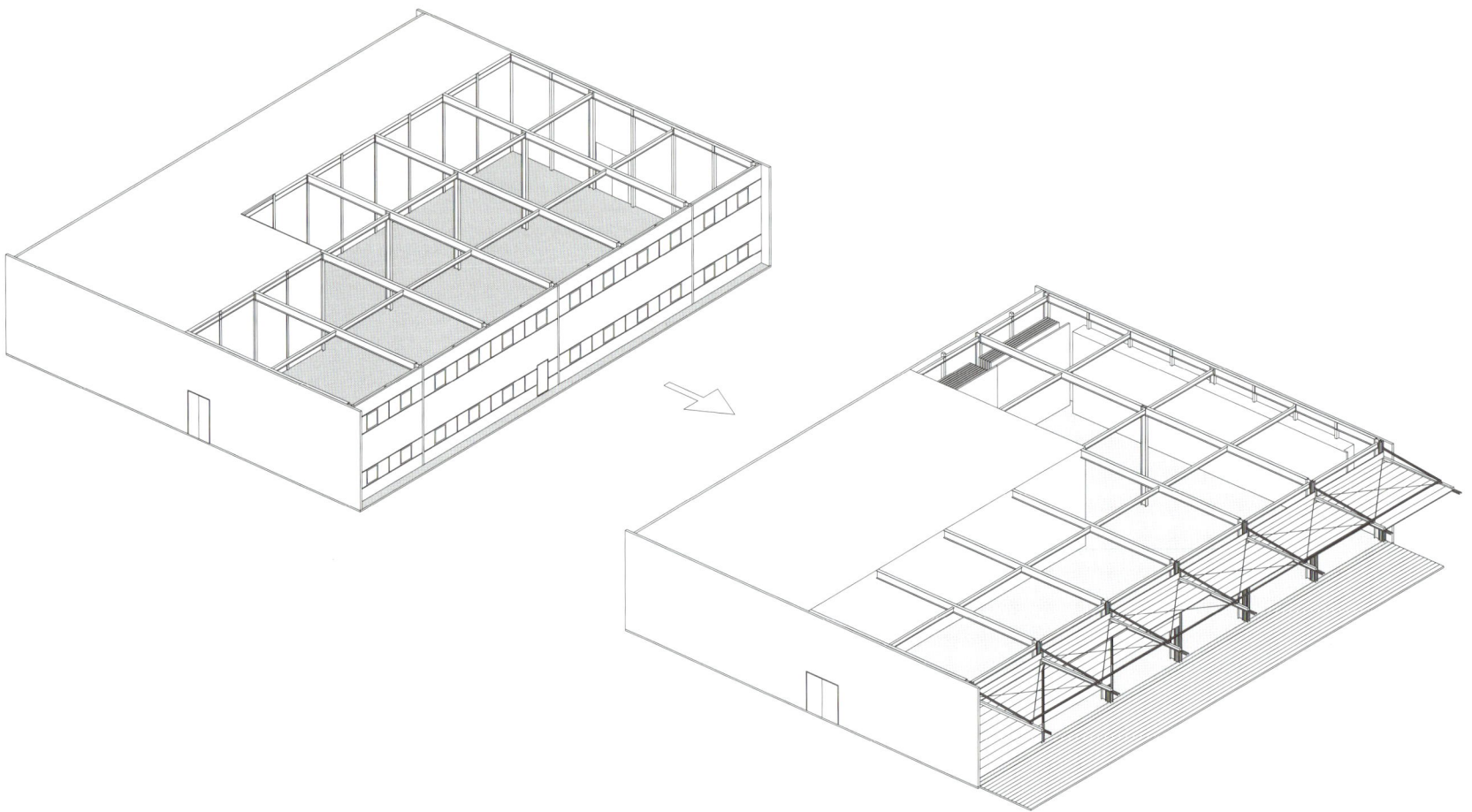

## New Technologies and Virtual Reality

Although today it may seem to have been impossible, twenty years ago, there were hardly any computers in architects' offices. The application of computer science has had enormous consequences on the way that the majority of architects work. It has possibly increased the number of plans that are now required when handing in a project. With animations and infographs, the representations of the architecture are intended to be closer and closer to reality. Renders are now indispensable in a presentation for any competition. For some architects, computers have also become efficient design tools and allow forms and complex systems to be developed more easily and efficiently. There are even some offices, such as Asympote, that have dedicated an important part of their activity to producing virtual architecture such as the Guggenheim Virtual Museum or the NYSE space.

## Investigation

Another common aspect of architecture is that of architecture as a process of investigation. The spatial development of the

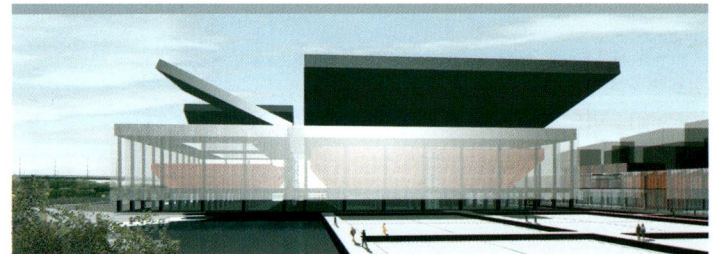

project, along with decisions as to how it should be constructed and the search for the most suitable and expressive materials, is perceived as an experimental process. Fruit of this attitude is the present interest in the many possibilities for the covering skins of the building.

## Urban Planning: from Local to Global

As has always been the case, the urban planner's work is directly related to political, economic and social factors. Nowadays, the tasks of an urban planer are diverse. Among these are found tasks such as localizing problems in the urban fabric and in the territory and offering local solutions that can be strategically integrated into a more general plan. Also, still of great importance and interest are the proposals that can be made by urban planners.

## Time

Time and its control is becoming a more and more important factor in the development of a project. As stated by Eduardo Souto de Moura: "The lack of time is the worst problem an architect has these days."

# Tadao Ando

He was born in Osaka, Japan in 1941 where he was brought up by his maternal grandmother. When he was ten, he became a carpenter's apprentice in his hometown. This fact must have triggered off his interest in construction and in use of materials. He is a self-taught architect: "I was never a good student. I always preferred to learn things for myself outside of class."

His education consisted of visiting a large number of examples of traditional Japanese architecture and of analyzing, in great detail, books on modern architecture such as one on Corbusier in which he redrew the designs from his first period: "I redrew the designs from his first period so many times that the pages become illegible," comments Ando.

His formation was completed with various trips to the United States, Europe and Africa between 1962 and 1969 after having been a boxer for a time.

Komyo-Ji Temple

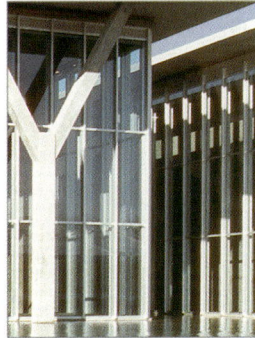

Modern Art Museum of Forth Worth

Pulitxer Foundation for the Arts

4x4 House

In 1969, he set up his own architectural studio *Tadao Ando Architect & Associates* in Osaka. In his own words: "I did not follow an apprenticeship with an architect because every time I tried to, I was fired for my stubbornness and bad temper"

Six years later, he won the annual prize from the Architectural Institute of Japan for Row House (1975-76). This house corresponds to a steel reinforced concrete box which isolates it from its chaotic urban context in the district of Sumiyoshi. His reputation was finally established with the residential complex Rokko Housing (1978-81), a composition of prisms in concrete over a steep slope, and with the construction of various buildings for religious meditation. Among those that stand out are the Chapel of Monte Rokko (1985-86), the Chapel of the Water (1985-88) and the Church of the light (1987).

At the beginning of the 1990's, he constructed his first two buildings outside of Japan, the Vitra Conference Pavilion in Vitra en

Weil am Rhein, Germany (1989-93) and the Japanese Pavilion for Expo 92 in Seville, Spain. Here, he raised a monumental construction entirely in wood, reminiscent of traditional Japanese architecture. From the last decade, the Suntory Museum (Osaka 1992-94), the Naoshima Contemporary Art Museum (1988-92), the Chiatsu-Asuka Museum (1985), the investigation center Benetton Factory in Treviso, Italy (1993-94) and the small meditation space in the UNESCO headquarters in Paris, France (1995) stand out.

Ando has been awarded with a large number of prestigious prizes such as the Alvar Aalto Medal in Finland (1985) and the Gold Medal of the French Academy of Architecture (1989).

In 1995, he received the **Pritzker Prize** for Architecture which was followed by the Gold Medal from the RIBA, Royal Institute of British Architects. He has also taught in the universities of Yale, Columbia and Harvard.

## Temple Komyo-ji
Sanjo, Japan

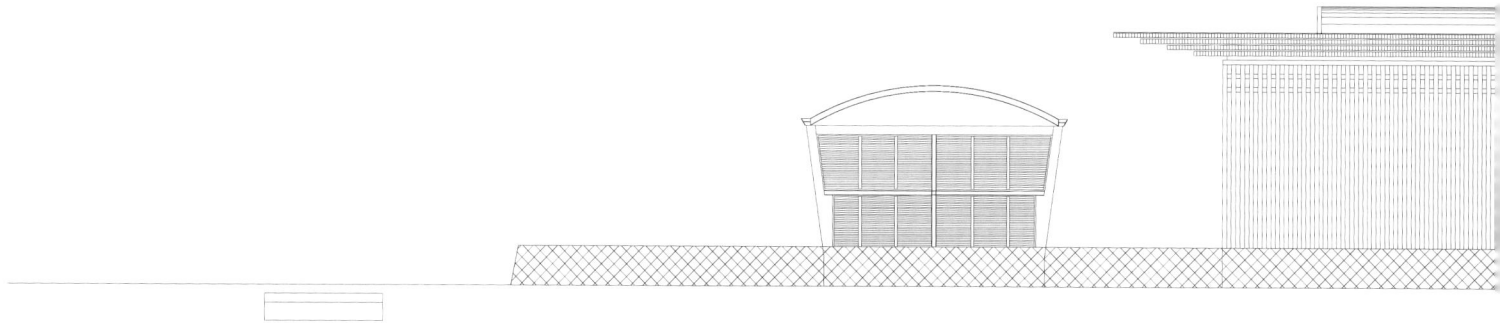

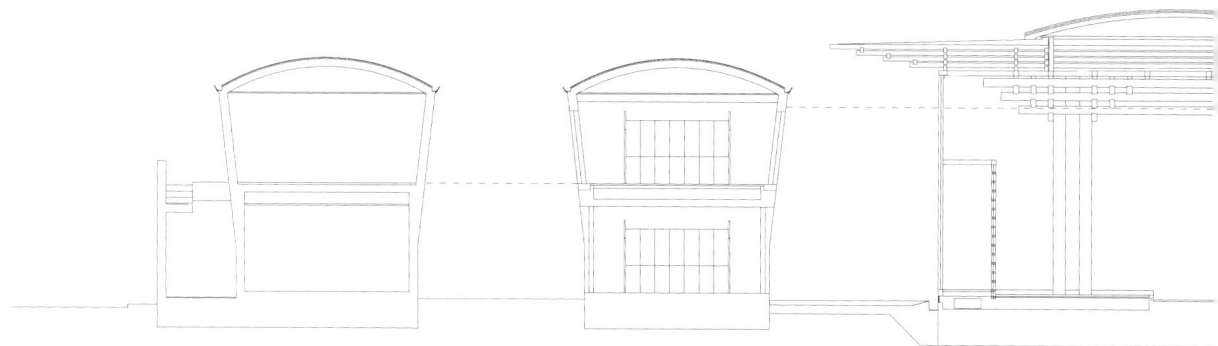

As much as in his work as in his life, Tadao Ando is an architect who has had a extraordinary course of development in which he has been guided by a search for spaces that awaken the sensitiv-

ities of man and in which he ignores fashions, schools of thought and styles. His work is an example of the search for a space for human inhabitance that allows for serenity and reflection while

10    20    30 F

2    4    6    8    10 M

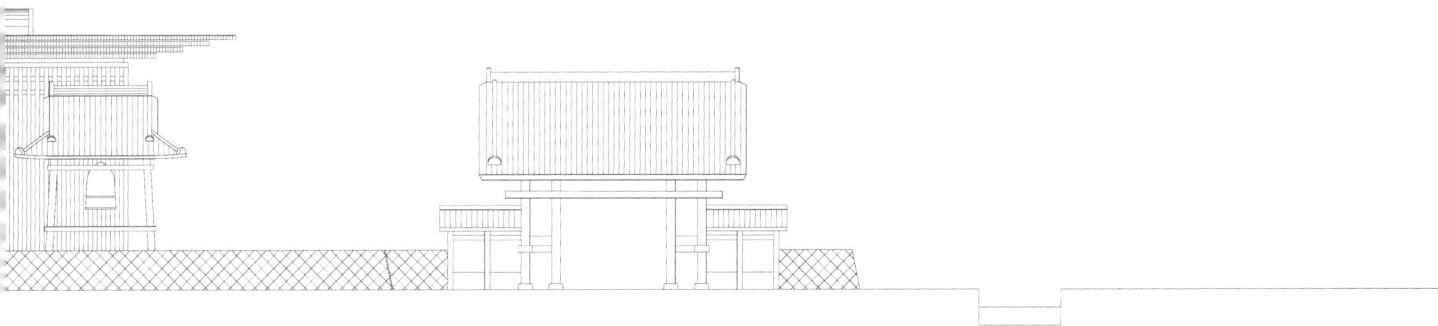

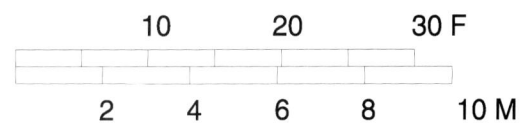

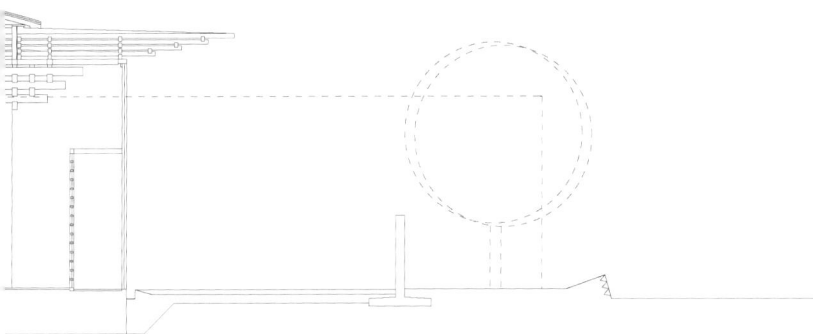

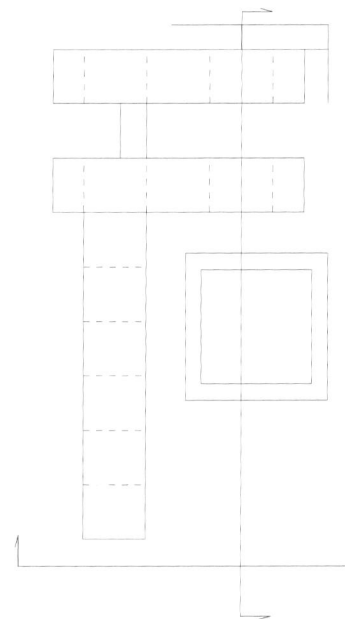

also revealing the spiritual dimension of everyday life. In the words of Tadao Ando himself: "In this world of rapidly changing values, my hope is to help promote an architecture that welcomes human-

ity with a lasting affect." In the architecture of Tadao Ando, a repertory of simple geometric forms articulate spaces with great subtle-

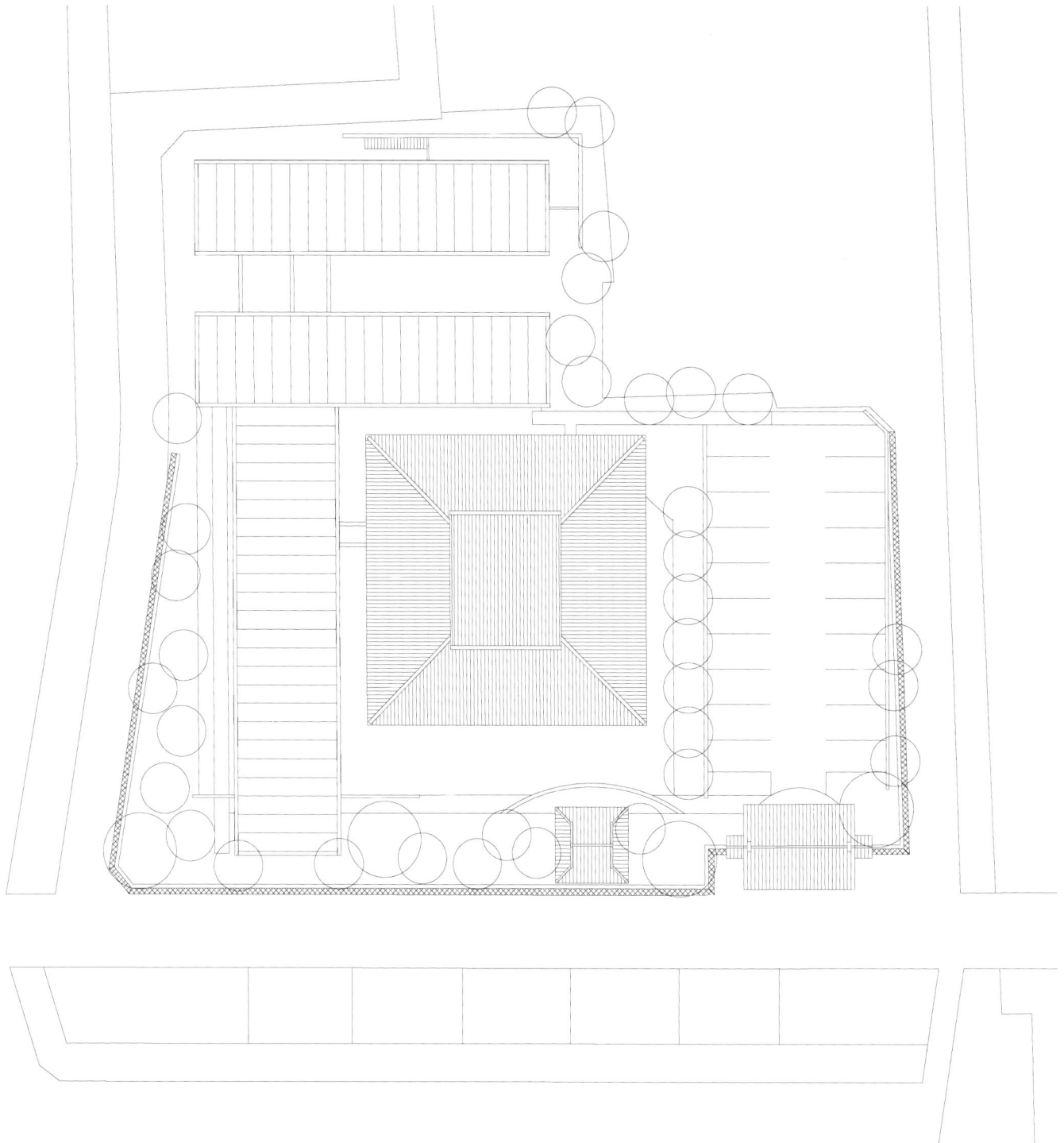

ty, complexity and dynamism. He sets against the fascination of form in some contemporary architectures, a fascination for space. Architecture eludes a box created with two objectives: One of the objectives is an ideal, the other, an ambition. The ideal of architec-

ture is to form a model of the world. Its ambition is to awaken man's sensitivities. His architecture possesses deep existential feelings. In it, the two dimensions of being are developed: space and time. The objective perception of time (the changes in light

with the passing of hours and seasons) is always measured by the subjective perception of an individual and by his or her memory. According to Ando, the work is the sum of what makes it up, what happens and what is perceived. It is through the passing of time, through the changes of light and the stations, of the movements of the inhabitants inside it that the architecture acquires its full meaning. As a result, in many of his works, such as in the Temple Komyo-ji in Sanjo, the movements of the shadows throughout the day have as much importance as the constructed elements.

"Architecture, which acquires stillness and balance thanks to geometric order, obtains dynamism thanks to natural phenomena and human movements," writes **Tadao Ando** in one of his articles.

Many of his works, such as the Church of the Water (1998), the Church of the Light (1998) and the Meditation Space, UNESCO, Paris (1995), reveal this desire to integrate natural phenomena into the architecture itself: light, shadows, the sky, water and wind.

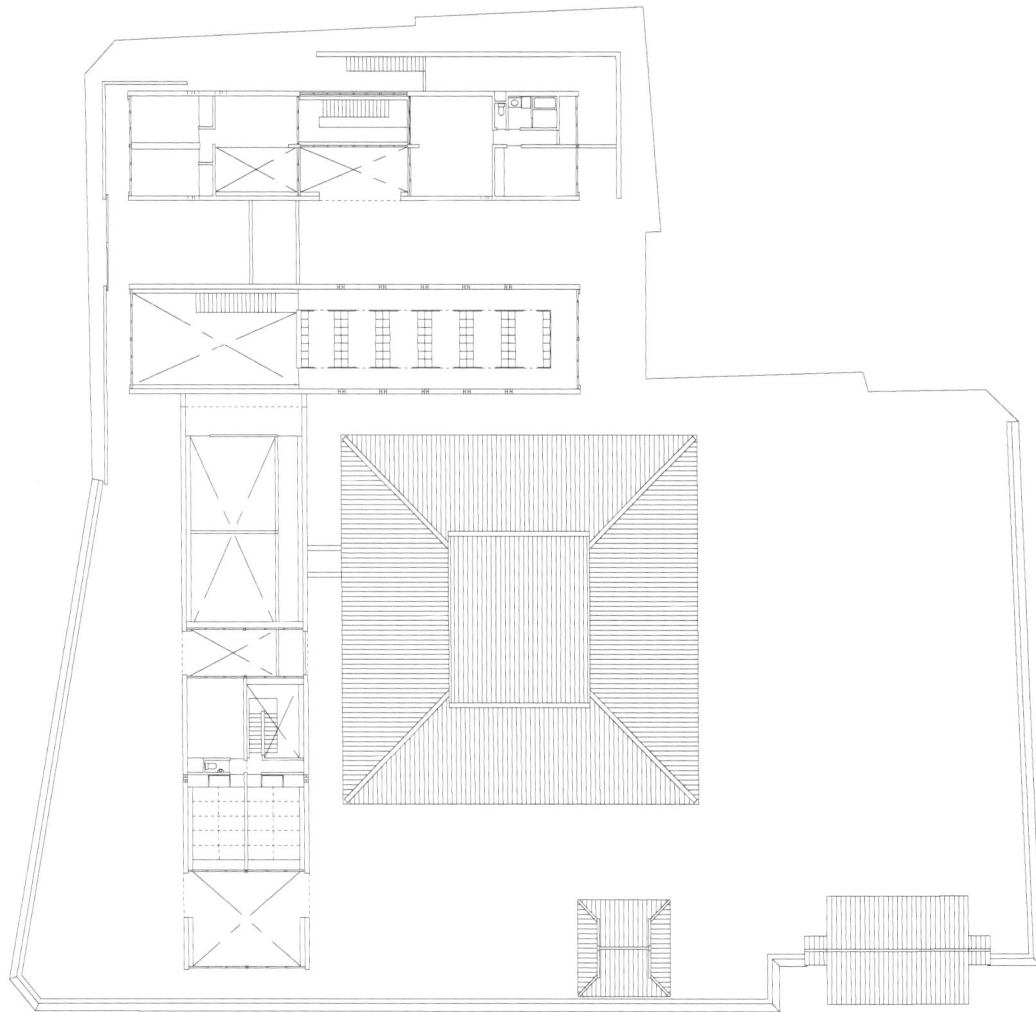

The sheets of water or the artificial lakes that reflect the sky and surroundings are common elements in his projects, as in the Water Temple on Awaji Island (1991) or in the recently built Modern Art Museum of Forth Worth, Texas, (2003).

So that nothing distracts from this spatial experience, the selection of building materials tends to be restrained. The majority of Tadao Ando's works are constructed in steel reinforced concrete and glass. Ando's concrete walls, due to their careful execution and

smooth textures, possess a special sensuousness. This is the case of the celebrated Koshino House (1984) or the Conference Center for Vitra en Weil am Rhein, Germany and in other buildings such as the Japanese Pavilion for Expo 92 or the Komyo-ji Temple constructed in wood within the Japanese tradition.

The phenomenological architecture of Ando has to be experienced to be fully appreciated. From a combination of the simplest of geometric forms and the effects of light on them, **Tadao Ando** manages to recreate the cosmos itself in the interiors of his buildings.

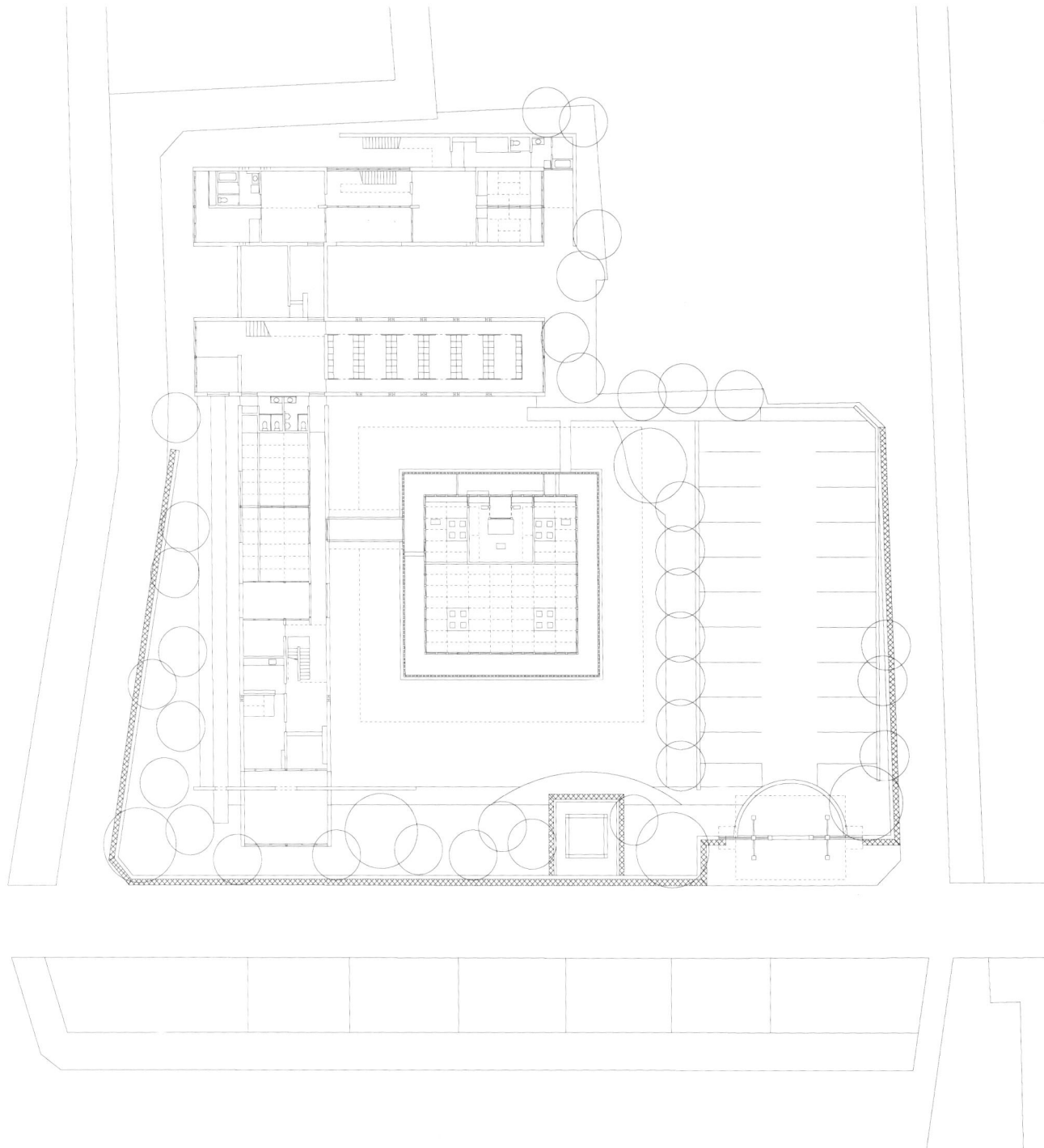

## Temple Komyo-ji

Sanjo, Japan

This project dealt with the reconstruction of an old temple of the Edo era situated in Sanjo. This is a coastal city close to Mount Ishizuchi (1,982 m), a place of exceptional landscape and numerous springs. The water element, as in other projects undertaken by Ando, is featured once again as the temple gives the impression that it is floating on an artificial lake.

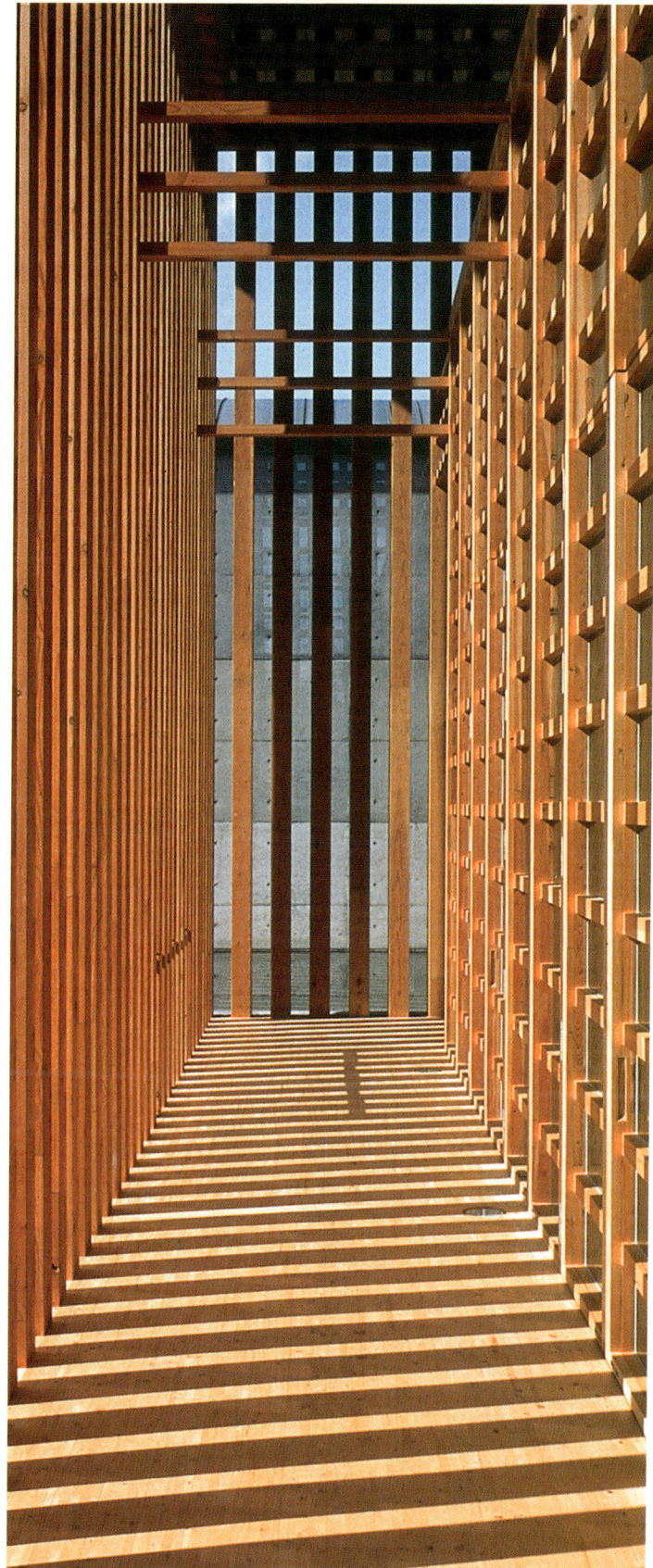

The inspiration for this project comes from traditional Japanese temples. In the same way that he did in the Japanese pavilion of the Expo 92, Ando abandoned steel reinforced concrete on this occasion and based his proposal for the construction on an assembly in wood. Being an author who knows how mix technological advances in construction with respect for history and tradition, Ando used laminated wood for its good structural qualities.

The result is a roomy square space with a double casing. The first layer of the casing consists of translucent glass and the second of wooden posts 15 x 21 cm that filter the natural light and create a ceremonial and luminous space. At night, the light filtered through the posts of the building itself is reflected in the lake.

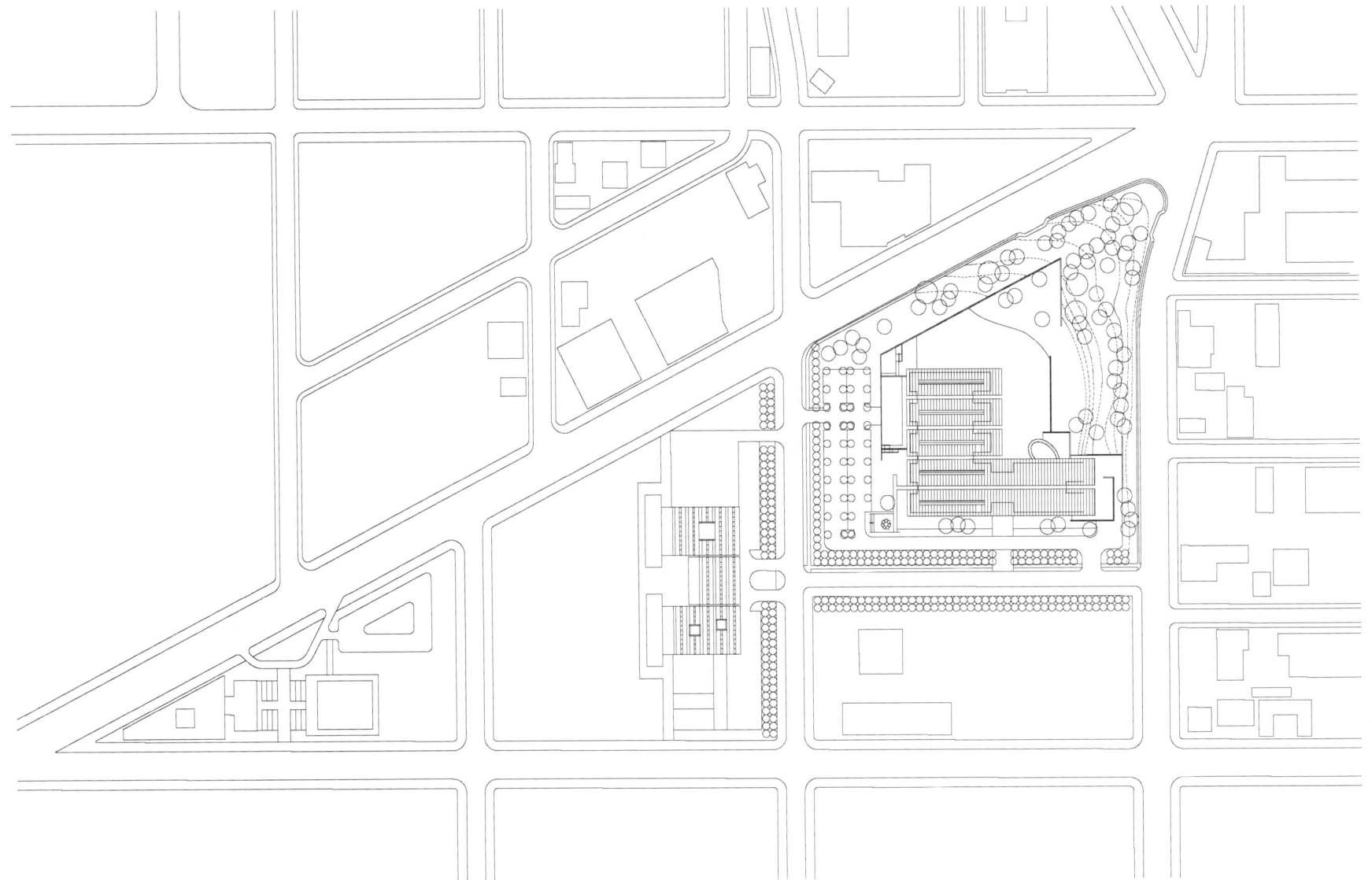

## Modern Art Museum Of Forth Worth
Forth Worth, Texas

The construction of this project, situated in the suburbs of Forth Worth, Texas, is the result of an international competition that was held in 1997. The building is adjacent to the Kimbell Art Mu-

seum, a masterpiece of the architect Louis Kahn and a classic of modern architecture.

The main challenges of the competition were to be the new building's relationship with Kimbell Museum and how to deal with the vastness of the plot, approximately 44,000 m², in which

WEST ELEVATION

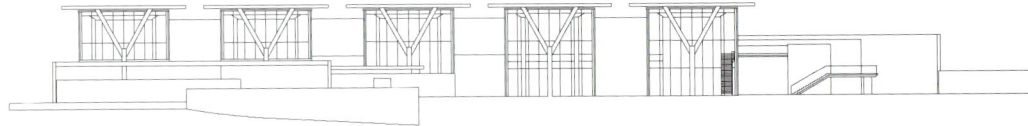

EAST ELEVATION

SOUTH ELEVATION

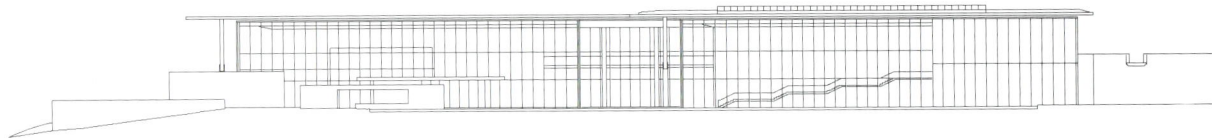

NORTH ELEVATION

MODERN ART MUSEUM OF FORT WORTH
EXTERIOR ELEVATIONS

a new garden with a large artificial lake has been sited. The design enters into dialog with Kahn's building with its powerfully simple spaces in which clear divisions between inside and outside are lost and which fill all those who visit it with inspiration.

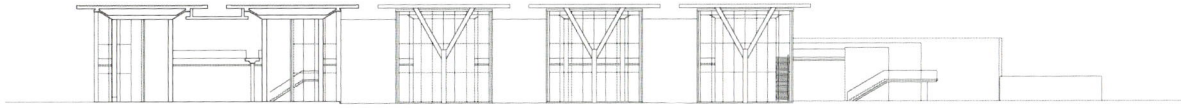

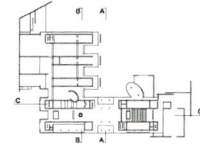

SECTION A

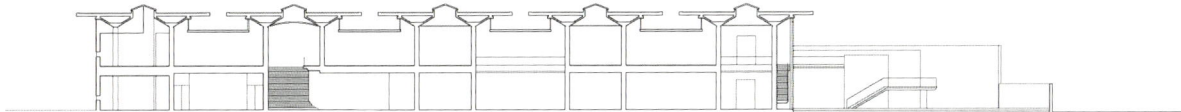

SECTION B

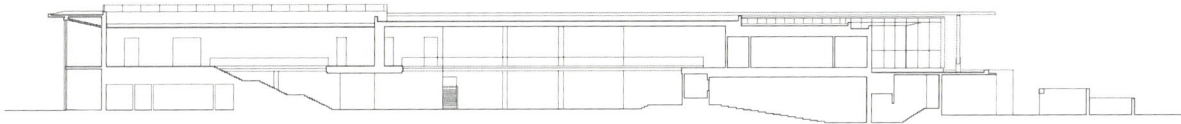

SECTION C

MODERN ART MUSEUM OF FORT WORTH
SECTIONS

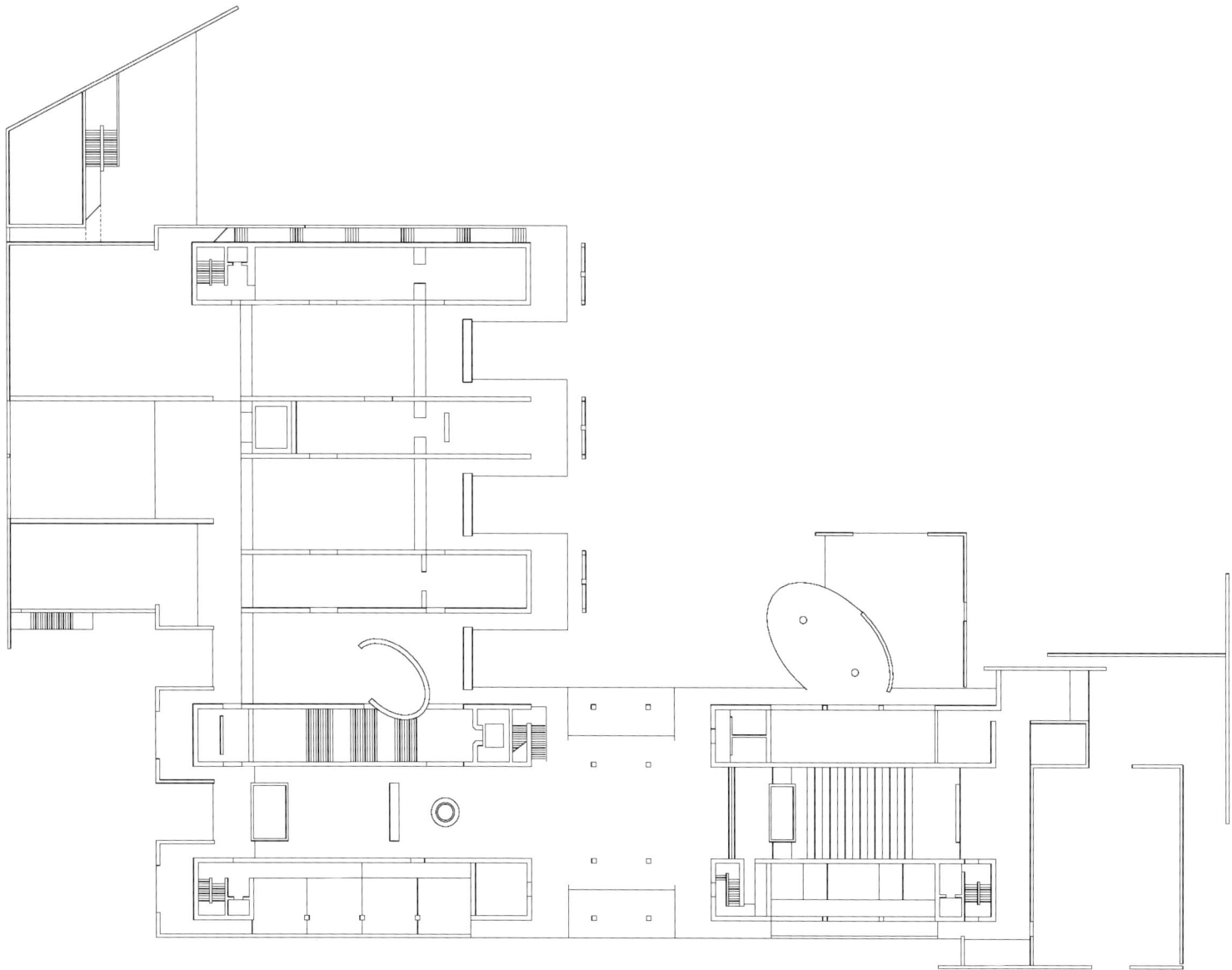

With the intention of creating an atmosphere favorable to artistic experience, six rectangular volumes have been set in line along the waterside of the artificial lakes, four for exhibition purposes and two longer ones to provide spaces for a variety of public activities. These elements have double casings. They are con-crete boxes covered with a second glass skin that presents a play between the qualities of each material: between lightness and heaviness, between transparency and opacity, between stability and the vision of a continually changing exterior landscape.

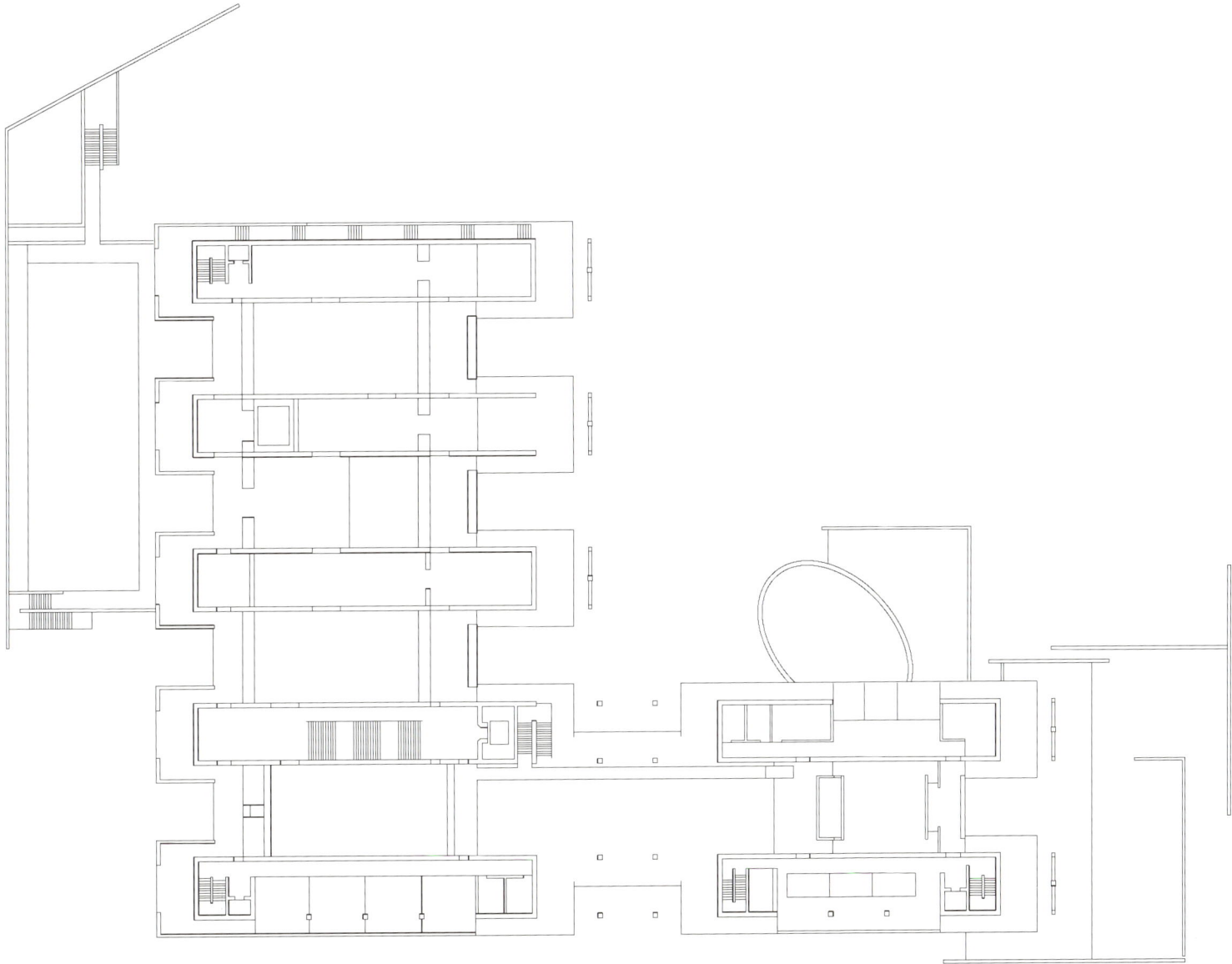

# Pulitzer Foundation for the Arts
## North American City of St. Louis

SECTION

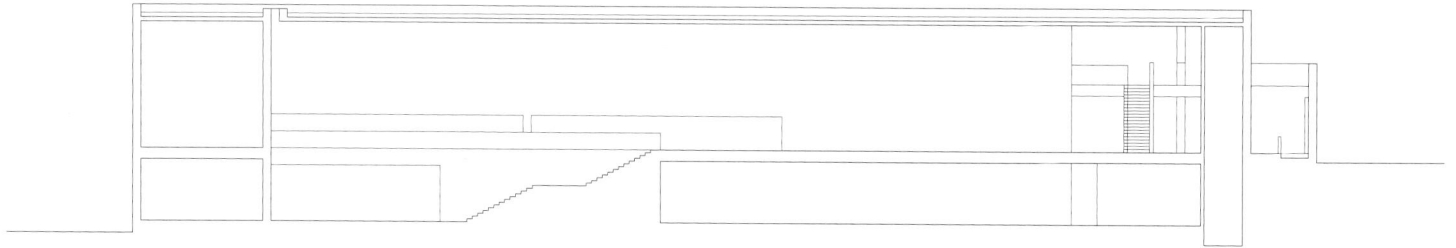

2F PLAN

BF PLAN

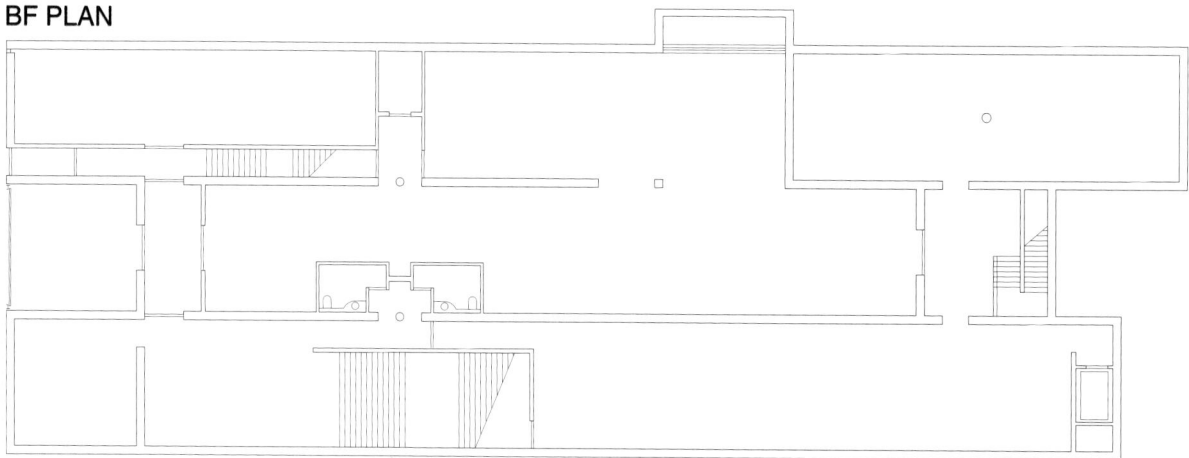

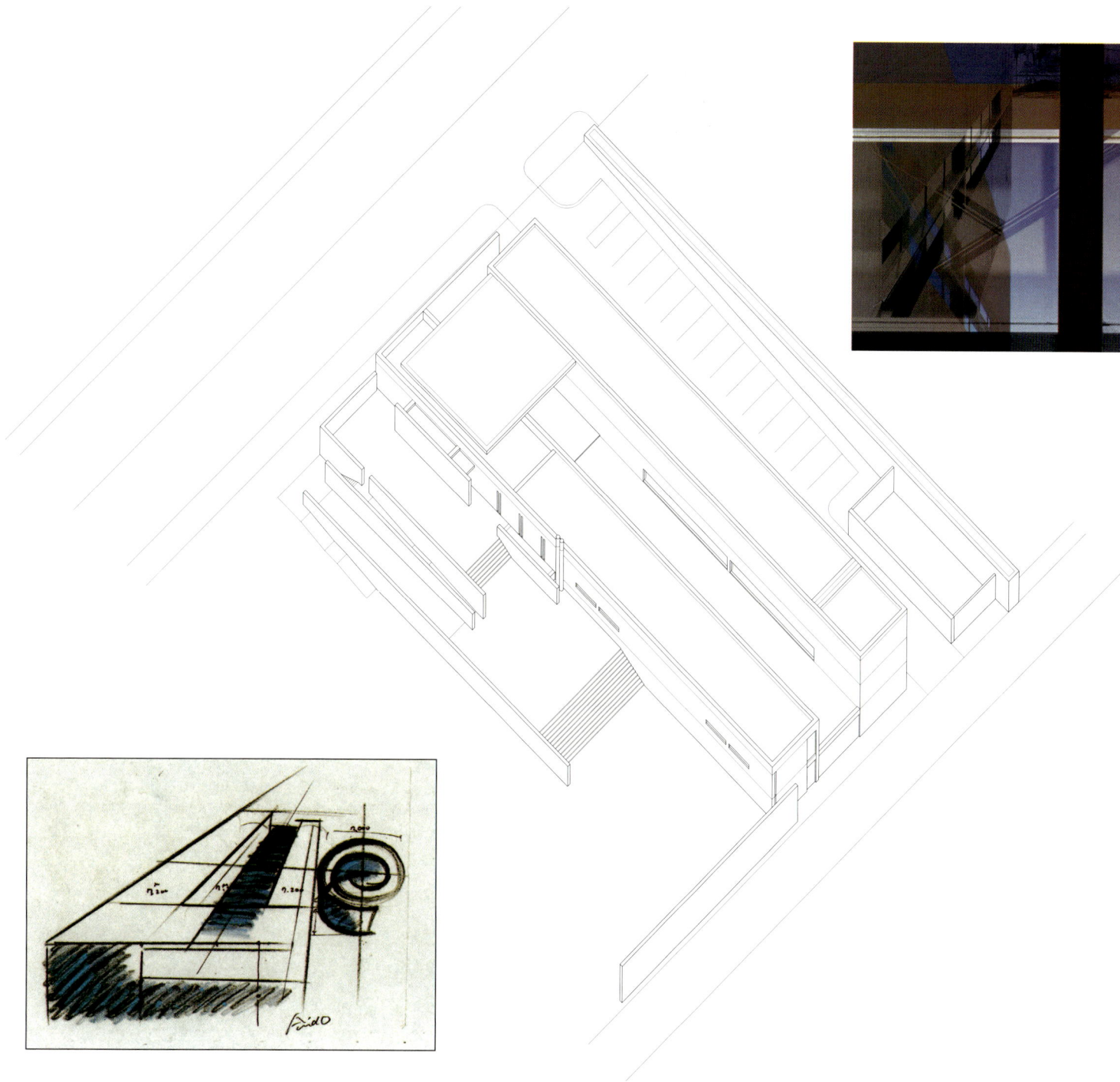

## Pulitzer Foundation for the Arts
North American City of St. Louis

This museum, located in the suburbs of the North American City of St. Louis, was constructed to house the collection belonging to the family of the founder of the Pulitzer Prize. It is a medium-sized cultural center for exhibitions of contemporary art desired to be a focal point for activities, as well as being a stimulus, within the district in which it is situated.

The museum is made up of two rectangular volumes 7.3 m (24 ft) wide which are of differing lengths and separated by an artificial lake of the same width. In the first, of a square section, the main gallery is located while the second is lower and presents a rooftop garden. With very few elements and by means of the balance in proportions between volumes and the openings in the concrete walls, Ando manages to create spaces that

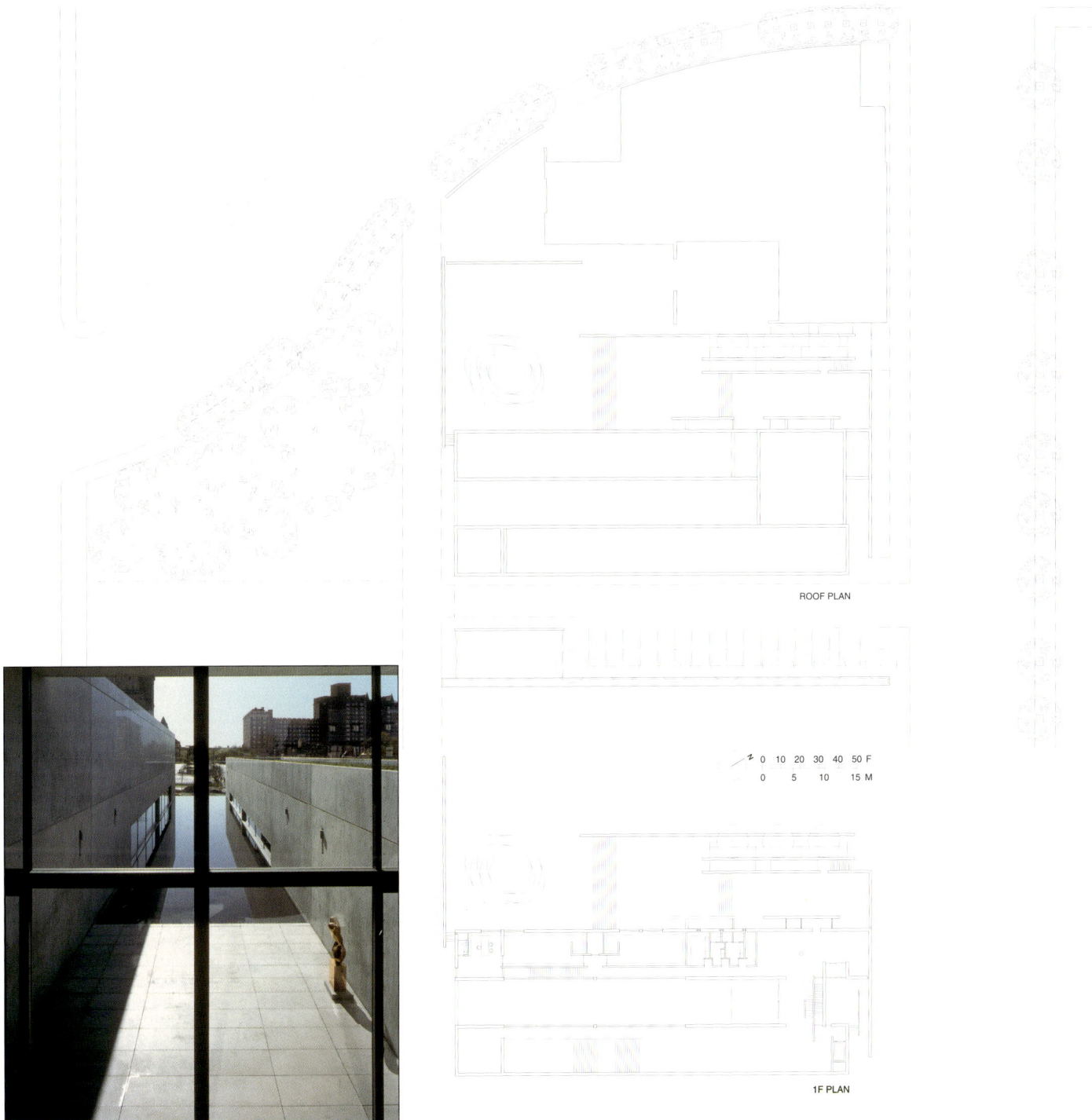

ROOF PLAN

0  10  20  30  40  50 F
0     5     10     15 M

1F PLAN

are full of tension between the interior and exterior areas in which the light indicates the passing of time and of the changing of the seasons. During the development of the project, Tadao Ando collaborated and exchanged ideas with some of the artists who have works exhibited in the center such as Ellsworth Kelly, Richard Serra...

## 4X4 House
### Costa de Kobe, Hyogo - Japón (2001-2003)

Situada en la tierra yerma de la costa de Kobe (Hyogo, Japón), en medio de un lugar inhóspito, entre una playa de extraña belleza y unas vías ferroviarias, esta casa de hormigón armado se erige como un refugio frente al huraño entorno inmediato. La complejidad del lugar determinó que ANDO proyectase la construcción verticalmente y con la mirada puesta en el hor-

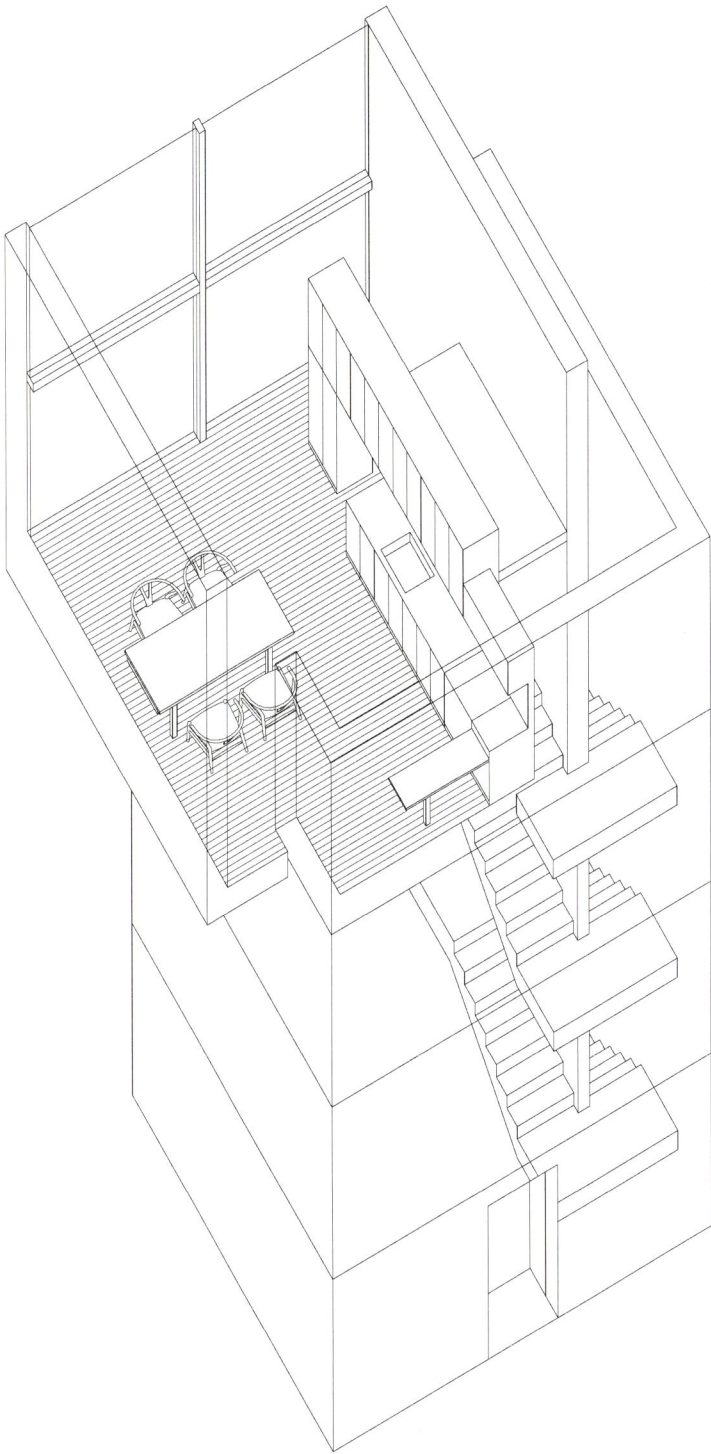

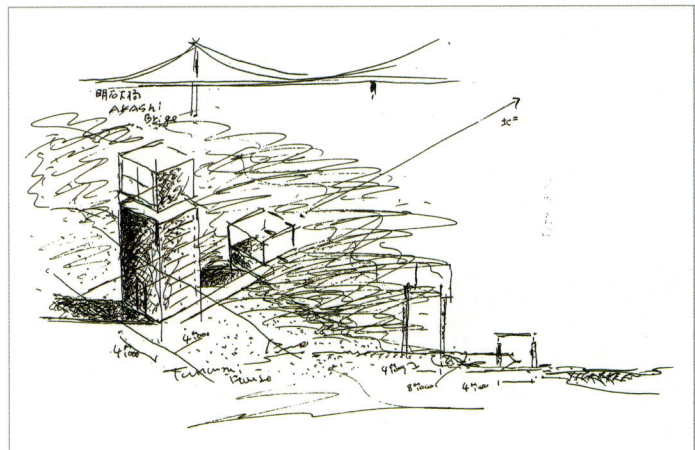

izonte, como si se tratase de un hito del paisaje. **TADAO ANDO** concibió este edificio de cuatro alturas y una planta de 4x4 metros como un mirador orientado hacia el mar de Seto,

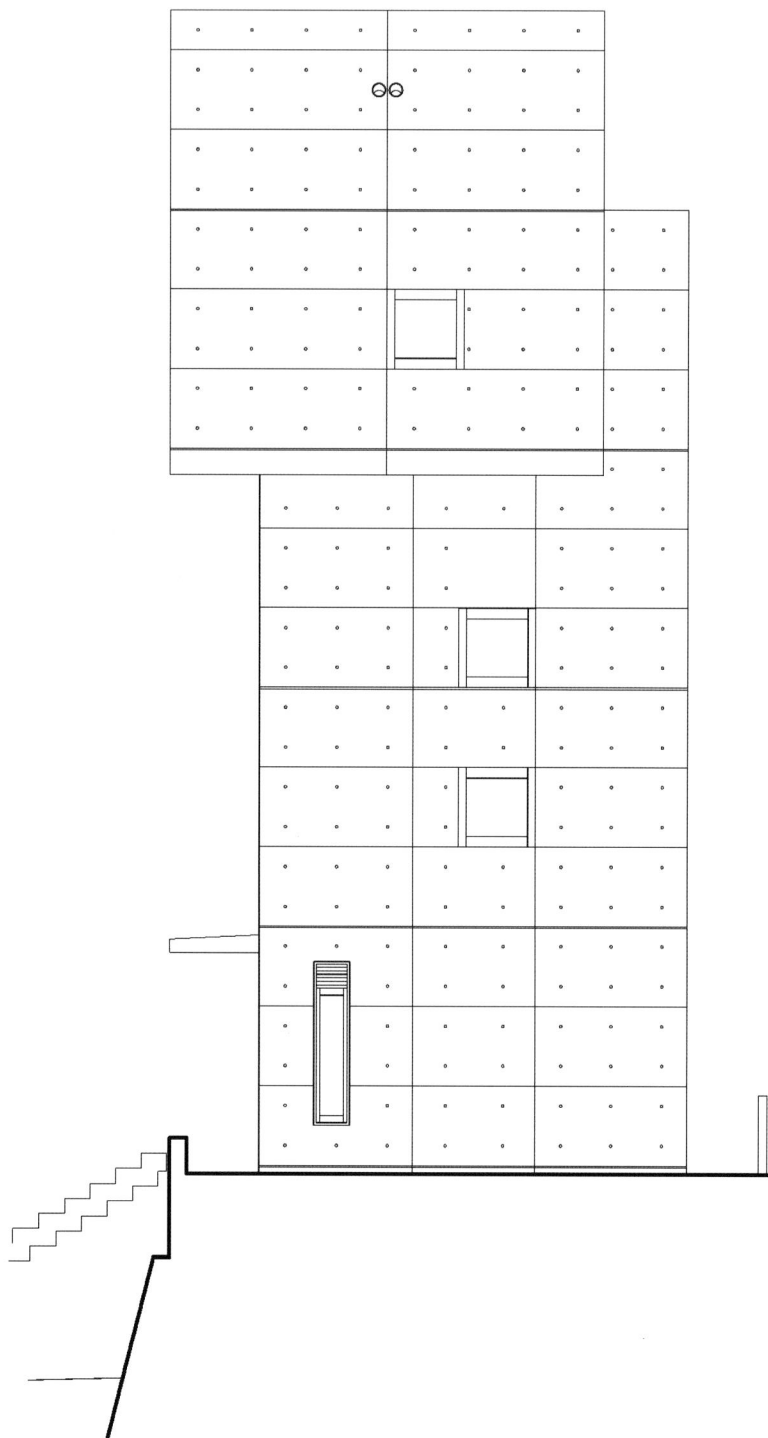

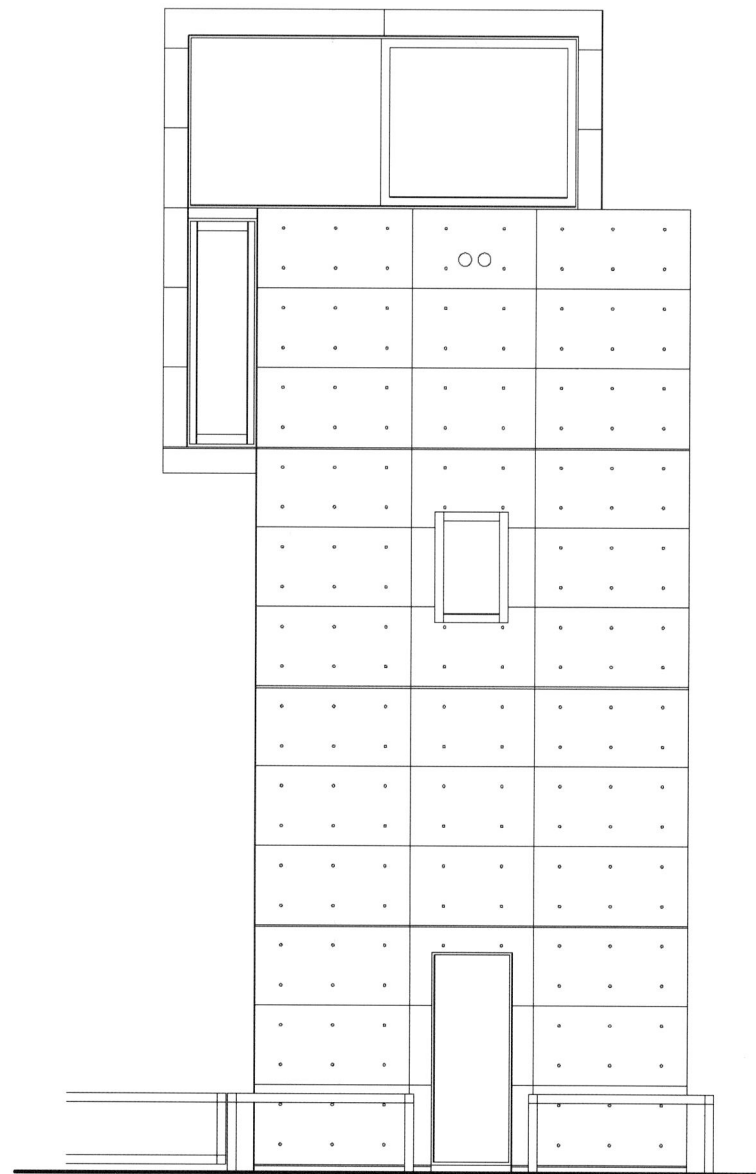

ya que las vistas al paisaje marítimo, la isla de Awaji y el puente de Akashi, uno de los símbolos de la ingeniería civil japonesa, constituyen el verdadero valor de este enclave.

En la planta superior, el volumen se desdobla en un cubo de las mismas dimensiones que el resto de la casa. Esta figura se desplaza un metro tanto hacia el sur como hacia el este, un bril-

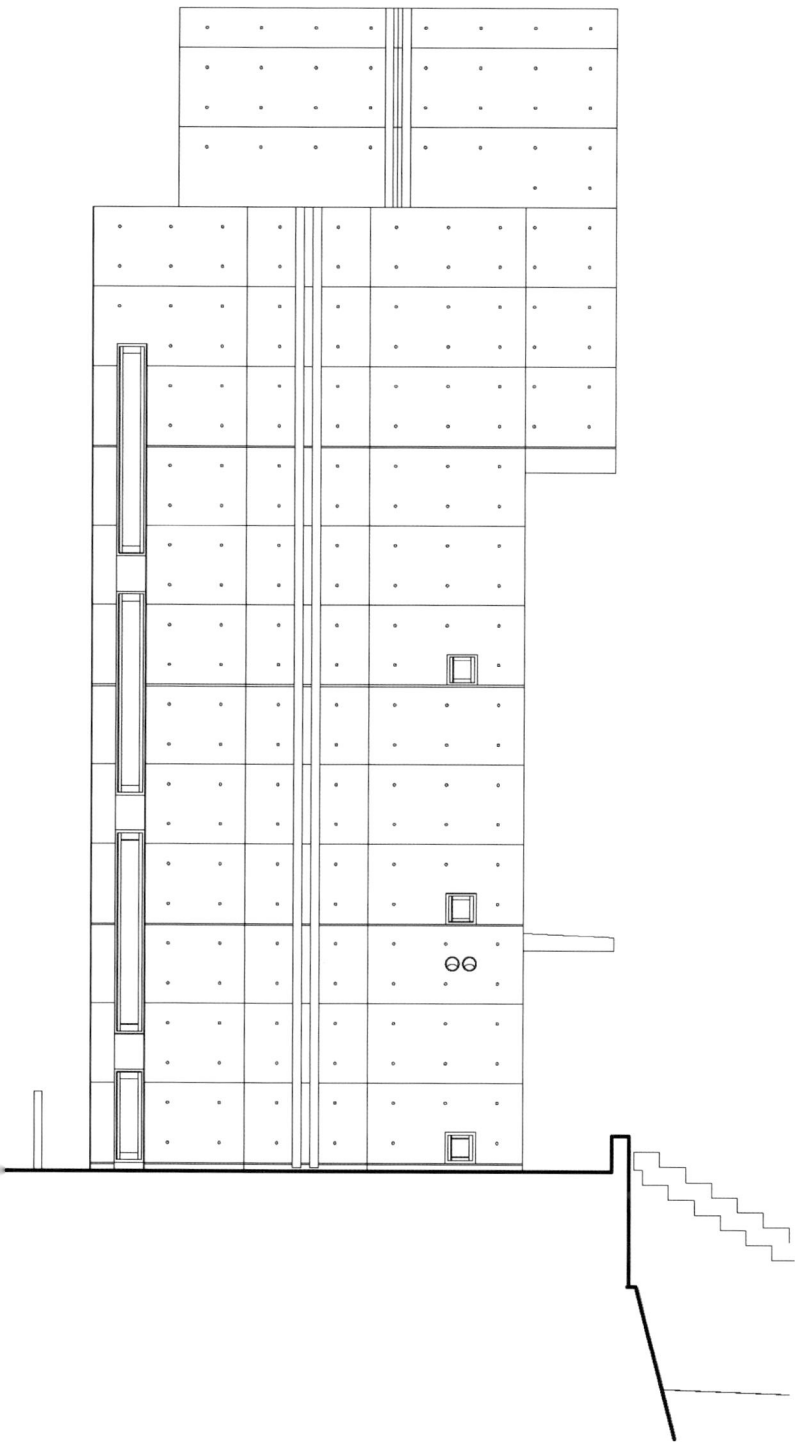

lante pero sencillo recurso formal, que enriquece el conjunto. La marcada verticalidad del edificio y su superficie reducida determinan la distribución de las diferentes zonas de la vivienda.

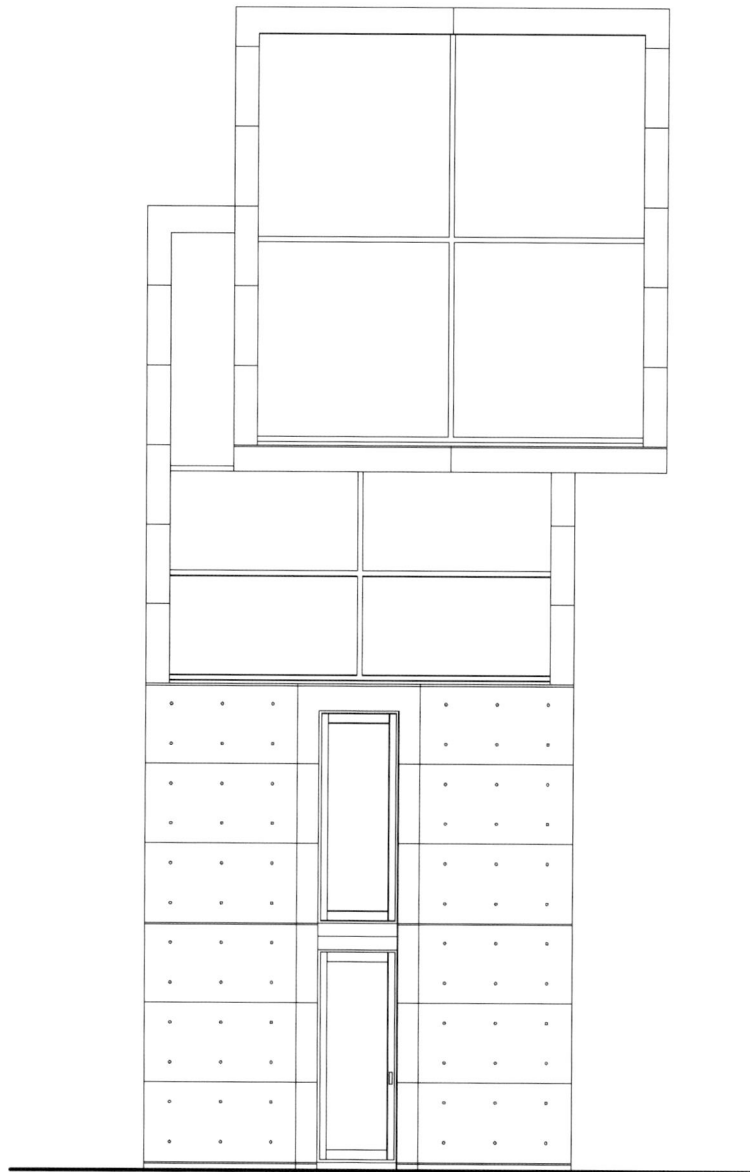

Cada planta se destina a una sola función y los diferentes espacios se comunican a través de una escalera. Los dos niveles inferiores se cierran al entorno para ganar privacidad, ya que al-

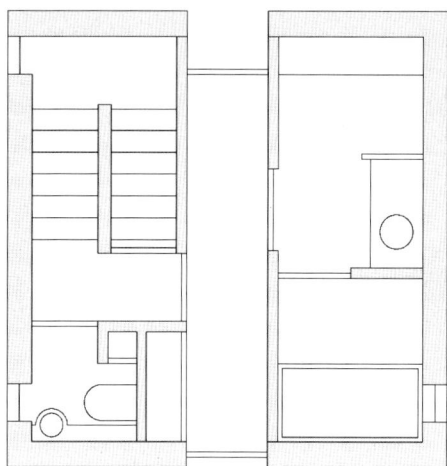

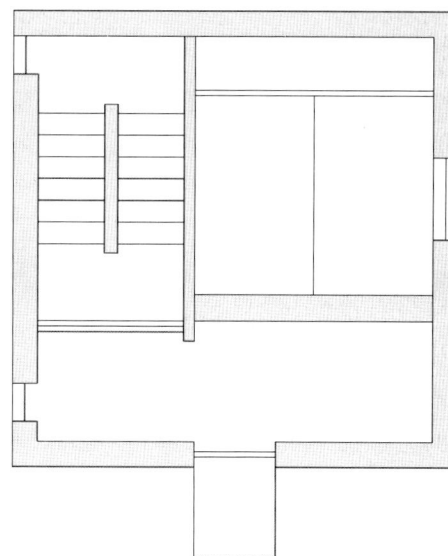

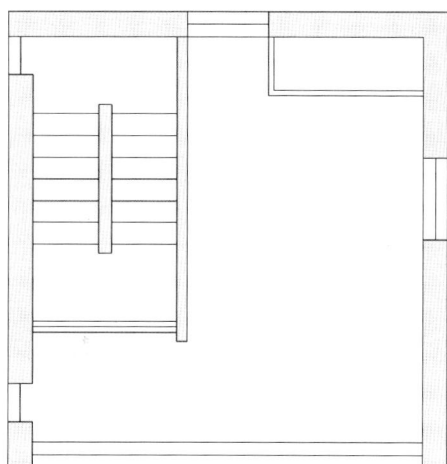

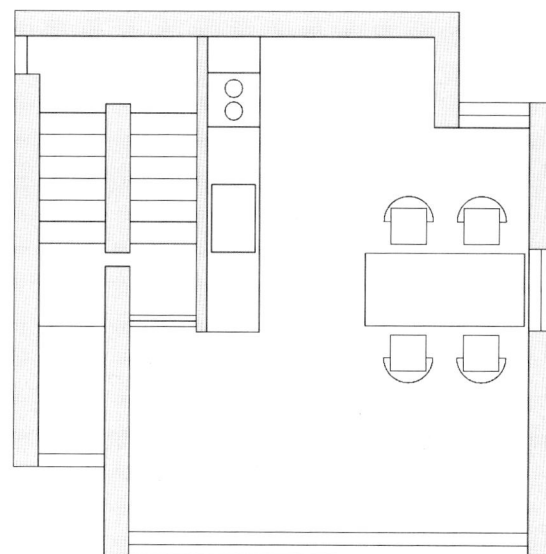

bergan el acceso y la zona de noche. En las plantas superiores, en cambio, el paisaje cobra protagonismo a través de grandes aberturas, donde tanto para el cliente como para el arquitecto japonés en el pedazo de paisaje que recorta el cubo "se incrustan pensamientos y recuerdos del terremoto", que en 1995 asoló la zona.

# Dominique
# Perrault

**W**as born in 1953 in Clérmont, Ferrand, France. He received diplomas in Architecture (1978) and in Urban Development (1979) in Paris where he also followed postgraduate studies in History. He set up his professional office in 1981 and, in 1989, he won the competition for the National Library of France, a work that received the Grand Prix National d'Architecture (1993), the Mies van der Rohe Prize (1997) and which led to his international recognition. In the 1990's, he won a number of competitions such as the Olympic Velodrome and Swimming Pool in Berlin (1991), the Extension to the European Law Courts (1996) or the Central Media Library of Vénissieux (1997). Dominique Perrault has taught in the School of Architecture of New Orleans, in Chicago, in the ETSAB in Barcelona and in the E.T.H. in Zurich.

Multifunctional Sports Complex

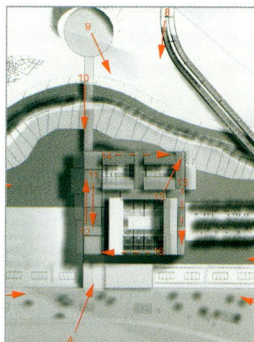

Central Media Library of Vénissieux

Masterplan Donau-City

Opera House Mariinsky II

In an interview, when asked about his work, **Dominique Perrault** answered: "It is not only the process or the finished building. I try, try and try again. It is experimentation. (…) It is an true scientific work."

As in scientific experimentation, the architect **Dominique Perrault** works with the intention of avoiding prejudice and values that are associated with a "**work of architecture**" and he rejects the notion of style, historic references or parallel narrations to the architecture itself. His work has often been described as minimalist architecture. However, this description could lead to a misunderstanding. It is not a question, in this case, of a formal style, but of a question of a far more radical nature: his strategy consists of obtaining forceful spatial results based on the arrangement of primary elements such as parallelepipeds and cylinders of large volumes in which the spaces between the elements take on a more important role than the volumes themselves, as in the case of the National Library of France. According to Frédéric Migayrou, author of various texts on **Perrault**, he deals with architecture of the neutral which is void of representations of external truths, free of references, codes or hierarchies. In some ways, his work is similar to sculptures by the North American minimalist artists Donald Judd and Carl André or the British artist Richard Long. In the words of **Dominique Perrault**: "The mechanism of minimalism interested me a lot: by the means of an installation I would define a spatiality; a spatial perception completely regulated with respect to a situation, to a determined reading."

In his latest projects, the layouts have become more and more complex and fortuitous as in the extension to the Landesmuseum in Zurich "we have based the project on the stacking of boxes in an extremely primitive way which is almost violent", in the proposal for the Mariinsky Theatre in St. Petersburg, or in the competition for the Pinault Foundation on the Ile Seguin, Paris. He moves away from the simplicity of his earlier compositions to give the buildings greater dynamism and a certain indetermination: "In the same way that in the beginning the layout was very regular, extremely immobile, very quiet and did away with the notion of movement, my current work is more rational, but of a more open, more volatile form of rationalism", says Perrault. It seems that he is being taken away along the road to experimentation rather than along the road to self-satisfaction.

He is interested in the concept of architecture as constructed landscape: "My objective now is not to construct buildings, but to construct landscape". This intention is clearly visible in some of his projects, such as the sports complex in Badalona (Spain). Also, in the competition for the University Center EWHA in Seoul (South Korea), won by the office in the summer of 2004, in which attitudes close to land art are displayed.

In his view, an inherent violence exists in architectural work, in the act of designing and constructing: "Violence is a vital quality, the first and primordial manifestation of the elements. (...) For me, violence is a question of assuming an act." However, he does not tend to privilege any moment in the design or construction process of a building. All of the moments are of the same importance to him. The relationships with the client, the industrialists and the construction companies also form part of the project which is a process that is open to any form of intervention. Because of this, he goes for quite an immediate first design. According to Parrault: "This does not take anything away from anything, but the design process becomes neutralized in as much as its duration is almost nonexistent. Later, great liberty is found when the working boundaries are changed

as what has been conceived quickly can be questioned with the same speed. If you work fast, you can change. If you are slow, it is impossible to change."

He considers that architects should intervene in industrial processes and convert them into fields of architectural investigation and to study the materials and their possible applications. His investigations into metal grating, glazed walls and multicoated ventilated facades have been full of novelties. The play on composition of these movable facades, with their continually changing skins, suggest an architecture that is not something finished and dead, but a variable object which seeks interaction from the user.

Many of these facades give the impression that the construction itself is disintegrating. This is the case of the glazed facade of the Hotel Industriel Berlier in which the light is filtered through rows of metal shelves. It is also the case of the cabin glazed in completely transparent glass that was installed in the Kolonihavehus, or that of the facade in shinning steel of the Aplix factory that reflects the surrounding landscape in broken segments. All of this leads to the 'disappearance' of architecture as a monument.

The burying of a large part of the construction often manifests this desire. This can been seen in the Olympic Velodrome and Swimming Pool in Berlin in which a significant part of the functional elements have been hidden below a disc and rectangle in metal mesh referred to by Perrault as two lakes in a orchard. It is also the case of the Conference Center Usinor in Saint Germain in Laye, and that of his own residence in Brittany, Villa One, in which he also decided to hide the presence of the architecture below the ground. Most of the house, Villa One, is hidden under a fold in the terrain and only opens onto the exterior on one side which is a glazed facade that looks out to sea.

The National Library of France was developed in a similar way. In the competition, Perrault stated that he wished to construct a place and not a building. In one of the collages for the competition, a photomontage of the Taj-Mahal appears in which the temple has disappeared and only the platform and minarets remain. In the project, the minarets of the image become the four towers where the books are stored and which define the empty space of the elevated plaza. In the center of this platform, on a lower level, we find a space that is a natural rectangle, an inaccessible forest to the users.

In Dominique Perrault's architecture, natural elements become construction materials. His way of negating any difference between natural and artificial elements brings strange airs to some of his spaces. At times, these elements are highly featured. For example, in his explanation of the Olympic Velodrome and Swimming Pool for Berlin, he insists that the main concept of the project is to construct an apple orchard in which, when walking, we discover two surfaces, two lakes, below which the entire scheme of the building is hidden. According to Fréderic Migayrou: "When Dominique Perrault defends this brutish use of natural elements, he does it as a direct expression of his unusual and sensitive energy against any apprehension that is too cultural, too architectural of the garden, of the green space." In his proposals, two types of 'nature', which range from wild and virgin to the artificial, coexist simultaneously.

Dominique Perrault seems to be an astute observer of his time. He is pragmatic and not very sentimental as demonstrated by his understanding of architecture as an activity based on collaboration, his way of seeing the expansion of urban zones "in which only the artificial exists" or the political use of large public buildings. In his proposals, he manages to give shape to his vision of reality in a strong and radical way.

## INTERVIEW

ATRIUM -I read that you studied Architecture and Urban Planning in Paris and that you are a post-graduate History. Some of your writings seem to be quite sceptical about traditional Urban Planning. In what way have your studies influenced your later professional work as an architect?
DP-More than sceptic, I think it is question of evolution. I studied the urban structures of the city in the 19th century, Paris especially. More specifically, I did my studies about the relation between the monument, the institution and the urban fabric.
My research involved a deep historical and urban analysis. Then I began to work as an architect, putting up buildings… and then it was another century. This analysis of the city in the 19th century is not operative anymore, though it allows you to learn about a lot of things. At that time, the plan of the city could be drawn.

ATRIUM - Isn't there some kind of will to still draw the city in Paris? I'm thinking of La Défense, and in the Parisian tradition of a strong axis.
DP - La Défense has been drawn and also the "périphérique" or ring road, but La Défense is more about composing a landscape.

ATRIUM -In some of your texts and interviews, you seem to reject the traditional role of architecture as a monument of institutional or economical power. What do you think about this matter? Anyway, some have seen some type of monumentality in some of your first big scale projects, your Olympic sports complex in Berlin, or in the Bibliothèque Nationale de France, for example). Do you feel your architecture has been misunderstood on some occasions?
DP- In the 19th century, the city had to be very stable, with good perspectives, etc…The positioning of institutional buildings was very important to control the people. They were a reference, a symbol, a tool of power. And about the Bibliothèque Nationale de France it is exactly the opposite. It must be a unique building, it must have a

presence, but it is not a monument, it is a cultural building at the end of the xx Century. The relationship between the people and this kind of building is different now. It's not necessary to build a fence around such a building, it should open to the city. It is an ambivalent situation, in a way it should be a monument, but a monument without a wall.

ATRIUM - A democratic monument?
DP- Yes, so you can go through.

ATRIUM - And what about your studies in History?
DP- At that time at school in Paris, it was normal to follow this process.
During this period architecture was very much centred on the history of the city, it was the trend.

ATRIUM - How do you approach a new project? Are there some subjects you are specially focused on?
DP- Each project is like a prototype. Each project should be specific. I'm very interested in the context, not only the immediate context around the project, but rather a global vision of the context: the quality of the client, the political situation, the site itself… I cook with those ingredients. I look for the specificity of the project. Sometimes a project demands a strong presence, because maybe the place needs something with a bit of character.
Then the project should be significant. Other times the situation is completely the opposite, where the idea is to introduce a system, the building can disappear in the landscape (for example in my project in Berlin, which is sunken into the ground).
Maybe it can also disappear in the landscape with the material of its outer surface, like in the Aplix Factory.

ATRIUM - What importance do you place on experimentation in your projects? Is it "scientific work"?
DP- When I say scientific work, I am speaking about the process, about starting from a hypothesis, not from a final idea you have to go to. When you work in a scientific process you don't know what the con-

clusion will be. I think it is more interesting when you are open to what can appear, and you are not looking for something definitive.

ATRIUM - Are you able to maintain this attitude when you are developing the project of a building?
DP- It is a research process, and then one must decide on something.

ATRIUM - So, the architect must always make a final decision.
DP- It's a decision that is taken inside the process, not a priori. It's a process of making the project richer. It is more about working with several hypotheses and verifying the validity of each element. Besides, one can begin to be more interested by one particular aspect; it can be the political one, or the geographical… and then make a decision on what is more relevant or has more potential, it's a matter of choice.

ATRIUM - In some of your latest projects there seems to be some kind of evolution. Your project for the Mariinsky Theatre, the proposal for the Landsmuseum in Zurich, or your competition for the Pinault Foundation on the Ile Seguin, all seem to be more dynamic and free. Do you think there has been an evolution from the beginning of your work until now, in your thoughts and in your projects?
DP- It's difficult to answer this question when you don't have enough distance. I think it's more the work of critics and journalists to answer this question, it doesn't really interest me. My answer, is let the critics do their work.

ATRIUM - About your architecture, does it have the ambition to be contemporary in the sense of following the beat of its time, or is it in some way timeless?
DP- This question doesn't interest me.

ATRIUM -I have read you are very interested in the work of some minimal artists and land artists like Donald Judd, Robert Morris or Richard Long. In what way have they influenced your work?
DP- These are important artists, they are interested in interventions in relation to a place. In particular Richard Long works in relation to the geography. With little elements he can transform the relationship with a place.

ATRIUM - Can you relate your work to some of the work of these artists?
DP- Yes, for example Robert Morris made a project with 4 glass blocks that is directly connected to the layout of the Bibliothèque Nationale de France. About Richard Long, maybe I can relate to his work, my studies with materials, the metal meshes…the material aspect. Maybe Donald Judd is more connected to the Hôtel Industriel in Paris. I am more influenced by artists than by architects.

ATRIUM - I've heard this comment from several architects recently. It seems, like Billie Tsien said, that architects are more interested in art than artists in architects, in most cases.
DP - Some architects interest me, it's just that they don't inspire me. The work of the architect is very much conditioned; it is a product of a lot of things. The work of the artist is more pure, intimate and personal.

ATRIUM - In some of your proposals, natural elements have a main role - for example Berlin. In your projects, do you make a difference between natural and artificial elements?
DP - There is no relation between natural and artificial. That doesn't exist. Nature is a material, because it is a material, you can manipulate it, because you can manipulate it, it becomes an artificial element. It is like the fact that we now live in cities, the countryside doesn't exist anymore. The society is urban. It is the same thing as saying that the world today is artificial, because nature is a nature we control and manipulate (Nature in the sense of the XVIII century doesn't exist anymore). The only factors that are still natural in that sense are natural disasters: cyclones, earthquakes, fires. Nature is for me a material like concrete, glass or metal.

ATRIUM - In what way do you think new technologies have changed the work of the architect?
DP- New technologies allow one to draw in a clean, perfect manner. Before, there were architects that knew how to draw and others who didn't. Today everyone knows how to draw. Today there are architects that are conscious of what they are drawing and others who aren't. Everyone can believe they are an architect and make a drawing with their computer by adding different images copied from the internet, making a superficial image. What is produced must be analysed in

terms of meaning: does the project have a specific relation with its place and context? This can't be solved by a collage of images from internet that is completely superficial. New technologies raise questions about the conscience the architect has vis-à-vis architecture, and these questions are cultural, ethical, political…It's a problem of authenticity, of truth. One can be a liar and a thief with the new technologies.

ATRIUM - Do you view the relationship with other collaborators, for example with different building industries, as part of the design process?
DP - This is related to the consideration that each building is a prototype. Each building has a need—more or less—of experimentation, a development in terms of material, form, design, light. This experimental research needs forms of collaboration with industry: the development of a façade, a metal mesh, a special glass…

ATRIUM - This way of collaborating closely with industry seems to me quite clever. In Spain, there is no respect in the construction phase for the construction details drawn by architects. Maybe this is a good way to create a better collaboration and a deeper compromise between the construction industry and architects.
DP - It is difficult to build in Spain. There's a lot of subcontracting, with many construction companies doing whatever they want, without any control.

ATRIUM - What do you like best about being an architect, and least?
DP - What I like best is the variety. You can be doing urban planning, and furniture, and a book, and a building; works of very different scales, one after the other or at the same time. It's not repetitive work. Every project is specific.

ATRIUM - What strategies do you use to obtain your clients' trust?
DP - I have no strategies, I only have strategies to get the work done. The only thing the client is interested in is having the project realised in a correct manner, on time.

ATRIUM - Do you think there has been an evolution in the type of client? I mean more projects with multiple clients, clients that are more specialized with more advisors?
DP- This is probably true, but it also depends where. Maybe this is truer for private developments, where there are enterprises that control different aspects of a project, financial or quality controllers… In public works it depends on the country. For example in France, public works—like the Bibliothèque—have a very good and efficient organisation. The transmission of information is clear between client and architect. In other countries this is more chaotic and disorganized.

ATRIUM - Do architects and urban planners have a role in the current evolution of cities?
DP - They do have a role, one of making proposals. The architect for his psychology (of focusing on the specific and on the general) is very good at making punctual proposals, which may fit into a wider, more comprehensive, idea of the city. There is an everyday view of the problems in a city, in the street, that is directly perceptible by the citizens, and a broader view. The way urban planners and architects are participating in the evolution of cities is by making partial proposals for some of its parts: sometimes zones that have a problem or don't work, sometimes acting in the limits of the city…

ATRIUM - How do you view Paris now, and Barcelona?
DP - There is currently some discussion in Paris about whether skyscrapers should be built in the city. There is also an international competition for redesigning les Halles. In Barcelona I took part in some of the conversations about the city with politicians and urban planners. Maybe the architect's role is is to open up a debate about the city. There must be some kind of general intentions behind the partial projects that are being built. There is an interaction between what is local and what is global, the bigger scale. It's a permanent laboratory. Today, you can't control a city with a drawing, but you can still have deeper thinking about it.

ATRIUM - What is your opinion about the existence of a "star system" of architects? Cities like Barcelona, Madrid or Florence seem actually more interested in acquiring buildings with a brand than in urban planning. The Spanish architect O. Tusquets said: "The architects of the 'star system' are political arms. They can help win elections." What do you think about this?
DP - Yes, you can win elections like that, and you can also lose them. What is true is that clients and politicians know better what they are expecting from the architect: something special or charismatic in some way, that helps them improve their political image.

ATRIUM - What changes do you observe in contemporary architecture? What would you like to see?
DP - One thing I see is that there is an intention to go back to the material quality of architecture. I think architects today are more attached to the territory and to the physical part of architecture ∎

## Multifunctional Sports Complex in the area of the River Manzanares

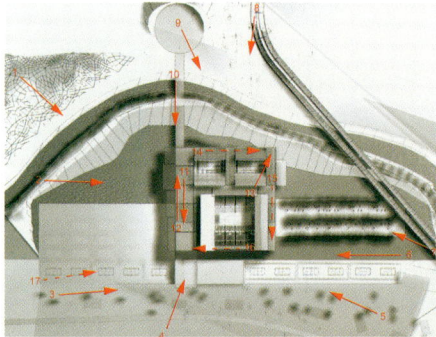

Madrid, Spain 2004-2008

The project encompasses a complex scheme which includes the Olympic Center, the Federation Headquarters, a large multifunctional stadium and an events center among other things. The proposal has of three objectives:

### To construct a landscape (diurnal and nocturnal)

The river is to be enlarged by creating an artificial lake: an immense surface that acts as a large natural mirror. In this lake, small islands to facilitate leisure and sport activities are to be created. The project will create various new itineraries: a walk around the 'lake', through the bridges, in the large plaza and so on.

## Install a Form of Architecture

The intention of the project is not to construct a building, but to install a form of architecture into a setting. The proposal is to encompass a magic box that accommodates the sports activities. This 'encompassing' opens and transforms, modifying its external aspect and the luminous and environmental conditions of the

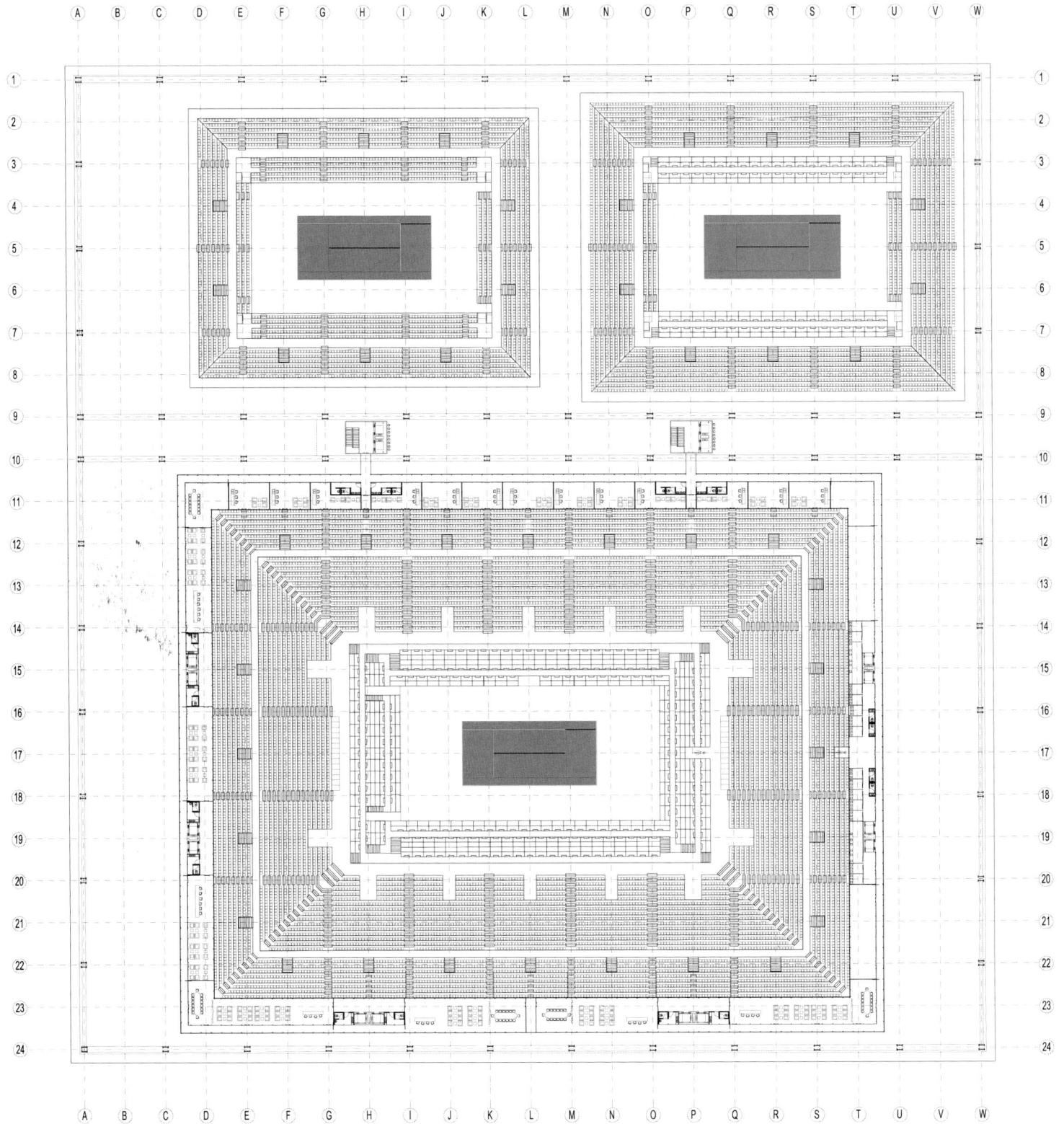

0  5          20                    50

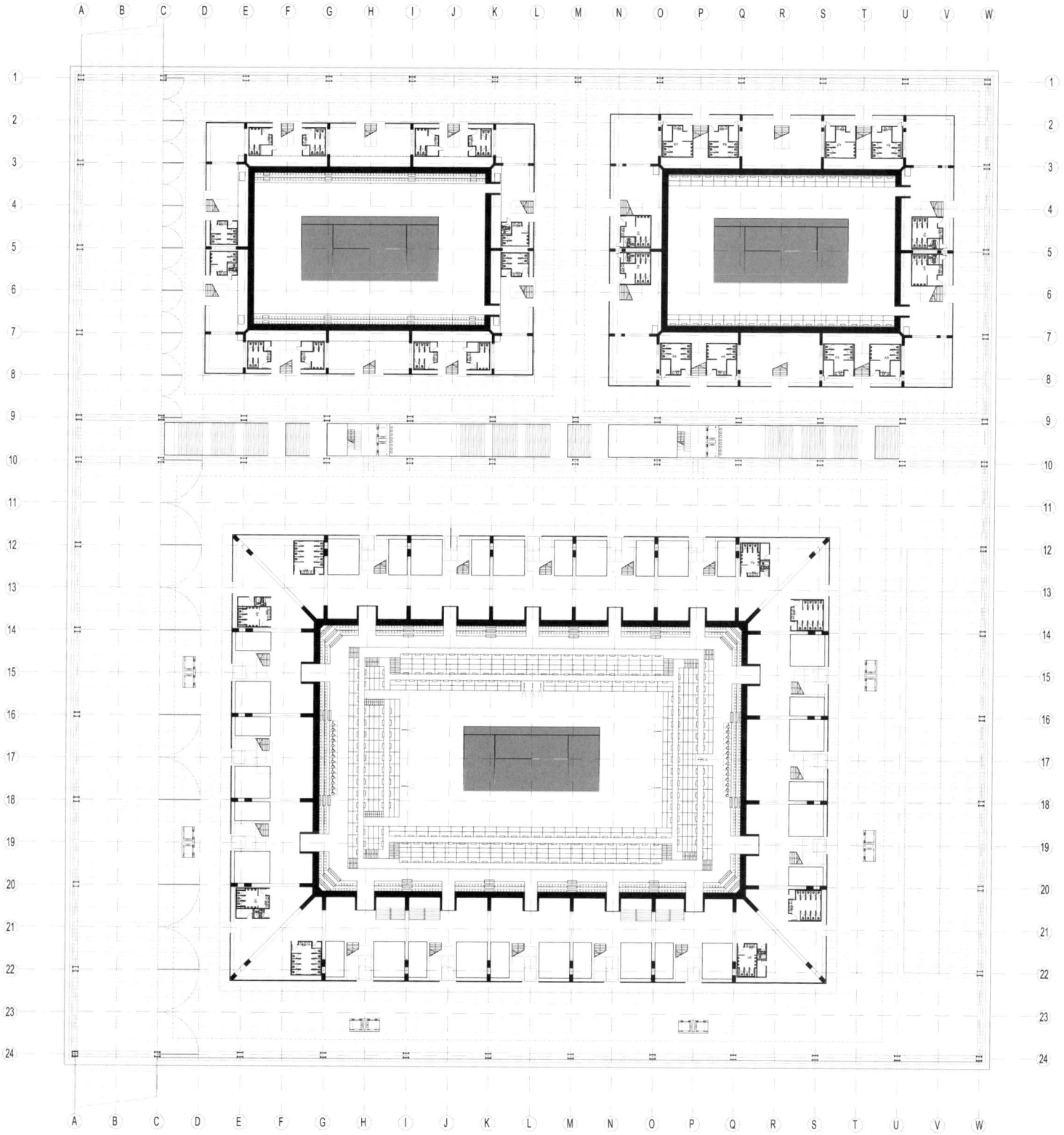

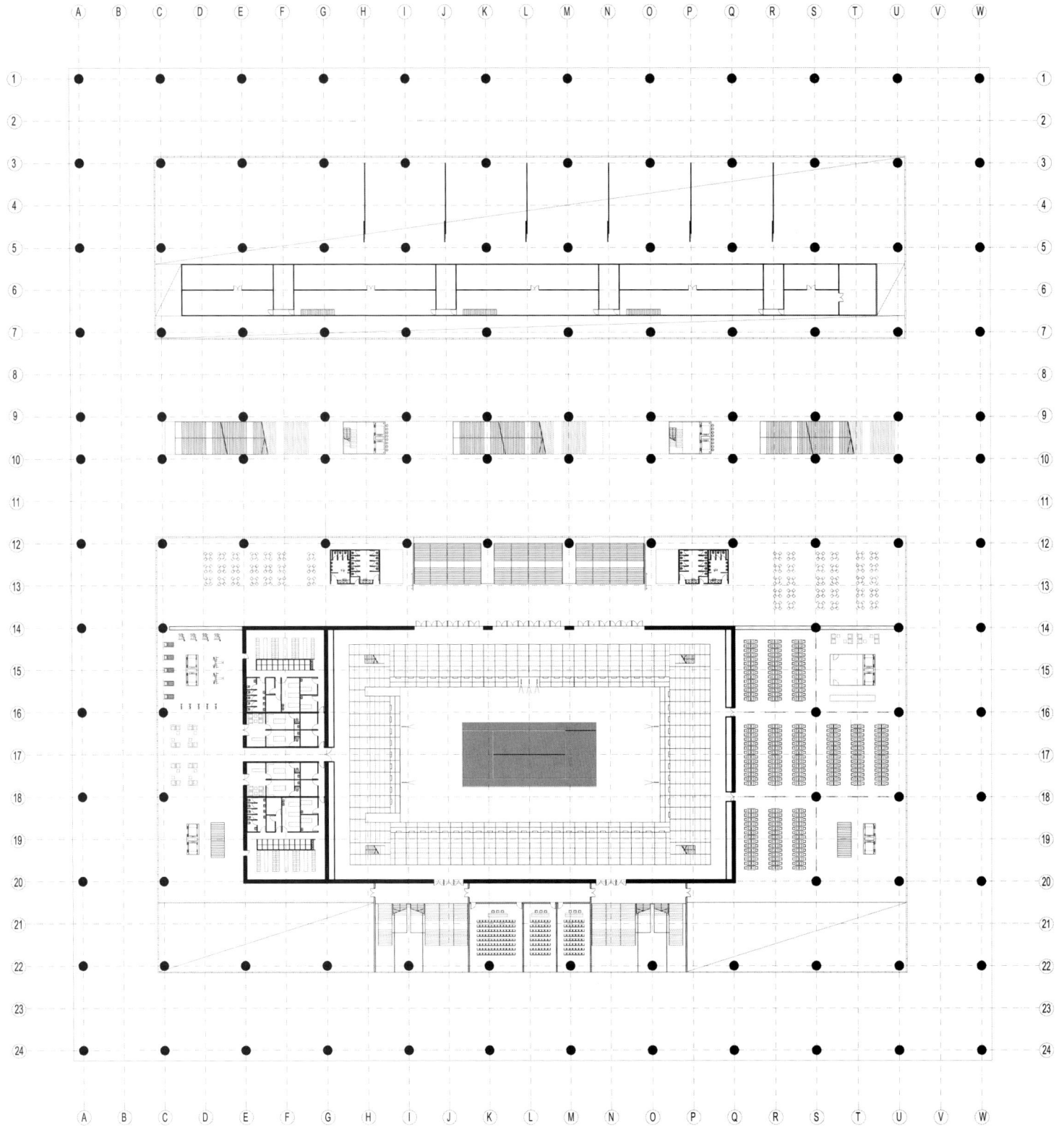

TOP ARCHITECTS OF THE WORLD

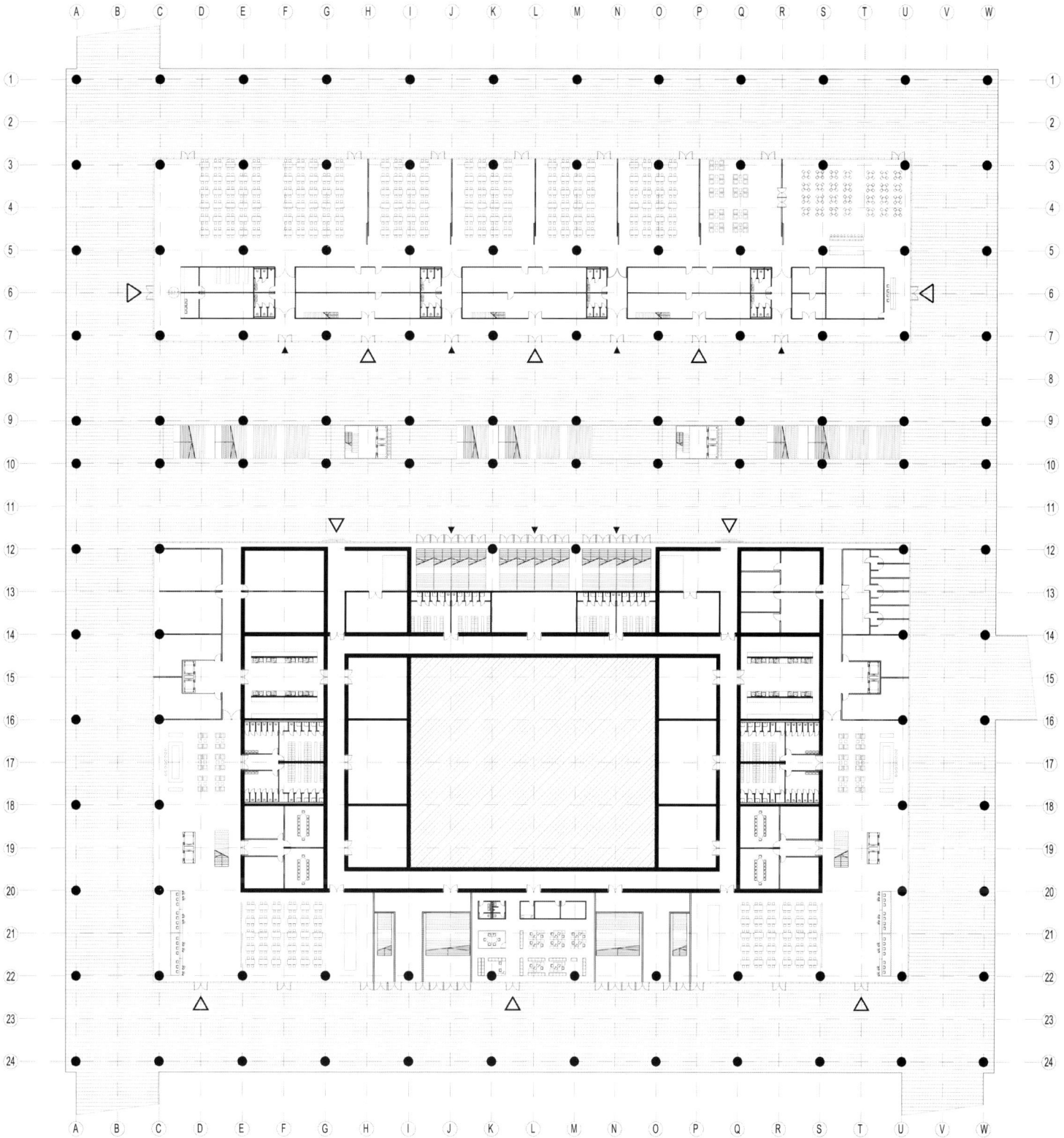

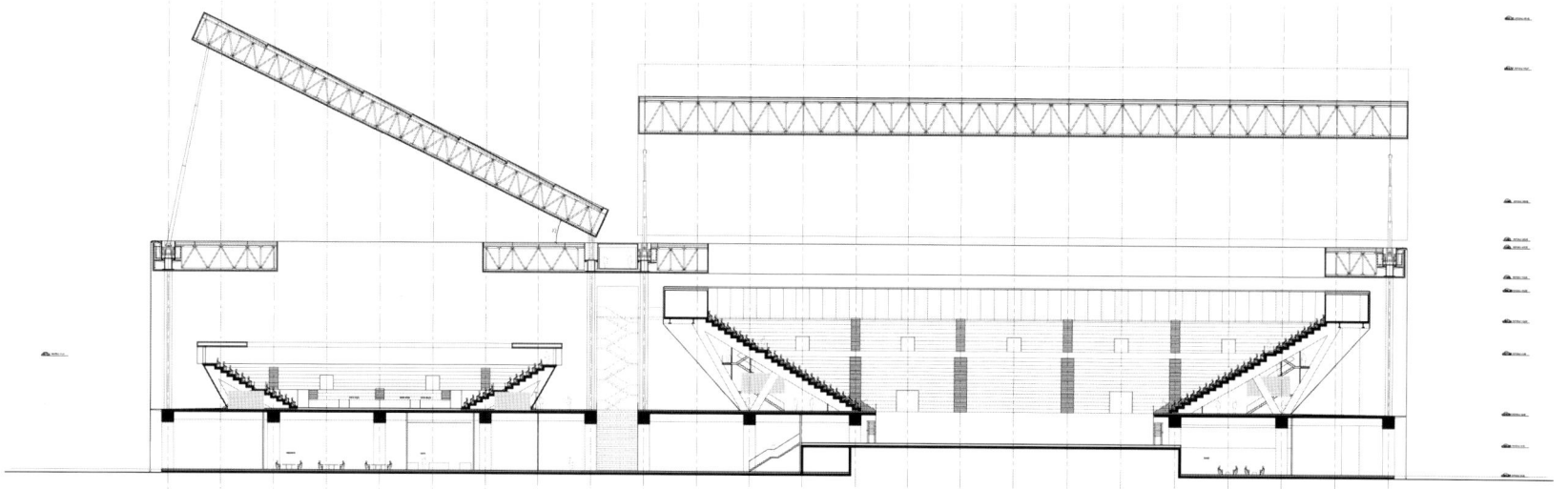

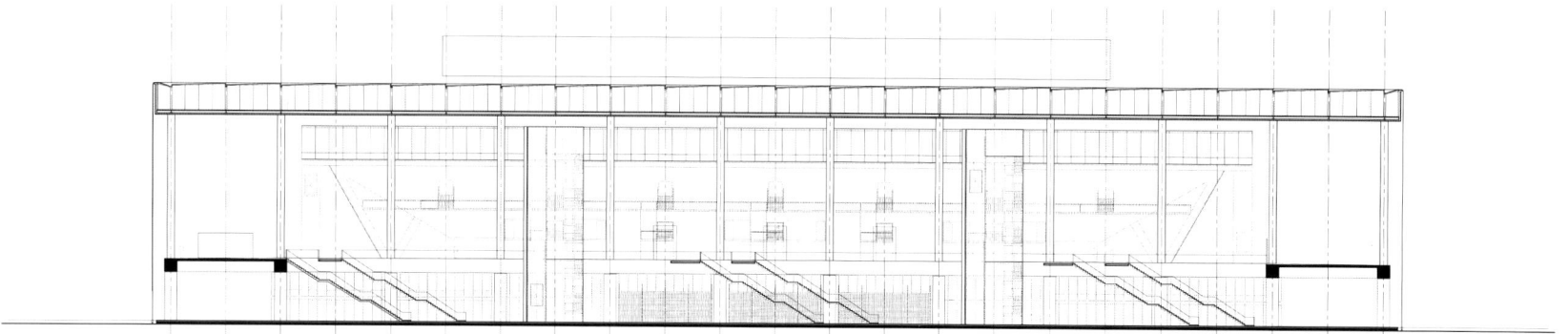

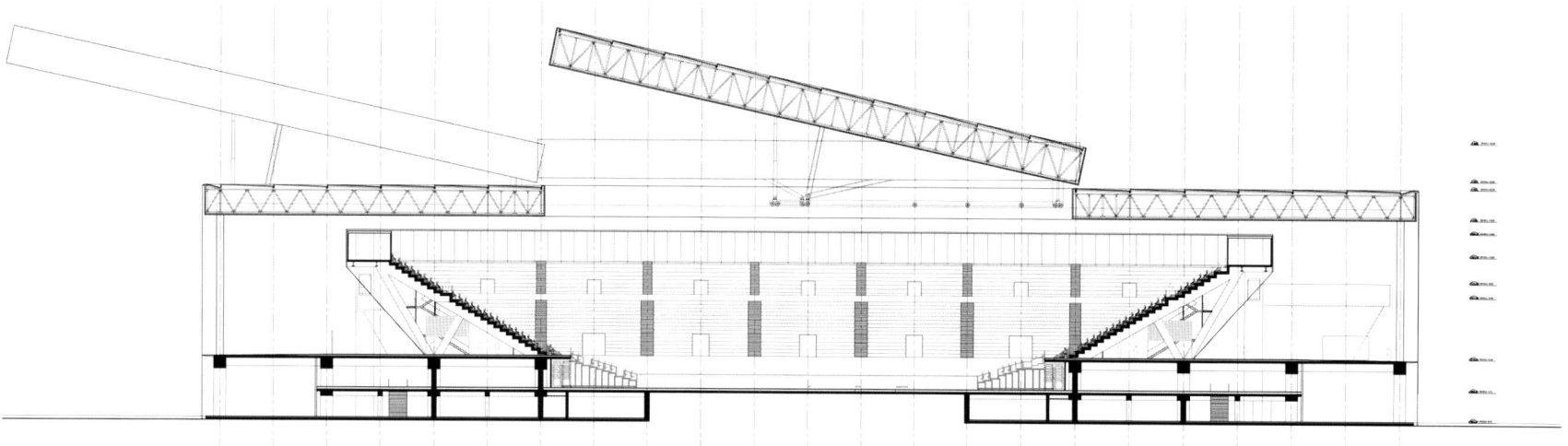

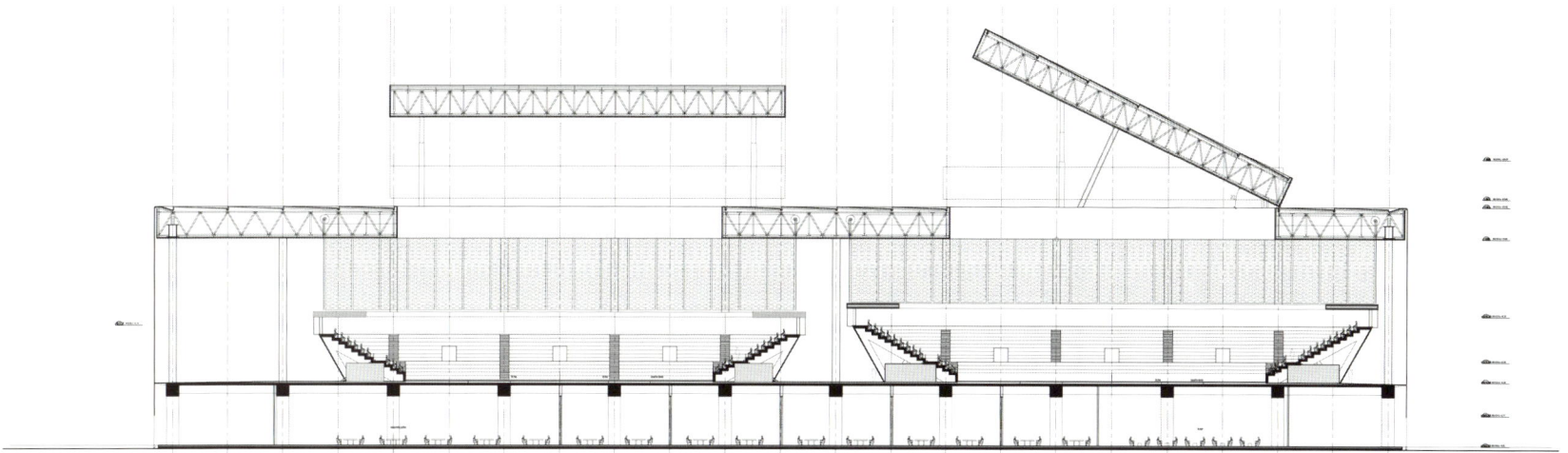

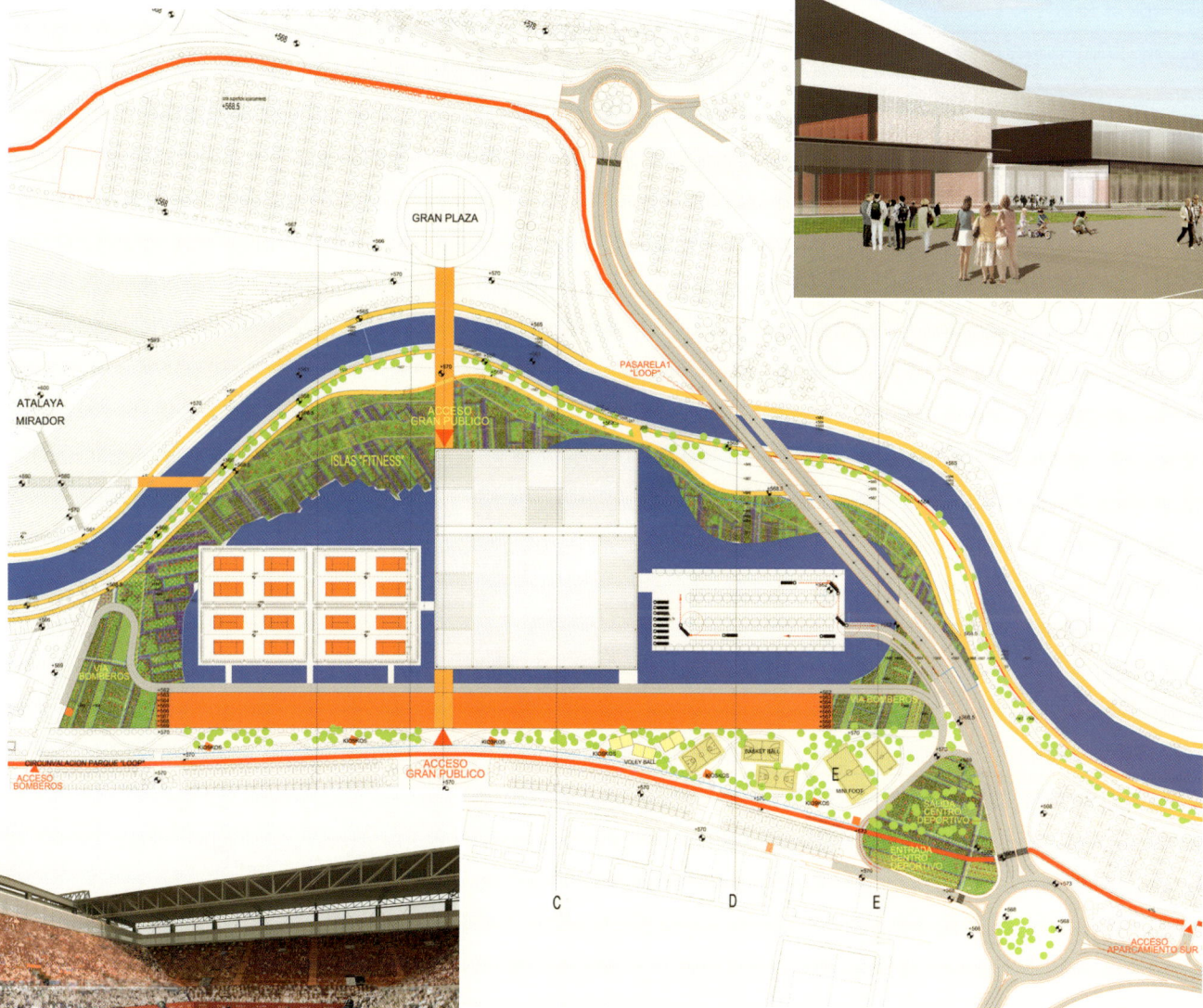

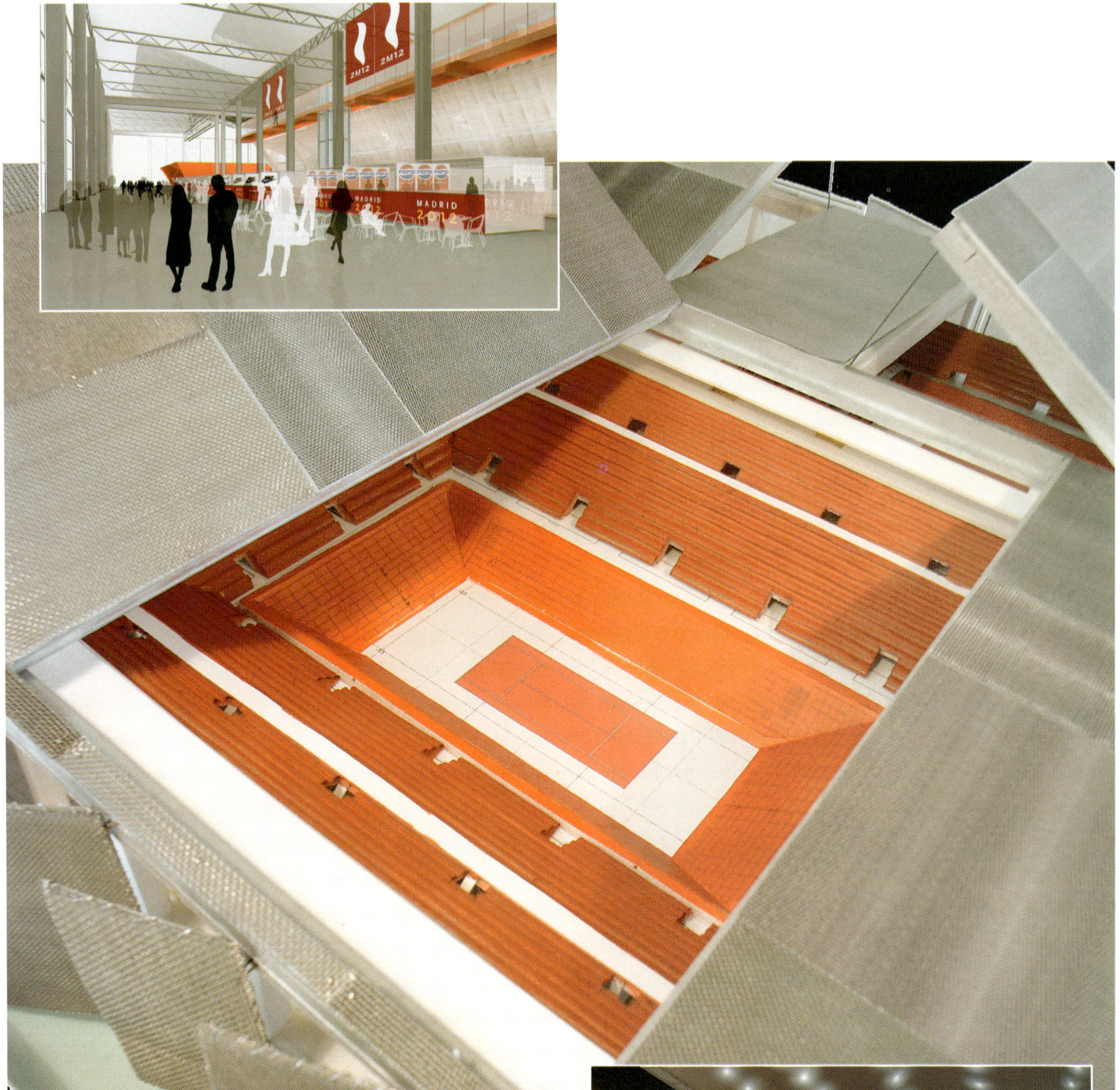

interior. The diverse fabrics that it is made up of give it a changing aspect: opaque and reflective during the day and brilliant at night.

## Superimposing Two Worlds

At the level of the artificial lake, all of the facilities and services required by sportspeople are to be installed: training centers, meeting rooms and reception areas as well as zones for the press, trainers and coaches. On the upper level, street level, the large plaza, areas for roller-skating and cycling along with the public accesses to the stadium are to be found.

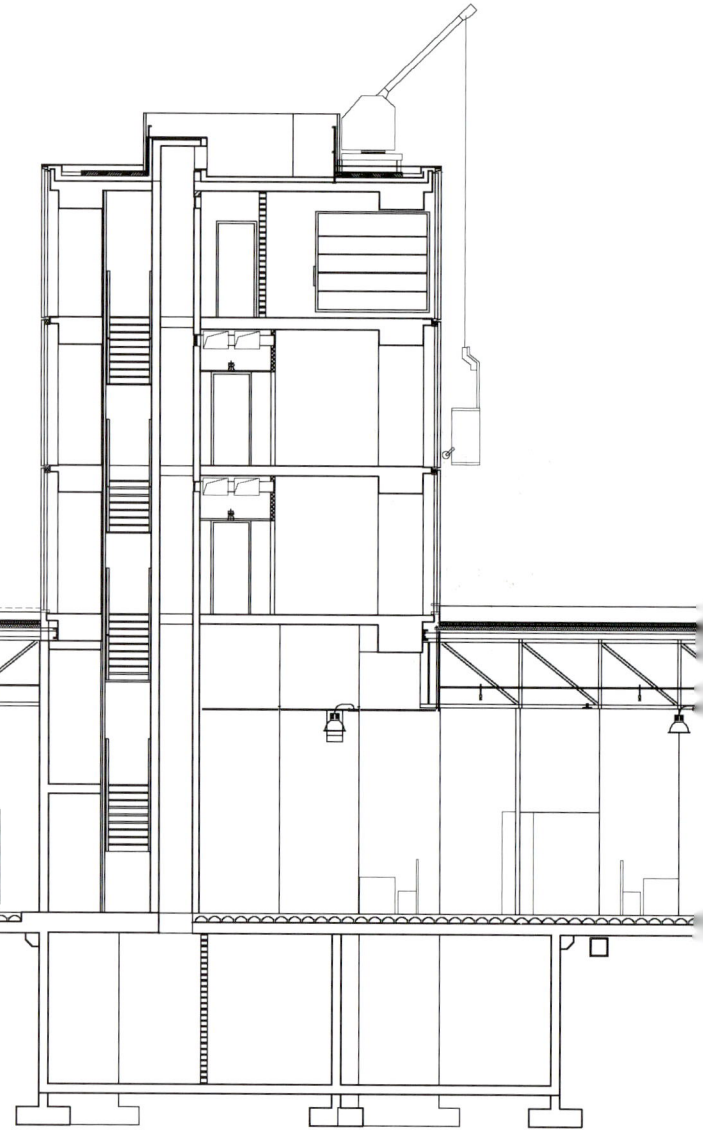

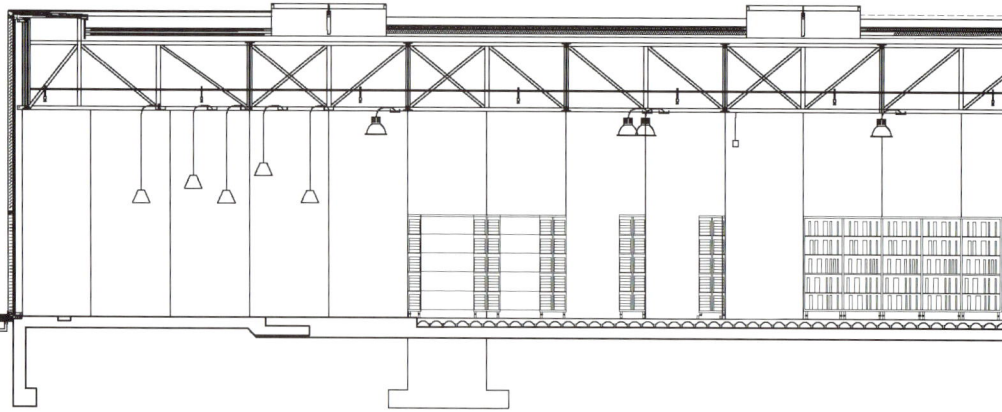

### The Central Media Library of Vénissieux
Vénissieux, France 1997-2001
The media library, of a total surface area of 4,000 m², is a 'large house': a multifunctional shelter which is open to the city and to worldwide knowledge. It is a place dedicated to the learning about different cultures and sensibilities. The proposal has been materialized in a glass box. Inside, all of the functions have been united on the same floor and surrounded by a gallery in peristyle. The

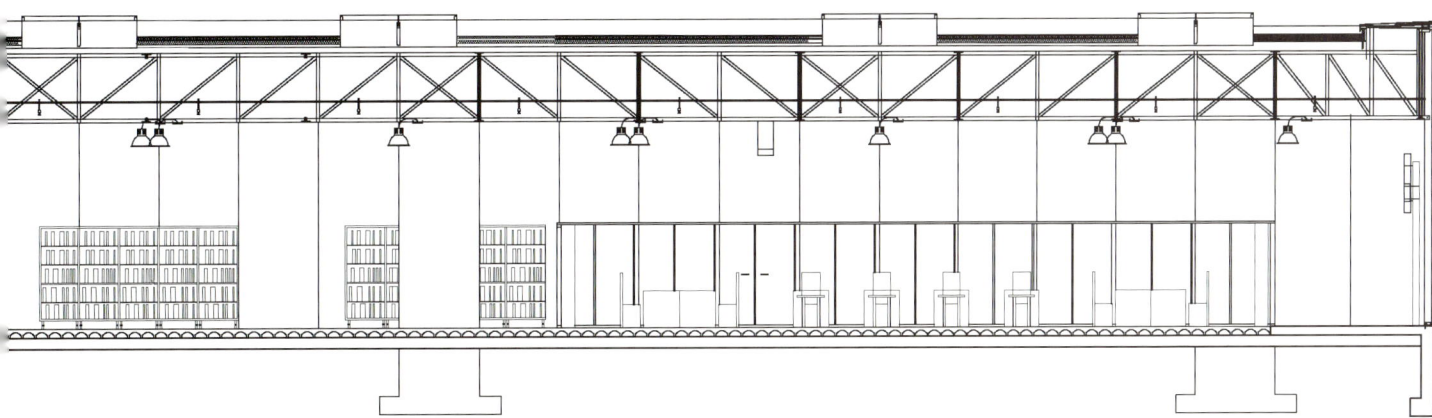

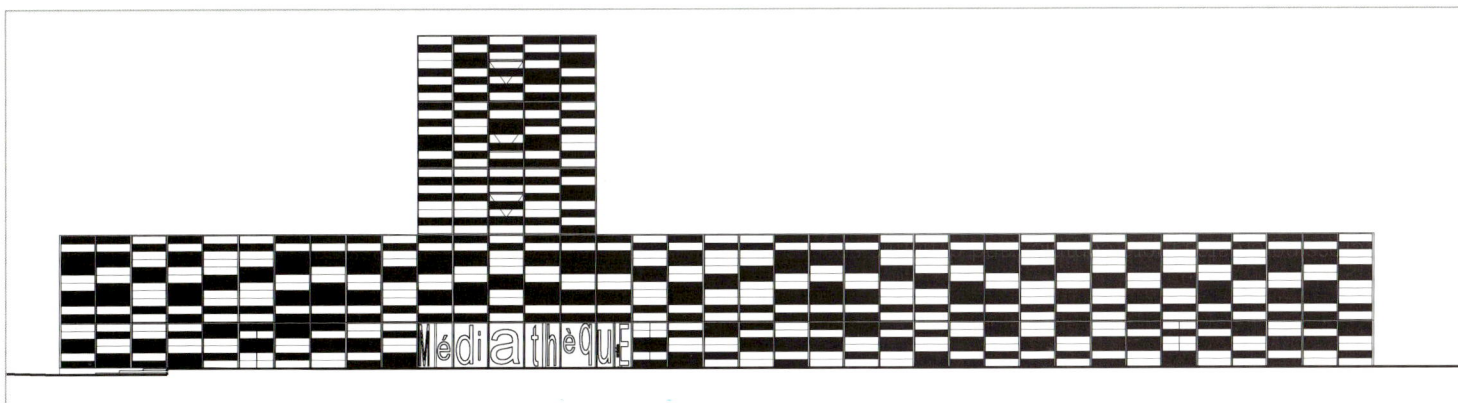

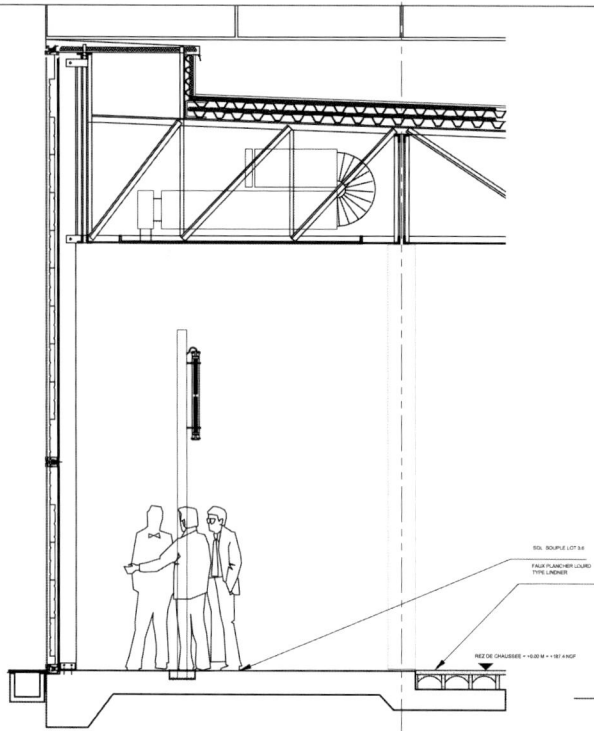

**1** COUPE DE PRINCIPE SUR LA FACADE RDC
ECH : 1/20

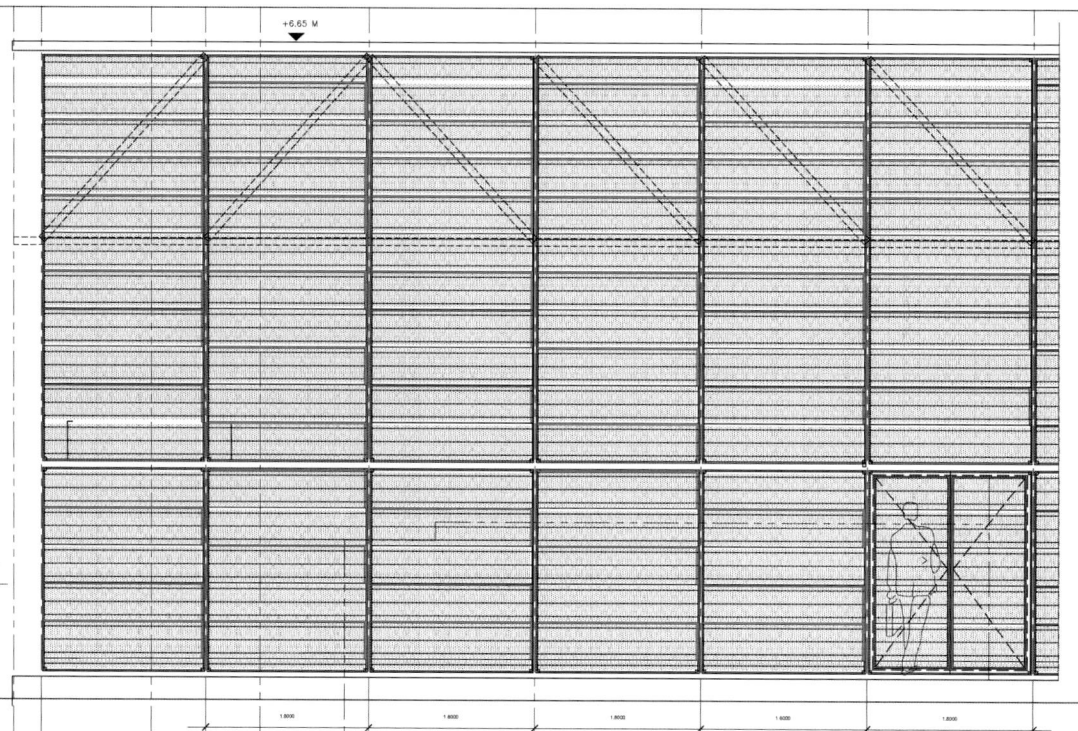

**2** ELEVATION DE LA FACADE RDC
ECH : 1/20

**3** PRINCIPE DE STRUCTURE

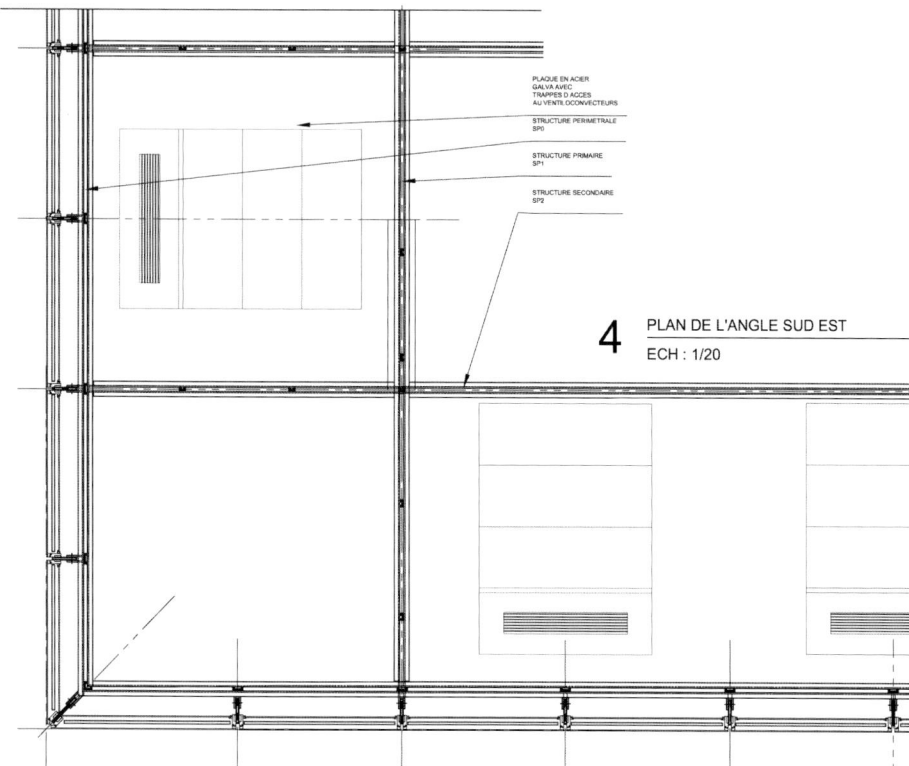

**4** PLAN DE L'ANGLE SUD EST
ECH : 1/20

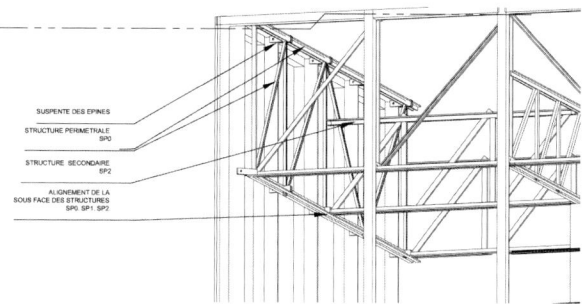

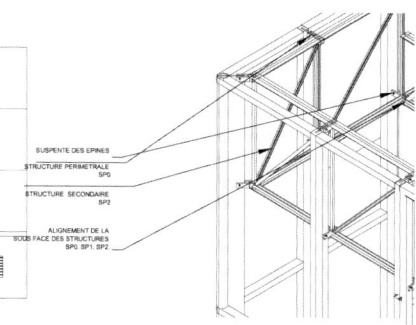

+6.65 M

PLAQUE EN ACIER
GALVA AVEC
TRAPPES D'ACCES
AU VENTS OCONVECTEURS

STRUCTURE PERIMETRALE
SP0

STRUCTURE PRIMAIRE
SP1

STRUCTURE SECONDAIRE
SP2

SUSPENTE DES EPINES
STRUCTURE PERIMETRALE
SP0
STRUCTURE SECONDAIRE
SP2
ALIGNEMENT DE LA
SOUS FACE DES STRUCTURES
SP0, SP1, SP2

SUSPENTE DES EPINES
STRUCTURE PERIMETRALE
SP0
STRUCTURE SECONDAIRE
SP2
ALIGNEMENT DE LA
SOUS FACE DES STRUCTURES
SP0, SP1, SP2

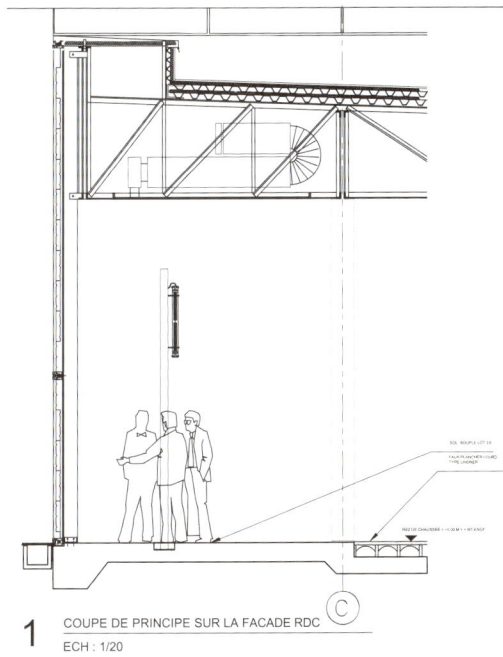

1  COUPE DE PRINCIPE SUR LA FACADE RDC ©

ECH : 1/20

# Plan Urbano Donau-City
## Viena, Austria

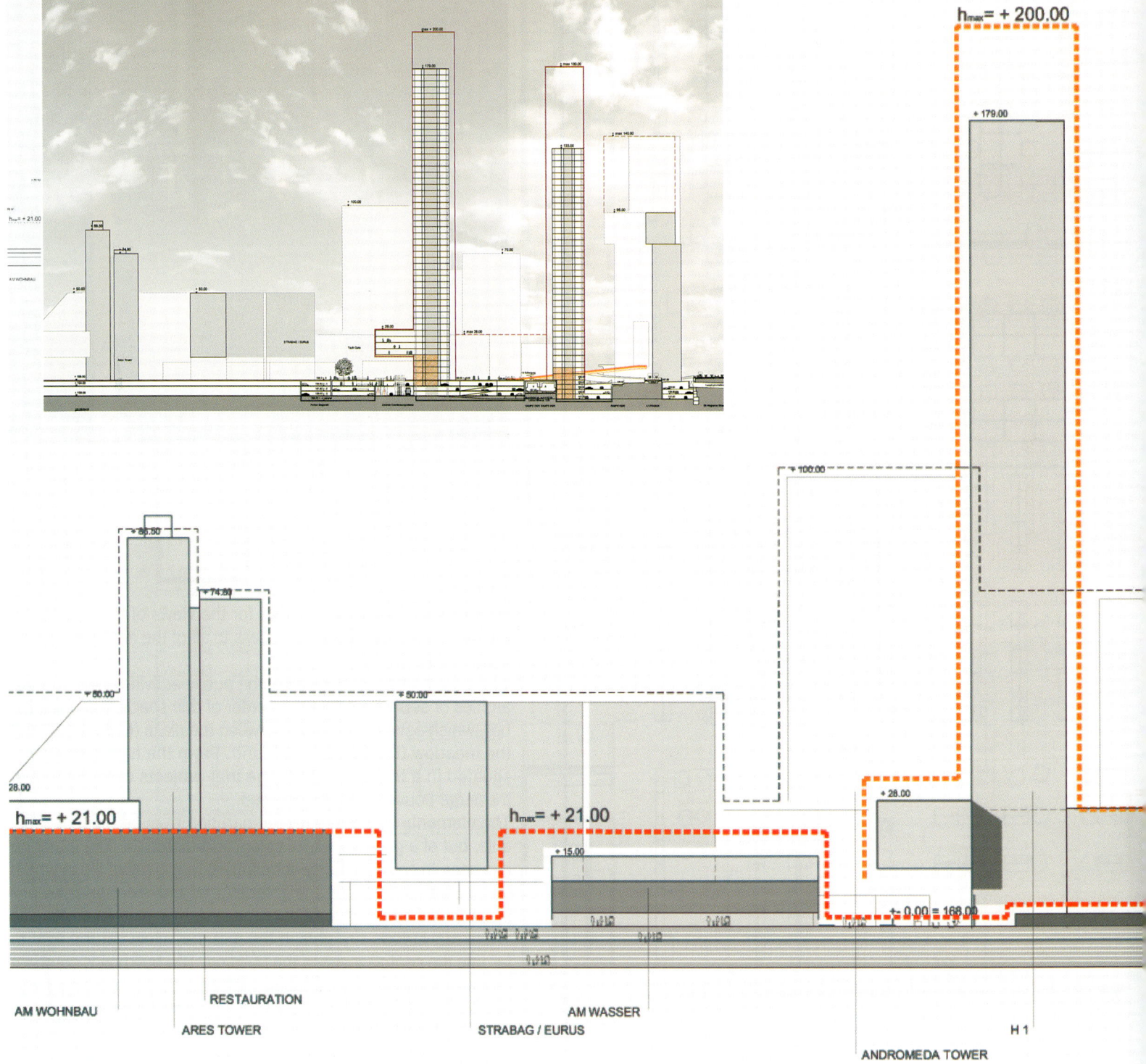

$h_{max} = + 200.00$

$h_{max} = + 21.00$

$h_{max} = + 21.00$

AM WOHNBAU

RESTAURATION

ARES TOWER

AM WASSER

STRABAG / EURUS

ANDROMEDA TOWER

H 1

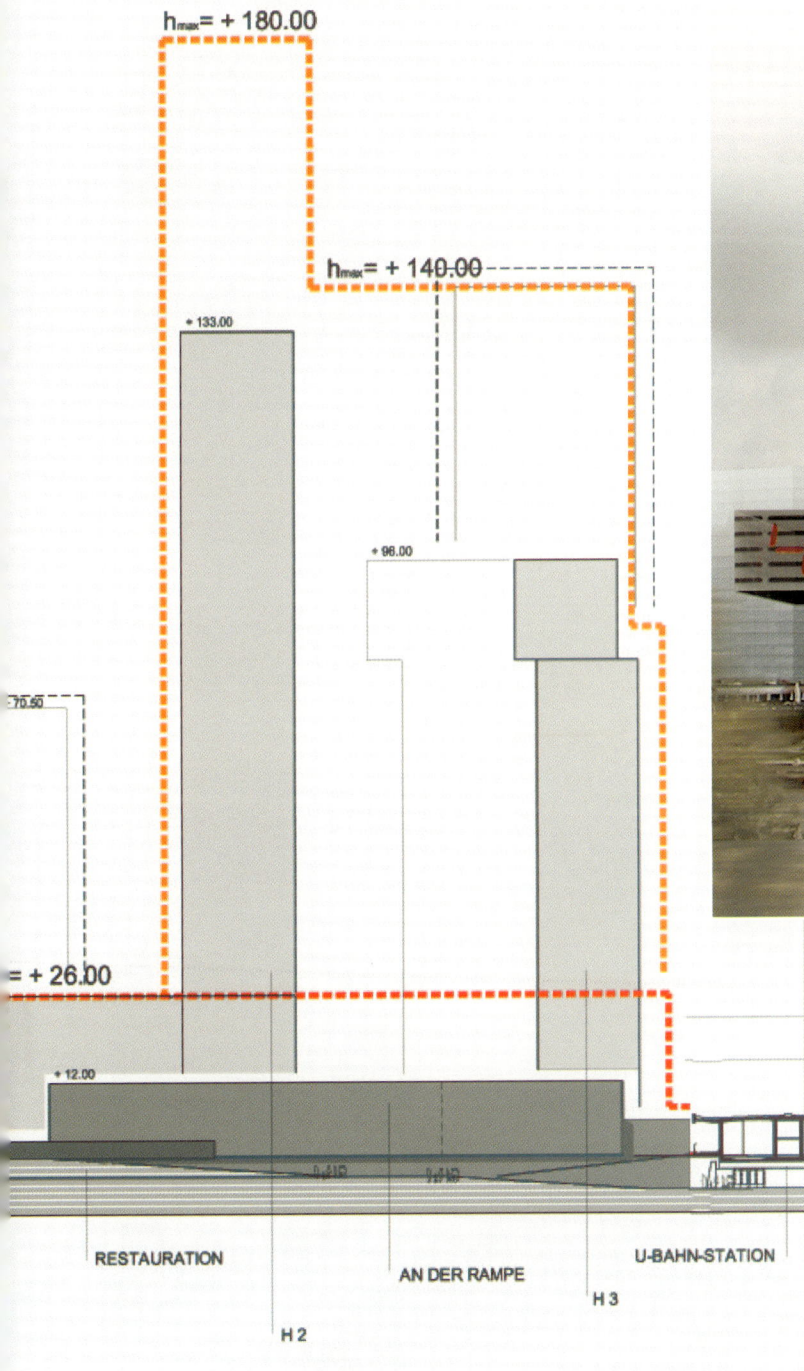

h_max= + 180.00

h_max= + 140.00

+ 133.00

+ 96.00

76.50

= + 26.00

+ 12.00

RESTAURATION

AN DER RAMPE

U-BAHN-STATION

H 3

H 2

## Masterplan Vienna Donau City

Vienna, Austria 2004-2008

This urban plan for the Donau City of Vienna, Austria, along side the Danube River, won the international competition in 2002. The proposal consists of a scheme for offices, residences, hotels, retail and cultural buildings, restaurants and parking facilities distributed over a total surface area of 750,000 m² constructed

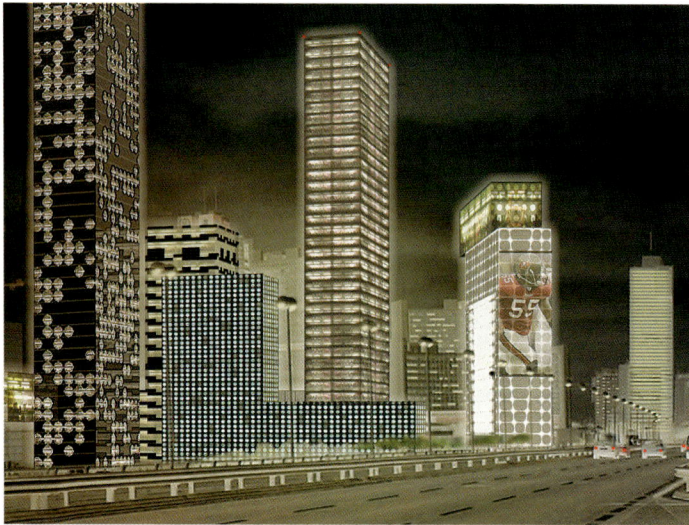

on a 160,000 m² plot. The plan proposes the construction of a new district of a futuristic aspect made up of a series of slender skyscrapers that will transform the Vienna skyline. The proposal will modernize the international image of the city.

# Opera House Mariinsky II

*Saint Petersburg, Russia 2003-2009*

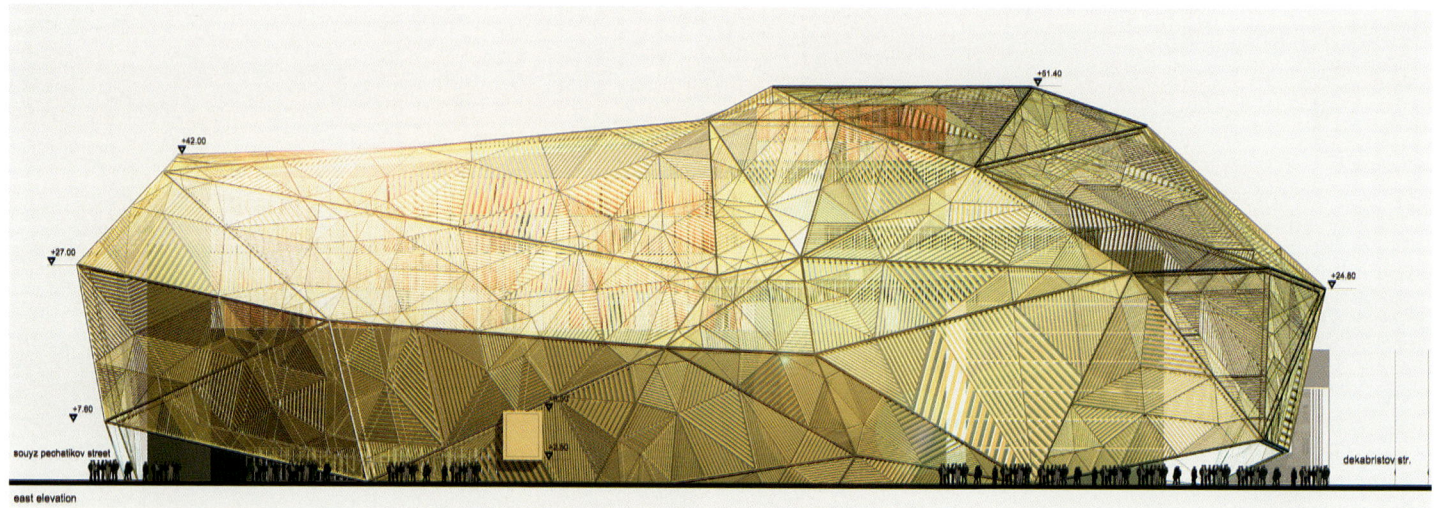

east elevation

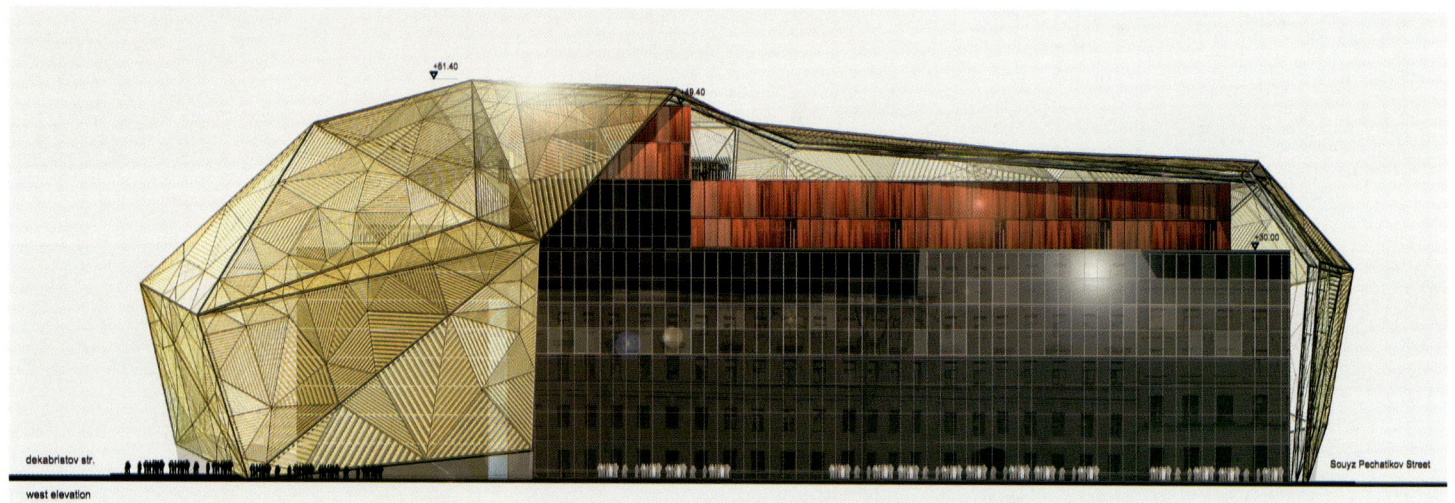

west elevation

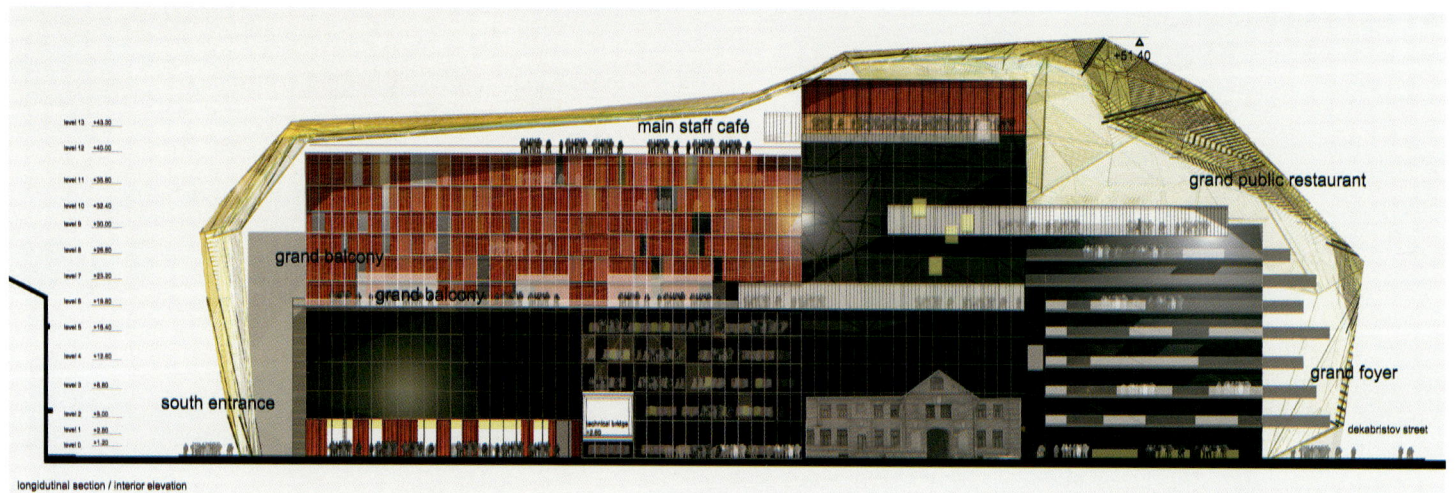

main staff café

grand public restaurant

grand balcony

grand balcony

grand foyer

south entrance

dekabristov street

longidutinal section / interior elevation

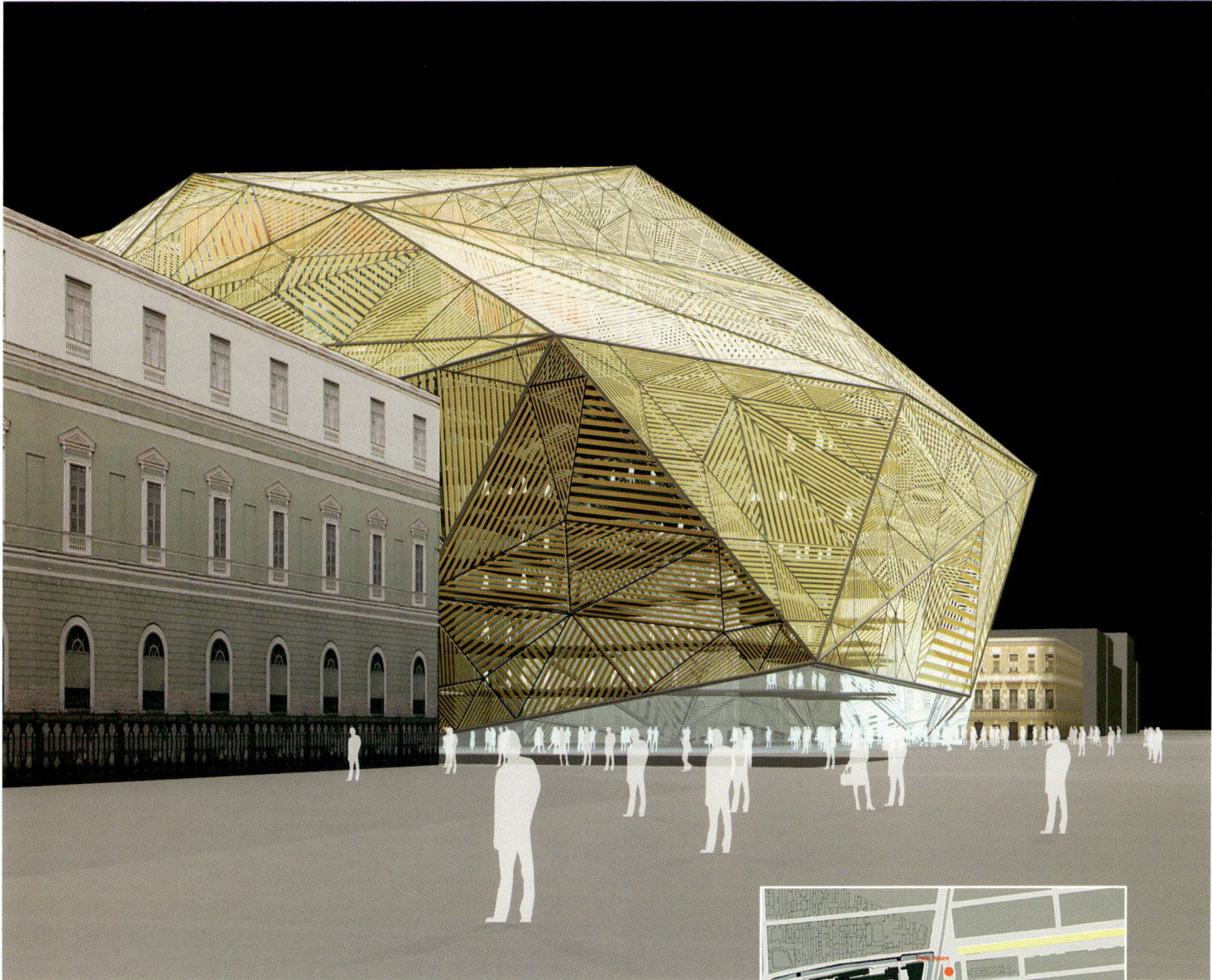

## Opera House Mariinsky II
Saint Petersburg, Russia 2003-2009

This proposal for the new Opera House in Saint Petersburg alongside the historic Mariinsky Theatre turned out to be the winner of the international competition carried out in 2003. The scheme consists of a large opera hall with a seating capacity for 2,000 people equipped with the corresponding services (changing rooms, scenery towers, rehearsal rooms, offices), a small auditorium with a capacity for 350 people, a large entrance hall,

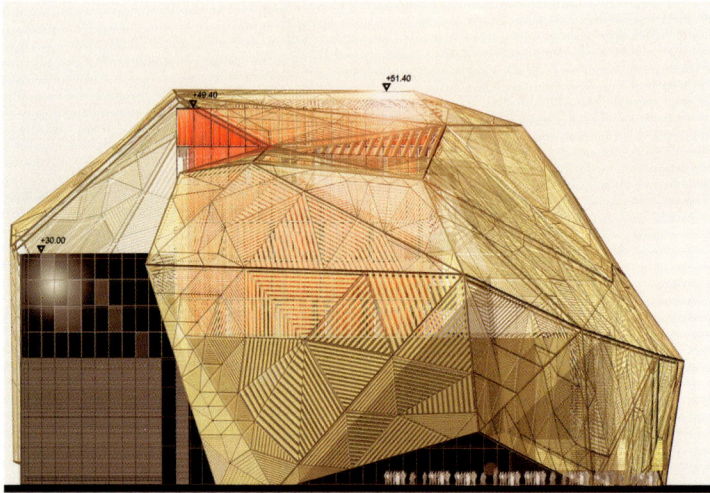

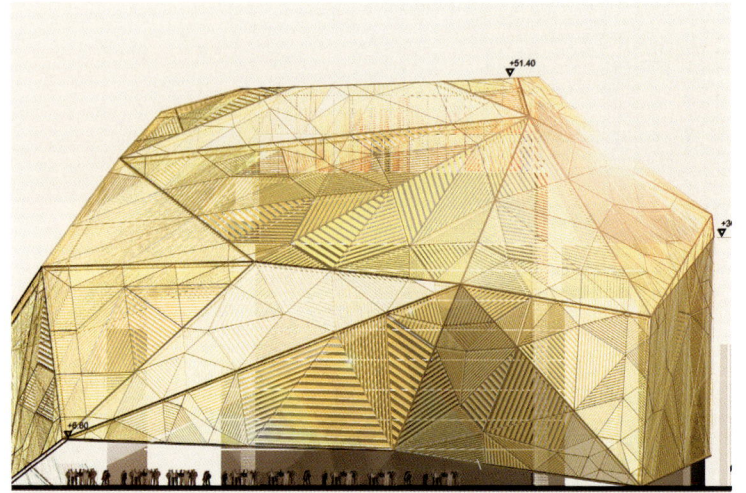

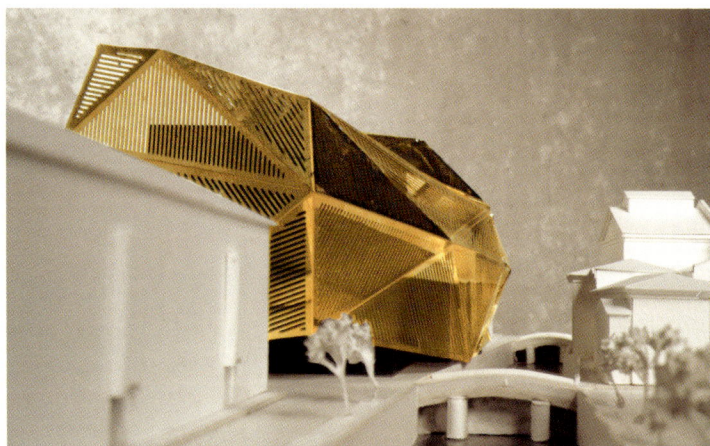

a foyer, an exhibition room, restaurants, offices and parking facilities. The project unites tradition, the forms of Saint Petersburg and its golden domes, with modernity. The relationship of the new theatre with the historic surroundings has been resolved by means of a large golden casing, a mesh that gives the building great mystery and interest.

Between the casing and the interior volume of the Opera House, a series of public foyers are found in which restaurants, stores, cafés and other services are situated. A series of balconies and lookout areas have been set at various heights in these large spaces. These elements visually connect these public areas with the activities of the theatre.

From behind the 'golden mask', a powerful volume of black marble, the Opera House, is entered. The main room has been presented as a dramatic space in black and intense red. Behind this, there are all of the spaces that serve it organized in such a way so as to optimize its efficiency and functionality.

The project foresees a telescopic bridge over the Kryukov Canal that will unite the new Opera House and the historic Marriinsky Theatre by connecting the foyers of both buildings.

# Zaha Hadid

**W**as born in Bagdad in 1950. She studied at the Architectural Association in London where she obtained her Diploma in Architecture with Merit in 1977. Later, she collaborated with the OMA, Rem Koolhaas and Elia Zenghelis' Office of Metropolitan Architecture, for a number of years.

**Hadid** also started her teaching activity at the AA in London. This aspect of her activity is something that she has not abandoned. She has taught at universities all over the world among which Columbia, Harvard (Kenzo Tange Chair, 1994), the University of Chicago (Sullivan Chair), the Hoschschule in Hamburg and the Knolton School of Architecture stand out. She presently teaches at the University of Applied Arts of Vienna and in Yale University, Connecticut.

In 1979, she opened her own architectural studio. She participated in various competitions, in some of which, for example her project for the Peak Club in Hong Kong (1983), her proposal for the Office Building in Berlin (1986), her Art and Media center in Dusseldolf (1989) and the Cardiff Bay Opera House (1994), she won first prize. Her drawings, perspectives that synthesize the

Rosenthal Center of Contemporary Art

Multimodal Stop at the North Terminus, Hoenheim

MAXXI: National Center of Contemporary Art

Phaeno Science Center Wolfsburg

Central Building – BMW Plant

complexity of her buildings with great expressiveness, represent a central instrument of investigation in her design process. They soon obtained considerable recognition and have been exhibited in the AA (1983) in London, in the Guggenheim Museum in New York (1978), in the MOMA and in the Central Station in New York (1995) and in the GA Gallery in Tokyo. In 1988, she received the commission for the Fire Station for the furniture company Vitra en Weil an Rhein (1991-93). This forceful building with aggressive aesthetics and shape angles is representative of her early period in which she worked the concept of plates and layers. The restaurant Monsoon in Sapporo (1990), the residential building IBA in Berlin and the series of temporary installations and exhibitions, such as the pavilion for the magazine Blueprint (1995), the Music Pavilion in Groningen, the pavilion for the Serpentine Gallery (2000), or the Meshworks installations in the Villa Medicci in Rome also date from this period.

In 1999, she constructed the LF One en Weil am Rhein, a space for exhibitions and activities for the Garden Festival. This same year, as a result of certain international competitions, she received some important commissions: the Rosenthal Center for Contemporary Art in Cincinnati, Bergisel Ski Jump in Innsbruck,

The Sea Ferry Terminal in Salerno, the Contemporary Art Museum in Rome and the Car Park and Terminus HoenheimNorth, in Strasbourg. For this last project, in which the boundaries between natural and artificial almost disappear, **Zaha Hadid** received the Mies van der Rohe Prize for European Architecture in 2003.

Over the last few years, she has been commissioned to undertake a large number of large-scale projects in Europe, America and Asia. Some of those that stand out are the National Library of Quebec, the Science Center in Wolfsburg, the Guggenheim Museum in Taichung, the Masterplans for Zorrozaurre in Bilbao, Soho City in Beijing, Science Hub in Singapore, her project for BMW in Leipzig and the Guangzhou Opera, China.

**Zaha Hadid** has participated in numerous exhibitions and conferences. She is an Honorary Member of Bund Deutches Architekten (1998), of the American Academy of Arts and Letters (2000), a Fellow of the American Institute of Architects (2000), and Commander of the British Empire (2002). For her intense and courageous career, **Hadid** received the **Pritzker Prize in 2004**. She is the first woman to have received this award.

# The Rosenthal Center of Contemporary Art

Cincinnati, USA 1997-2003

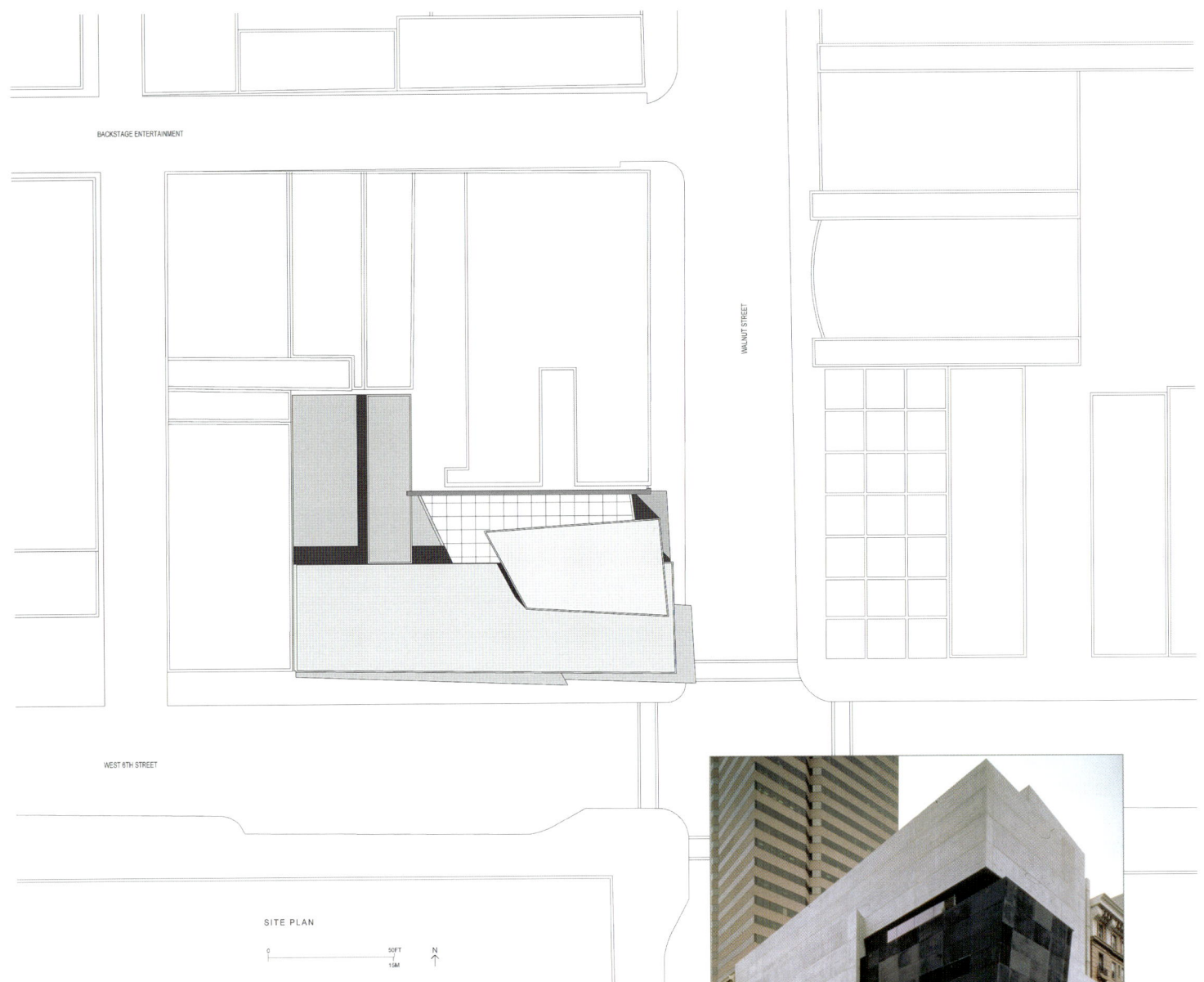

BACKSTAGE ENTERTAINMENT

WALNUT STREET

WEST 6TH STREET

SITE PLAN

0    50FT
     15M    N

The architect **Zaha Hadid** is presently one of the most successful professionals working with the concept of architecture being a field of flows and forces with which artificial landscapes can be created. Many of her works can be understood as what she refers to as 'manipulations of the ground' in which factors of all natures (programmatic, urban flows, special investigation) touch upon the theme of how to produce complex deformations in surfaces and seek the greatest dynamism in terms of spatial itineraries. It is, to sum up, a form of architecture that incites the movement of the visitor-user through itself.

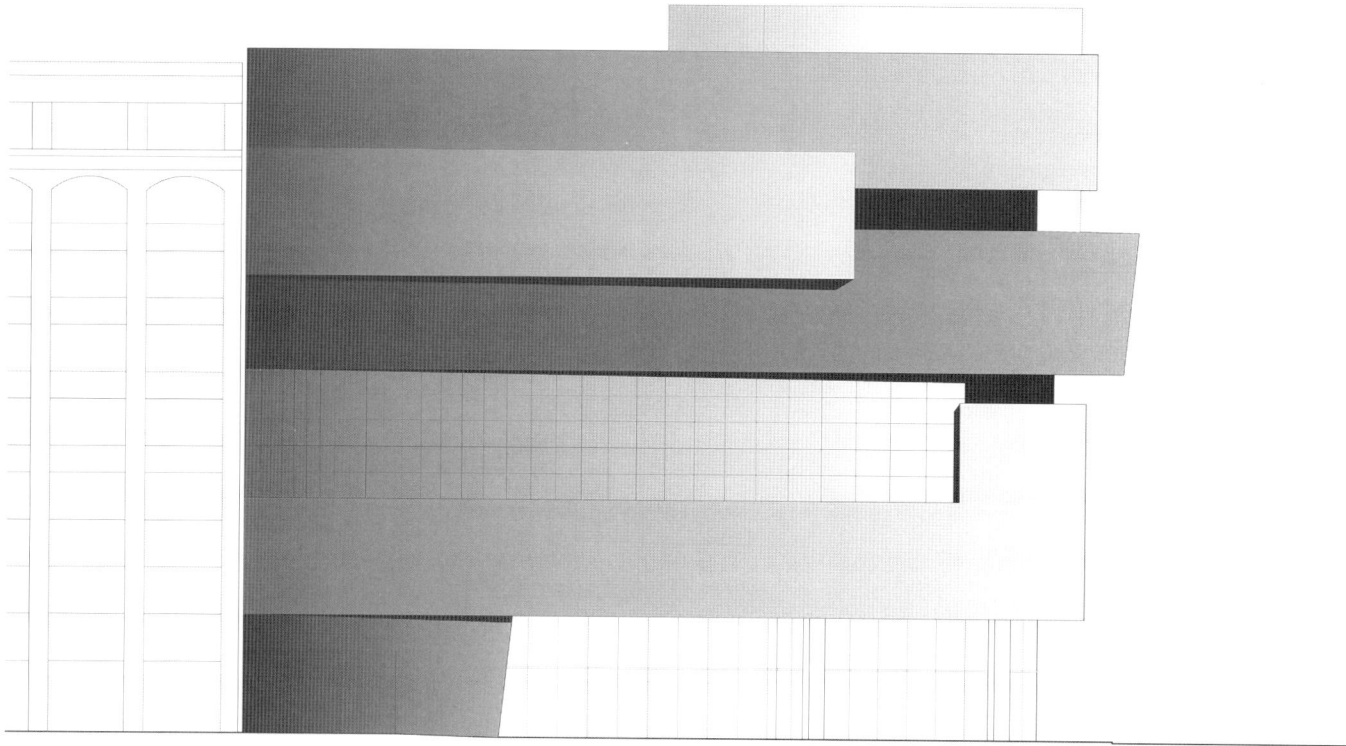

Zaha Hadid has developed a professional career marked by coherence and tenacity. She is a pioneer in the way in which she produces architecture. It is close to the fluid but powerful forms of Eero Saarinen. For many years, her proposals, full of dynamism and expressiveness, were considered to be too audacious to be constructed. As a result, in her beginnings she was endlessly presenting proposals for competitions, in which she obtained a number of first prizes, but hardly constructing anything. In 1994, she won the competition for the Cardiff Opera House, but Norman Foster was finally commissioned to carry out the project.

From the beginning of her professional career, Zaha Hadid has been a 'cult' architect and has presented exhibitions of her projects and drawings all over the world. She soon acquired great recognition and exhibited at the AA in London (1983). She has also exhibited in the Guggenheim Museum in New York (1978), in the MOMA, in Central Station, New York (1995) and in the GA Gallery, Tokyo. Her drawings and paintings have always represented a central instrument for investigation in her design process. They synthesize the complexity of her buildings with great expressiveness: "Three-dimensional representation additionally demands deformations and distortions. Not only is the floor plan a prominent aspect, but the section is also decisive and should be developed at the same time," says Hadid. To begin with, her proposals stood out because of their spatial dynamism and their expressionistic and angular forms. At the time, the critics were inclined to place her within the architectural tendency of the deconstruction, although according to Hadid: "I have never fully understood all of this about deconstruction. For me, it all consisted of adapting myself to historic and postmodern architecture."

In 1993, Zaha Hadid, constructed a fire station for the furniture company Vitra en Weil am Rhien. This forceful building with aggressive aesthetics and shape angles is representative of

her early period in which she worked the concept of plates and layers. She has developed her architecture toward spaces of greater fluidity, without spatial interior-exterior barriers, and has managed to construct markedly urban buildings in which the route of the visitor-user is not interrupted upon arrival at a 'fortress-monument'. According to **Zaha Hadid**: "The first works were much more shamelessly aggressive… Later, it was those hidden spaces which came to be more important than those which were more evident (…) The discussion moved on from the plan or volume to the spatial."

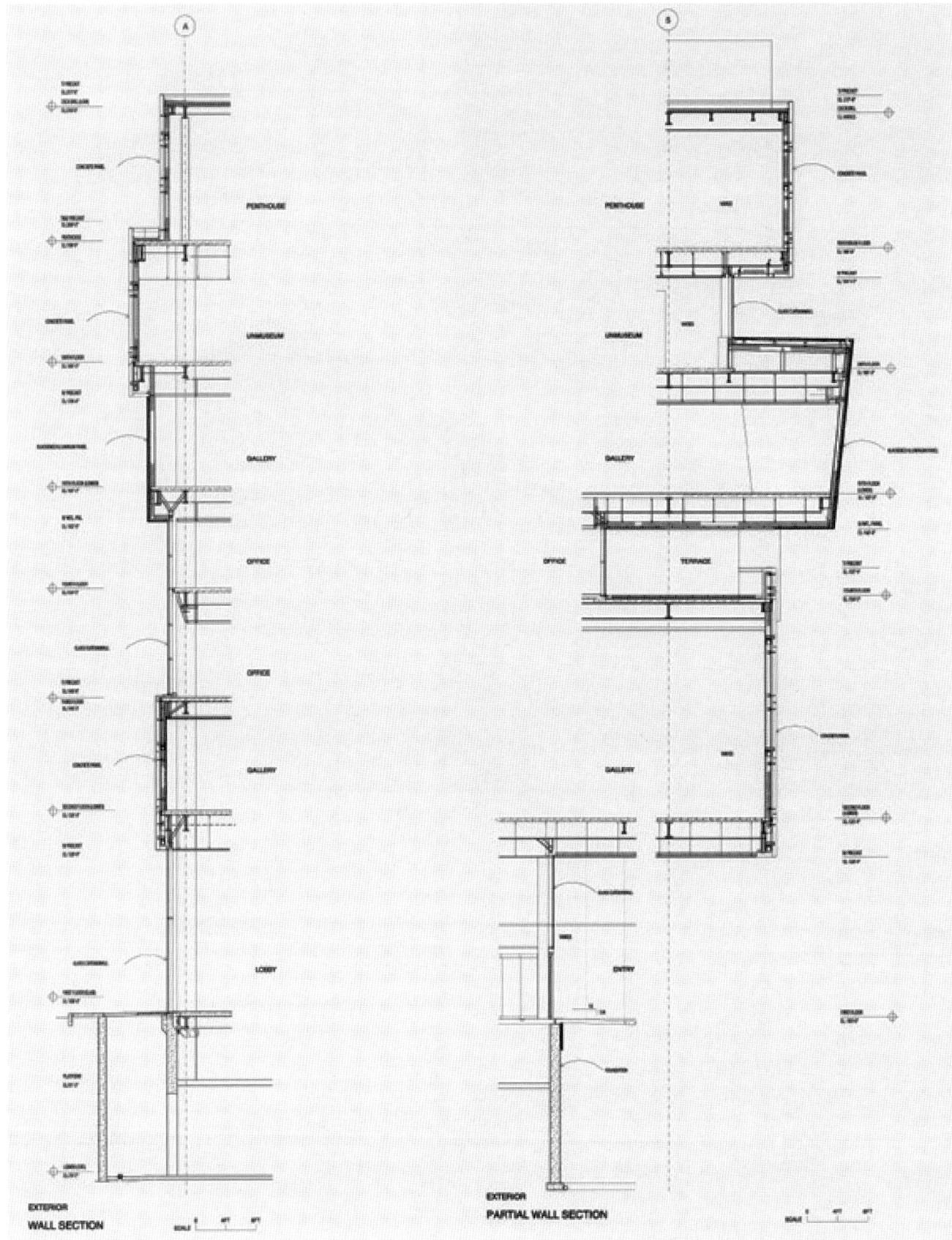

EXTERIOR
WALL SECTION

EXTERIOR
PARTIAL WALL SECTION

R FOR CONTEMPORARY ART

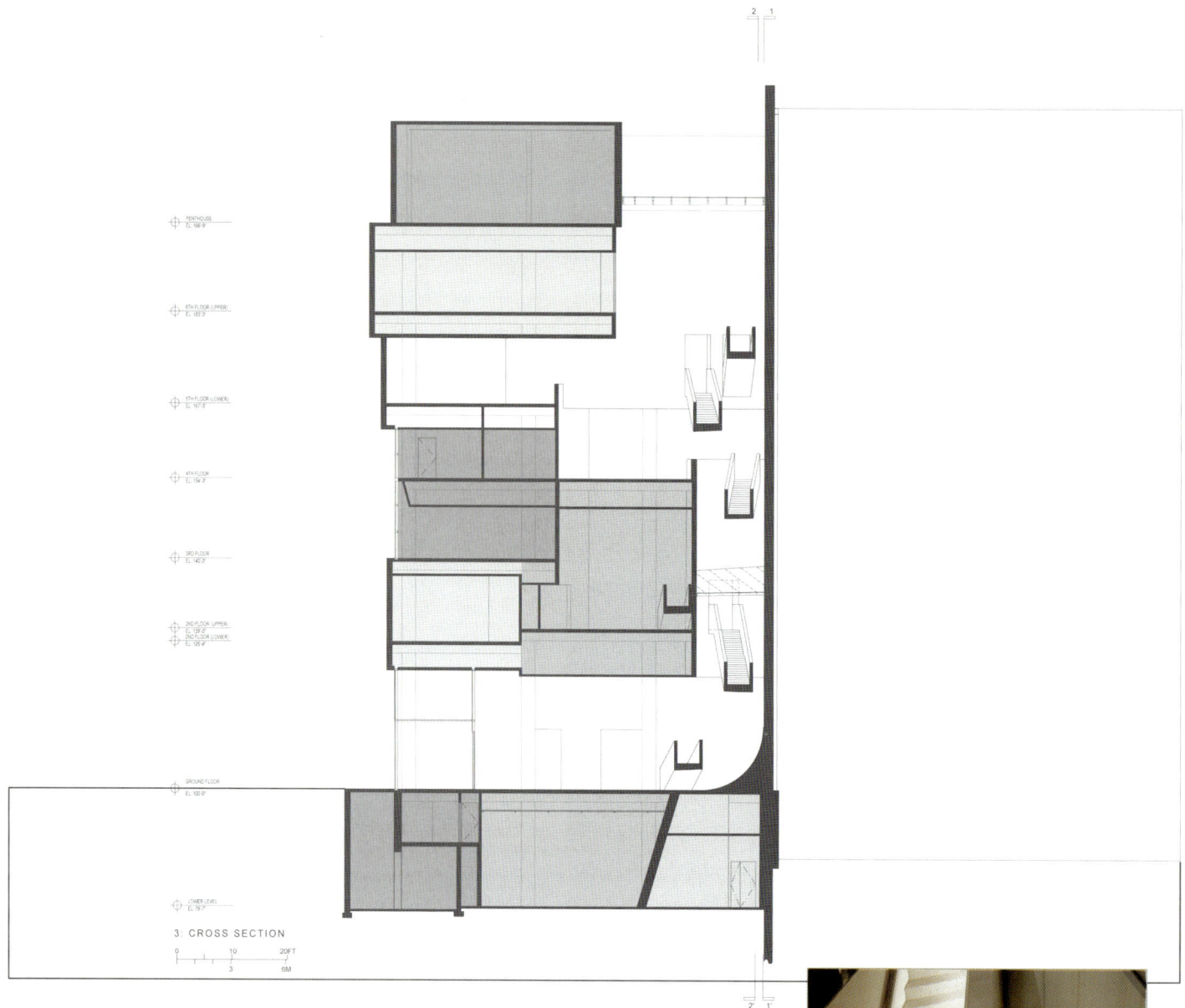

3: CROSS SECTION

0      10     20FT
     3     6M

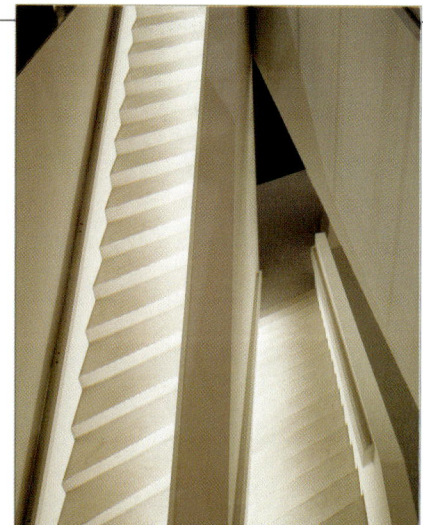

In 1999, she constructed the LF One en Weil am Rhine. This is a space that was created to accommodate exhibitions and activities for the Garden Festival. Conceptually, the building looks like an overlapping of three pedestrian pathways that materialize by emerging from the ground and interlacing one with the other:

> "The connections and adjacencies that this creates, or the different layers of people who cross each other's paths are all different experiences of the building that confirms some of my intuition about a possibly public space".

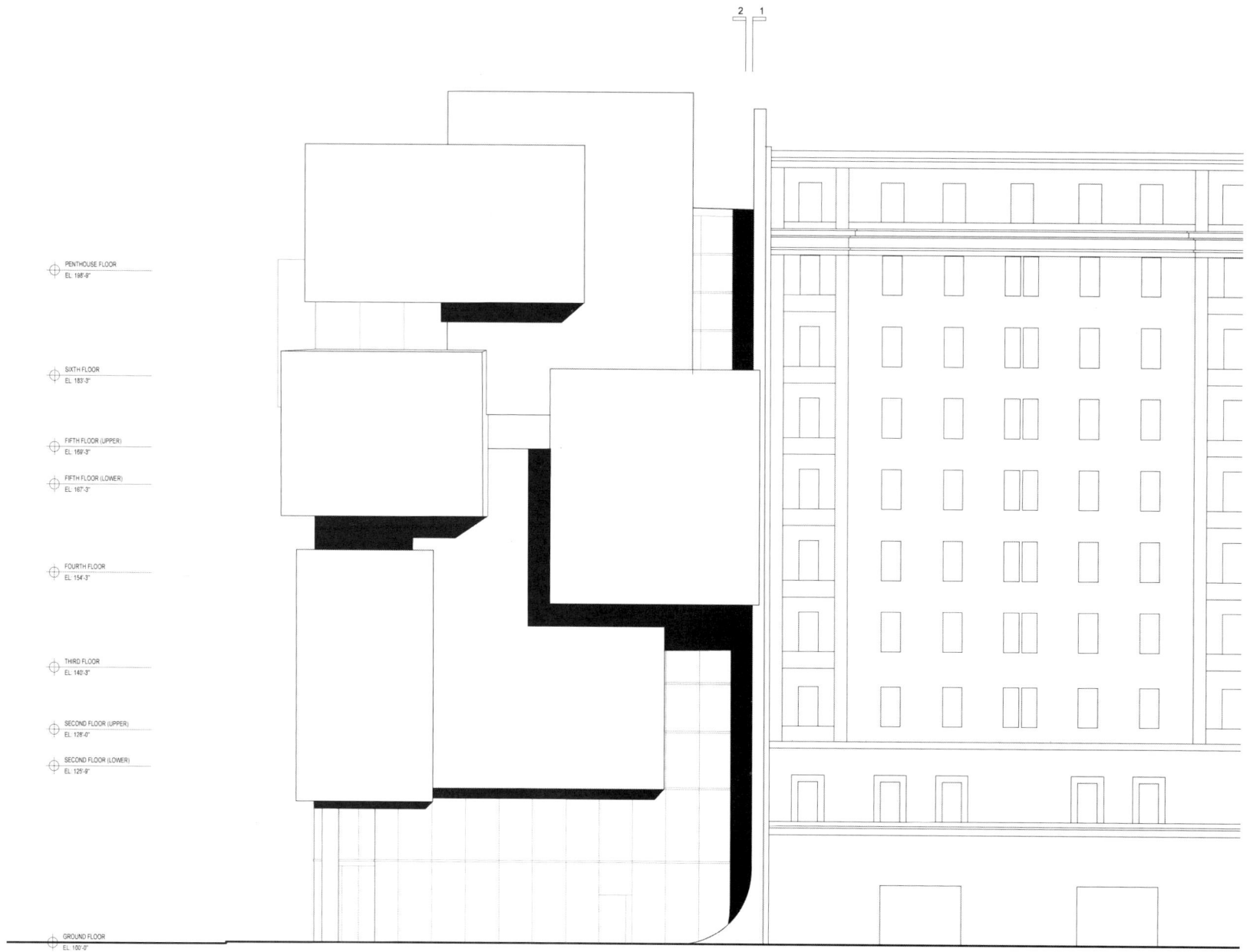

PENTHOUSE FLOOR
EL 185'-9"

SIXTH FLOOR
EL 183'-3"

FIFTH FLOOR (UPPER)
EL 169'-3"

FIFTH FLOOR (LOWER)
EL 167'-3"

FOURTH FLOOR
EL 154'-3"

THIRD FLOOR
EL 142'-3"

SECOND FLOOR (UPPER)
EL 128'-0"

SECOND FLOOR (LOWER)
EL 125'-9"

GROUND FLOOR
EL 100'-0"

**EAST ELEVATION**

0        10        20FT
3        6M

This intercrossing creates more complex and dynamic spaces. She continues to develop the idea of the building as a public urban space in all of her later works. Following the success of the buildings constructed by Zaha Hadid Architects in the 1990's, the rhythm of commissions, mostly obtained through competitions, incremented at a considerable rate. Those that stand out from recent years are her projects for the National Library of Quebec and a project for a Science Center in Wolfs-

TOP ARCHITECTS OF THE WORLD

burg, Germany. Both projects deepen into the concept of architectural landscapes and are inspired in the natural topography of the sites and, even, in the geology. In these, the concept of spatial progression is developed as multiple dynamic routes or pathways that are offered from every point of the building. Looking at Zaha Hadid's work, we get the feeling that her proposals and investigations are way ahead of any criticism or intellectualism of her work. This tends to fall short of the enjoyment obtained from the powerful living experience of her buildings. Hadid wrote: "The intention is not only to question the way in which people use space –their way of life or the form in which they work– but also to provide a feeling of wellbeing. I believe that at times, we lose sight of the question, 'What does all this lead too?' The truly primordial consists of adding something to our lives."

TOP ARCHITECTS OF THE WORLD

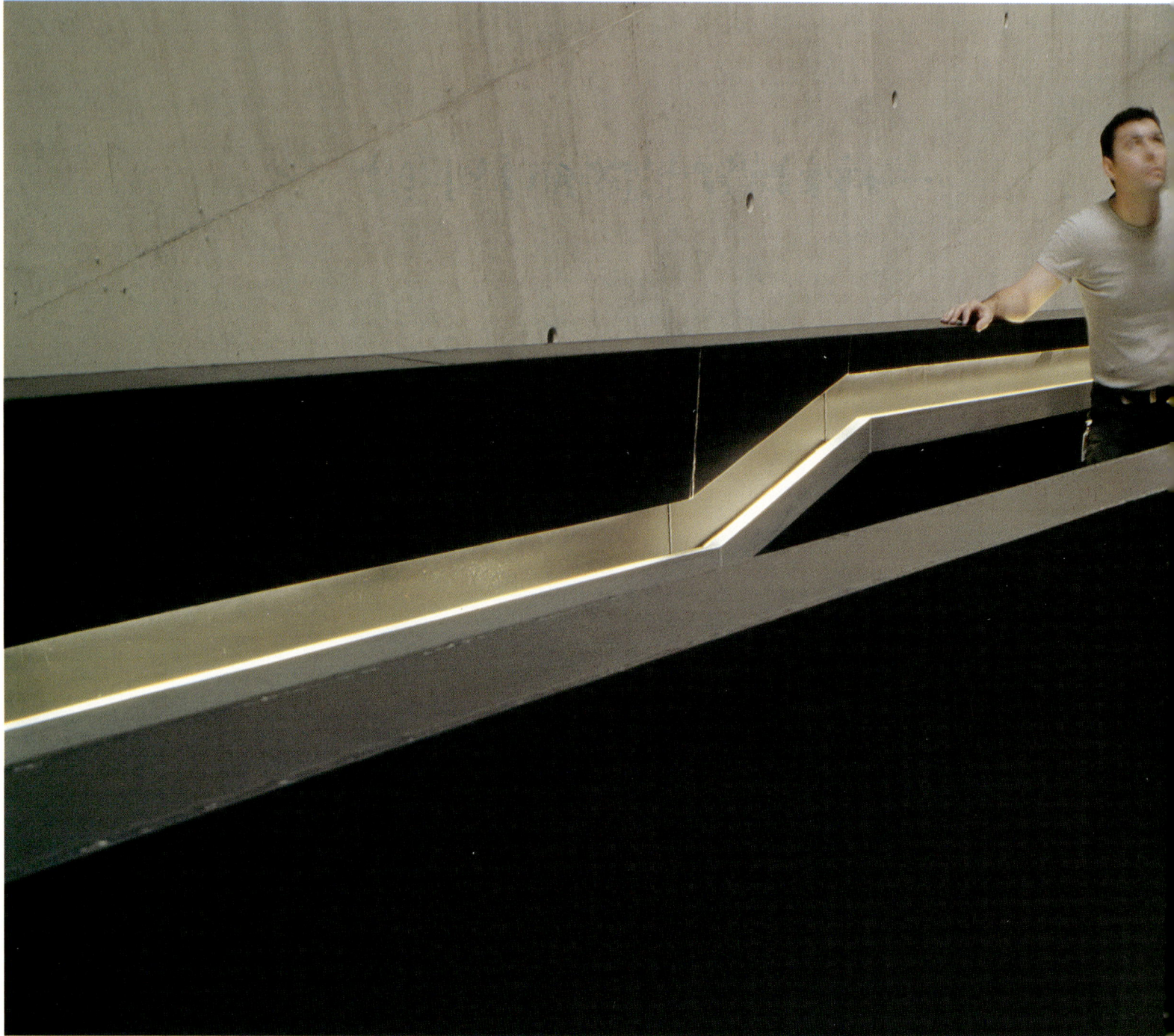

## The Rosenthal Center of Contemporary Art
Cincinnati, USA 1997-2003

The Rosenthal Center of Contemporary Art in Cincinnati, which has recently been completed, accommodates temporary exhibitions, installations specifically developed for the setting and performances, but not a permanent collection. Other aspects of the scheme include classes, offices, workshops and public areas such as the café, the hall and the store. The Art Center is made up of two complementary concepts: the 'urban carpet' and 'stacking boxes'. In order to attract those in the surroundings into the interior of the building

and create dynamism, the entrance and hall on the ground floor have been organized as an 'urban carpet'. As a result, a gradient has been created in the paving that runs from the corner of Sixth Street with Walnut Street and curves round into the building until becoming the back wall. From this space, a ramp that runs through the entire hall starts. The ramp leads to the galleries. In contrast to the 'urban carpet' with its smooth undulating surfaces, the galleries seem to have been dug out of a unique block of concrete that floats over the space of the hall. The views between both systems are unpredictable, as is what can be seen from the ramps climbing up in

zigzag in the rear part of the building. The galleries have different forms, dimensions and characteristics as far as lighting is concerned to cater for the greatest variety of artistic proposals possible. They fit together as if they were a puzzle of interlocking shapes. The situation of the building in a corner implied each of the two fa-cades being developed separately, but in a complementary way. The south face (Sixth Street) is formed of a translucent skin through which the activity of the center can be seen. The east face is expressed as a sculptural volume, a relief in negative of the interior of the galleries.

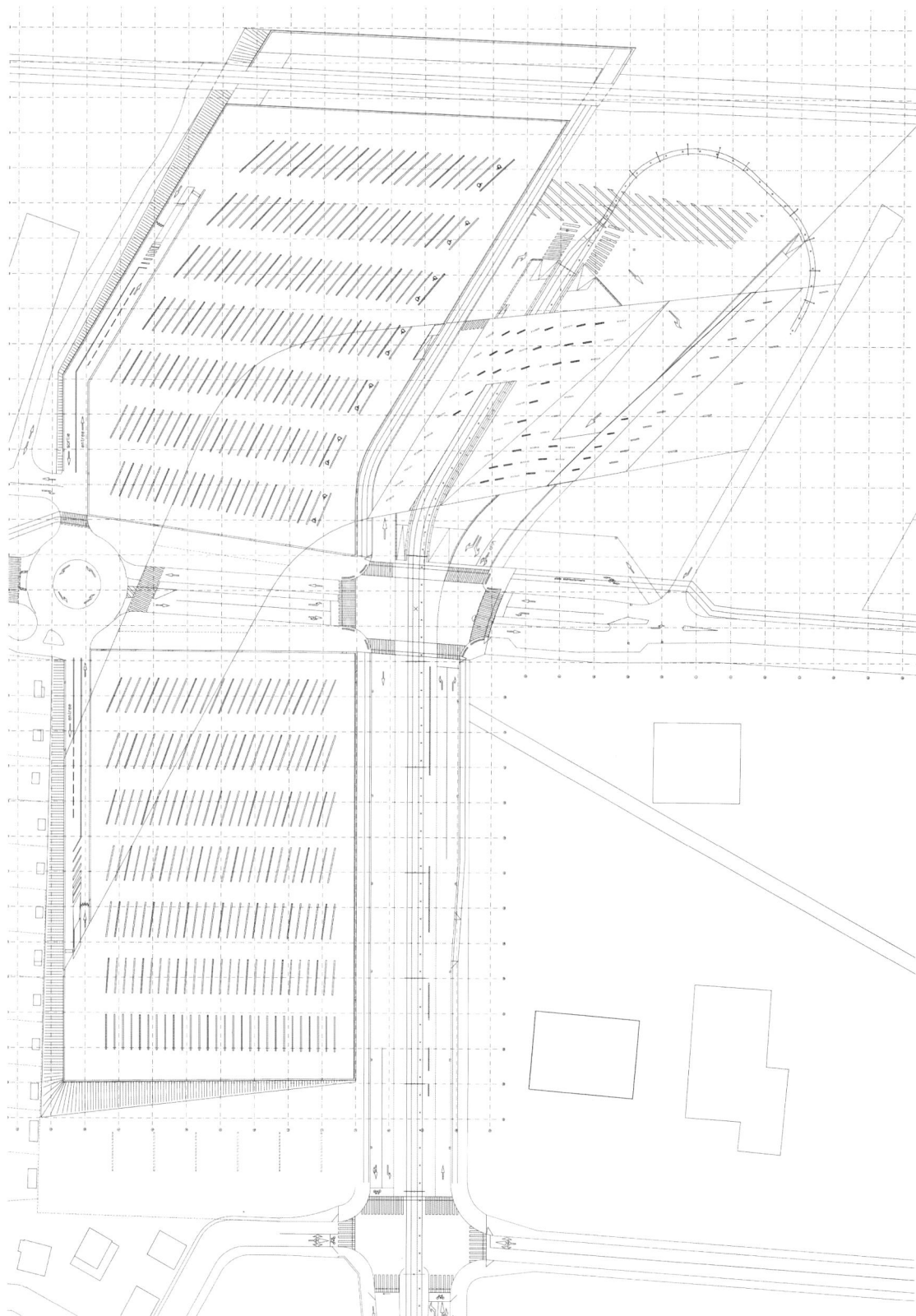

TOP ARCHITECTS OF THE WORLD

## Multimodal Stop at the North Terminus, Hoenheim

Strasbourg, France 1999-2001

Car parking facilities and the tramway terminal in Strasbourg were constructed with the intention of fomenting public transport. The idea was to encourage the public to leave their private vehicles at home and to use the tramway. Zaha Hadid was invited to participate within a series of interventions that included various artists in the design of the station and car park for 800 vehicles on the northern vertex of the line. The concept of the proposal was based on the interaction of certain fields and lines which inter-crossed one another to make up the whole. These fields corre-

spond to the lines of movement created by cars, trams, bicycles and pedestrians. The transition between different forms of transport materializes.

The station accommodates a waiting area, bicycle racks, public conveniences and a store. The space, full of attraction and ener-

gy, has been treated in such a way that it defines how everything circulates within it. The car park, for 800 cars, has been divided into two zones.

**Zaha Hadid** deals with the car park as if it were a piece of land-art in which the graphology of the brand names painted on

the ground along with the street lamps with their fiber glass threads make up a truly dynamic space. The reciprocity between the static and dynamic elements of the proposal on their different scales stands out. A large slab of concrete with cut edges and which is folded back in some of its extremes forms the roof of the terminal. For this project, in which the boundaries between natural and artificial almost disappear, Zaha Hadid received the Mies van der Rohe Prize for European Architecture in 2003.

## MAXXI

National Center of Contemporary Art Rome, Italy 2003-2005
This project was the winner of the international competition held
in February 1999 and is currently under construction. The Museum of Contemporary Art and Architecture of Rome is situated
on a large plot in the district of Flaminia on the northern limits of

the city's historic center. It is the first national museum of contemporary art in Italy. The center includes spaces for permanent and temporary exhibitions, commercial galleries, an architectural center, bars and restaurants, a conference center and a li-

brary. The overall concept of the project is based on the idea of 'irrigating' the site with surfaces of lineal exhibition and weaving a dense texture of interior and exterior spaces. The routes and pathways that cross the site, along with the desire to accompa-

ny the visitor along new paths, organize the form of the building (guidelines for existing and desired movements). It is an urban construction in which the barriers between the surroundings and the building between the interior and exterior and between one pathway and another disappear. The Center acts like an 'urban field' irrigated by continuous walls that intersect and interrupt one another and which thus create a multitude of spaces. Many of these are illuminated by natural light that comes in through the ribbed ceilings that follow the undulations of the walls and emphasize and filter the aforementioned entrance of light.

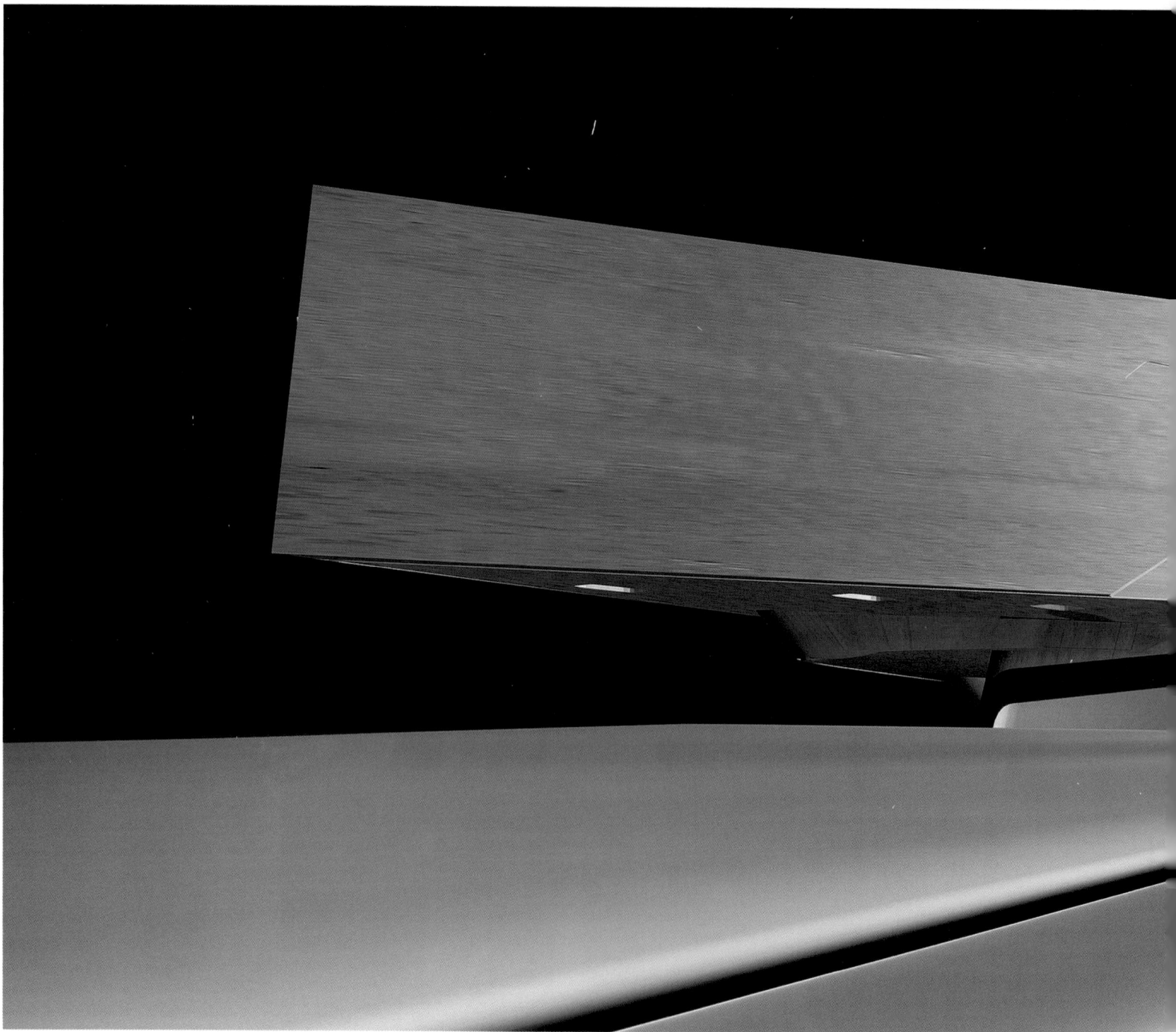

## Phaeno Science Center Wolfsburg
Wolfsburg, Germany 2000-2005 (in construction)
The science center, the first of this type in Germany, appears as a mysterious object that awakens the curiosity of those that come

close to the center. The visitor finds him or herself faced with a strange place that possesses a certain level of complexity, but which is, however, controlled by a strict system of structural organization. Situated in a representative zone of the city of Wolfs-

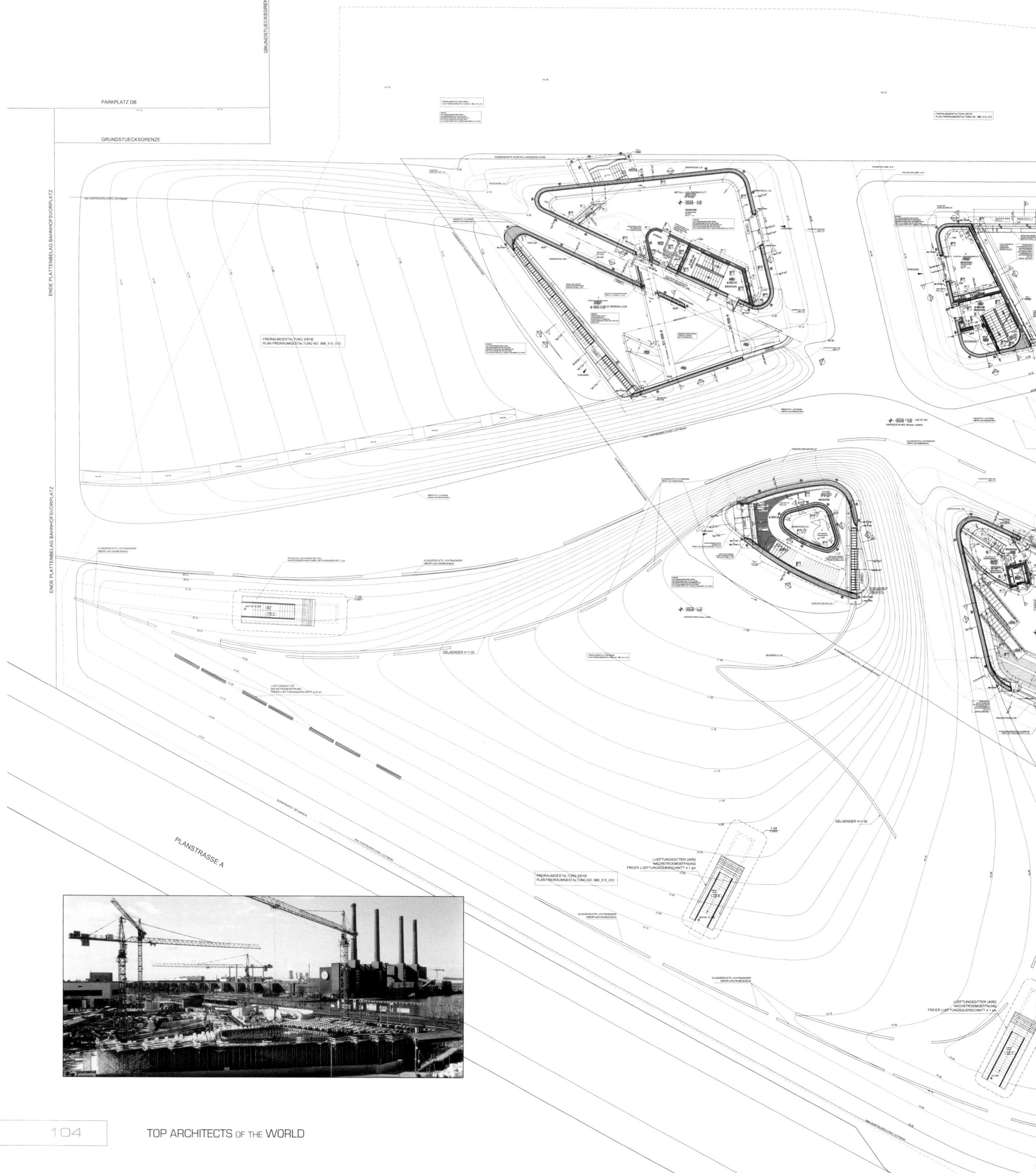

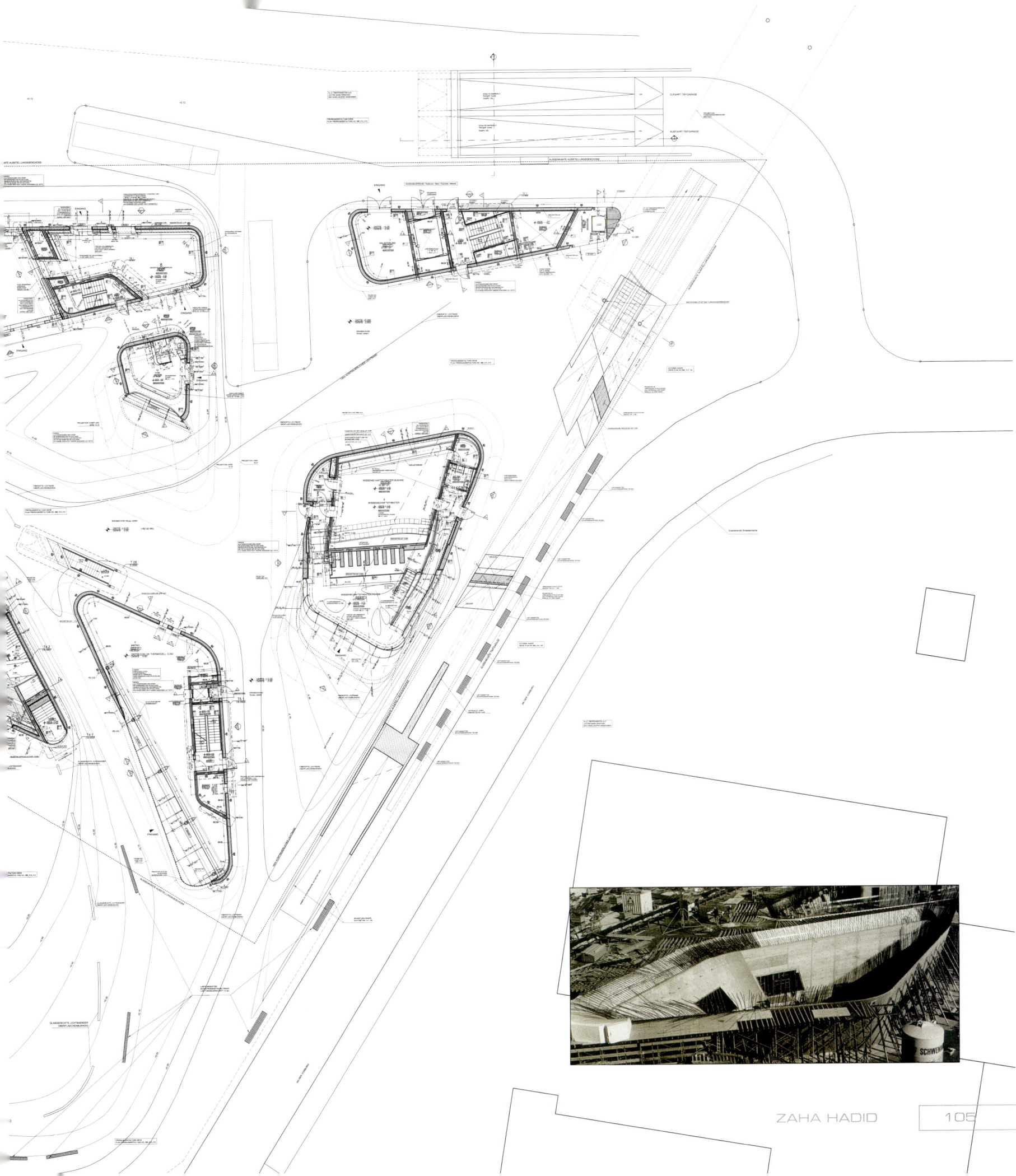

ZAHA HADID     105

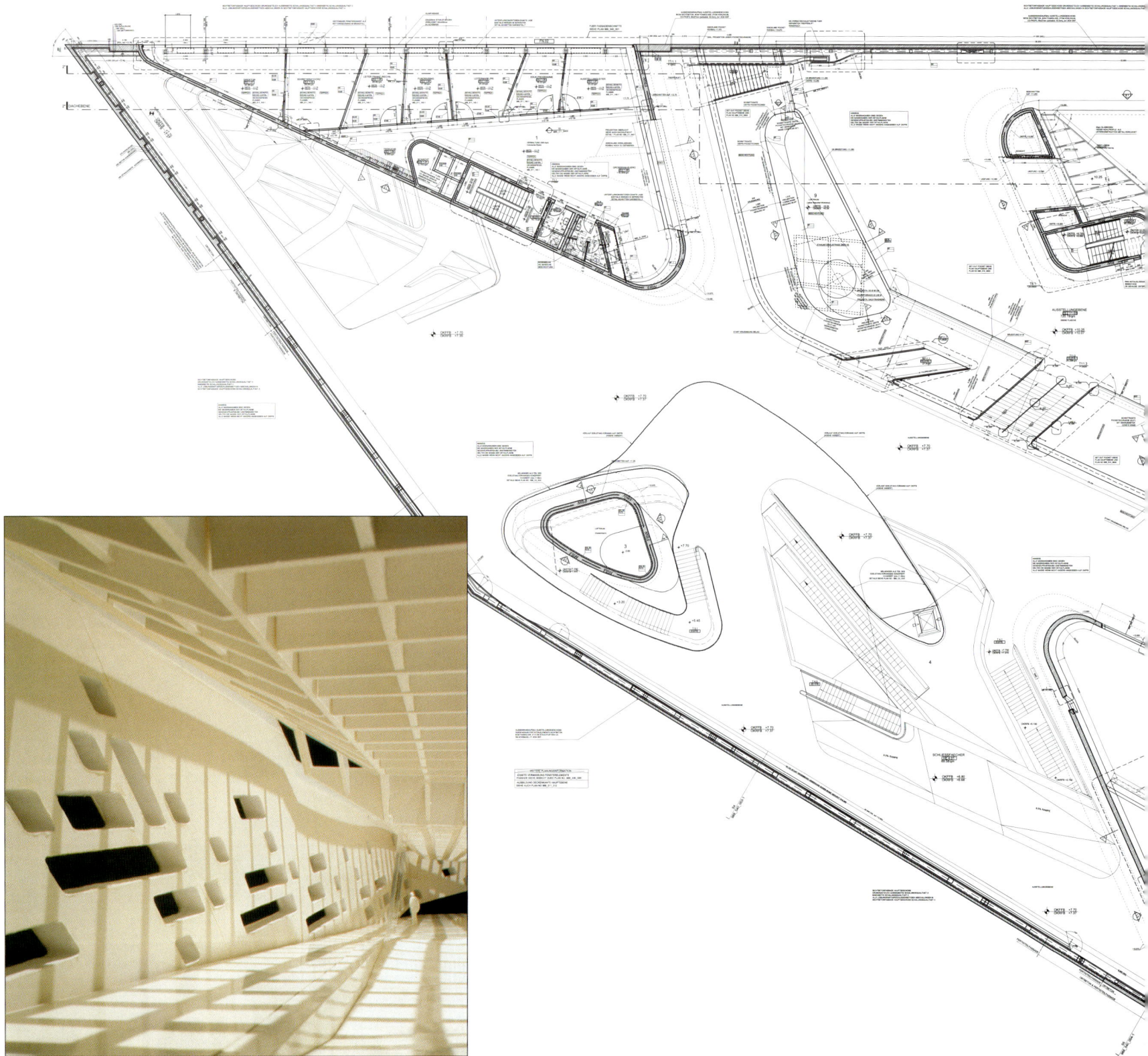

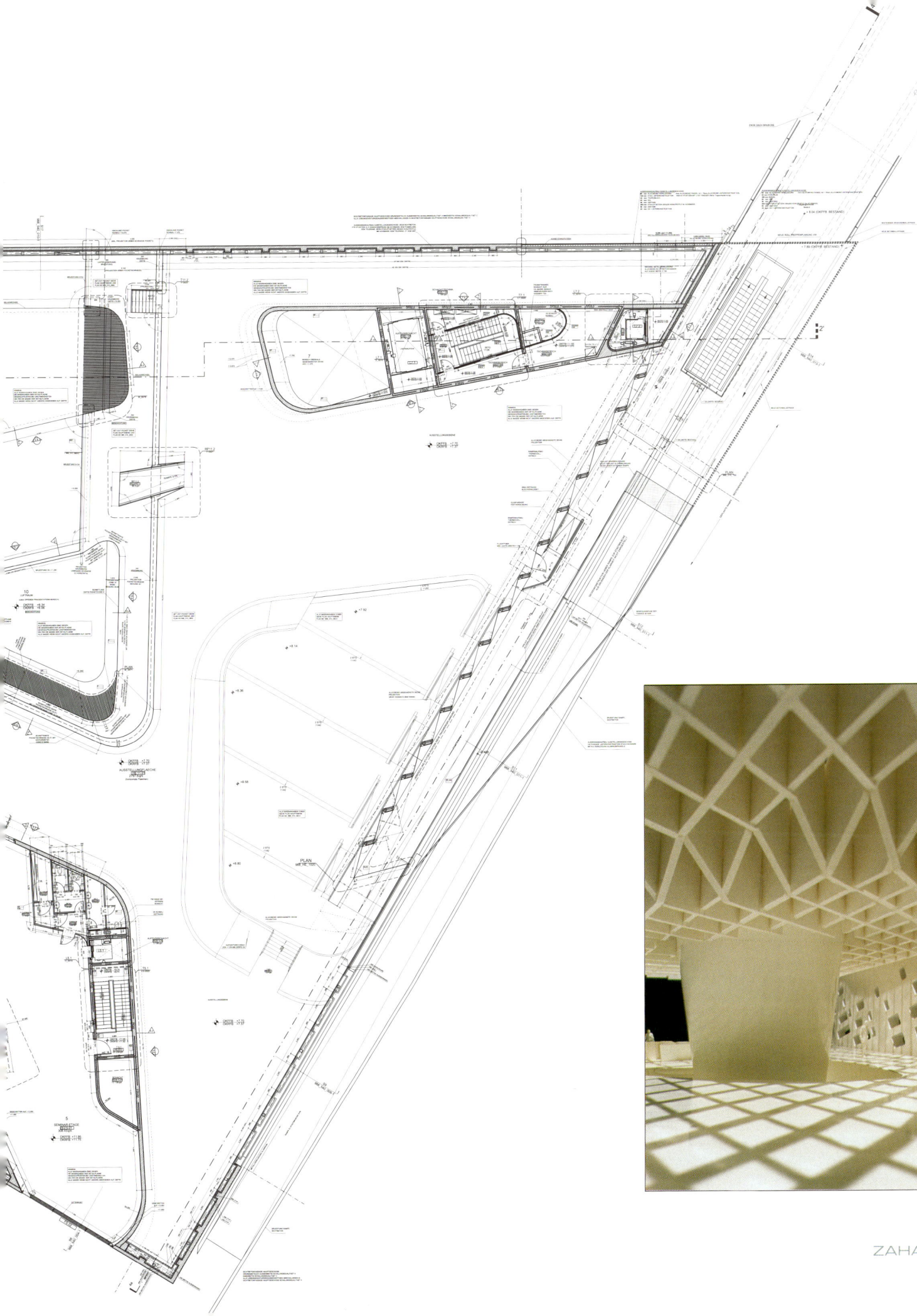

burg, it finalizes the route of a series of important cultural buildings (Aalto, Scharoun y Schweger) and also constitutes a nexus with the north bank of the Mittelland Canal – Volkswagen City.

The proposal integrates a large number of itineraries for pedestrians and vehicles across the site as much at the level of the ground floor as on higher levels. The access level maintains great

transparency and porosity given that the principal volume – the exhibition space – is raised a floor to cover the public plaza. This volume is supported by some steel reinforced concrete structur-

al cones and accommodates retail and various cultural functions. The prism of the exhibition zone, reasonably plane and sensitively triangular, is found in its interior completely eroded by 'craters'.

These elements, in addition to providing the structure to support the prism building, allow light to enter and offer access to the roof. According to **Zaha Hadid**, 'The result of all of this is a volcanic landscape which, although strange, is coherent.'

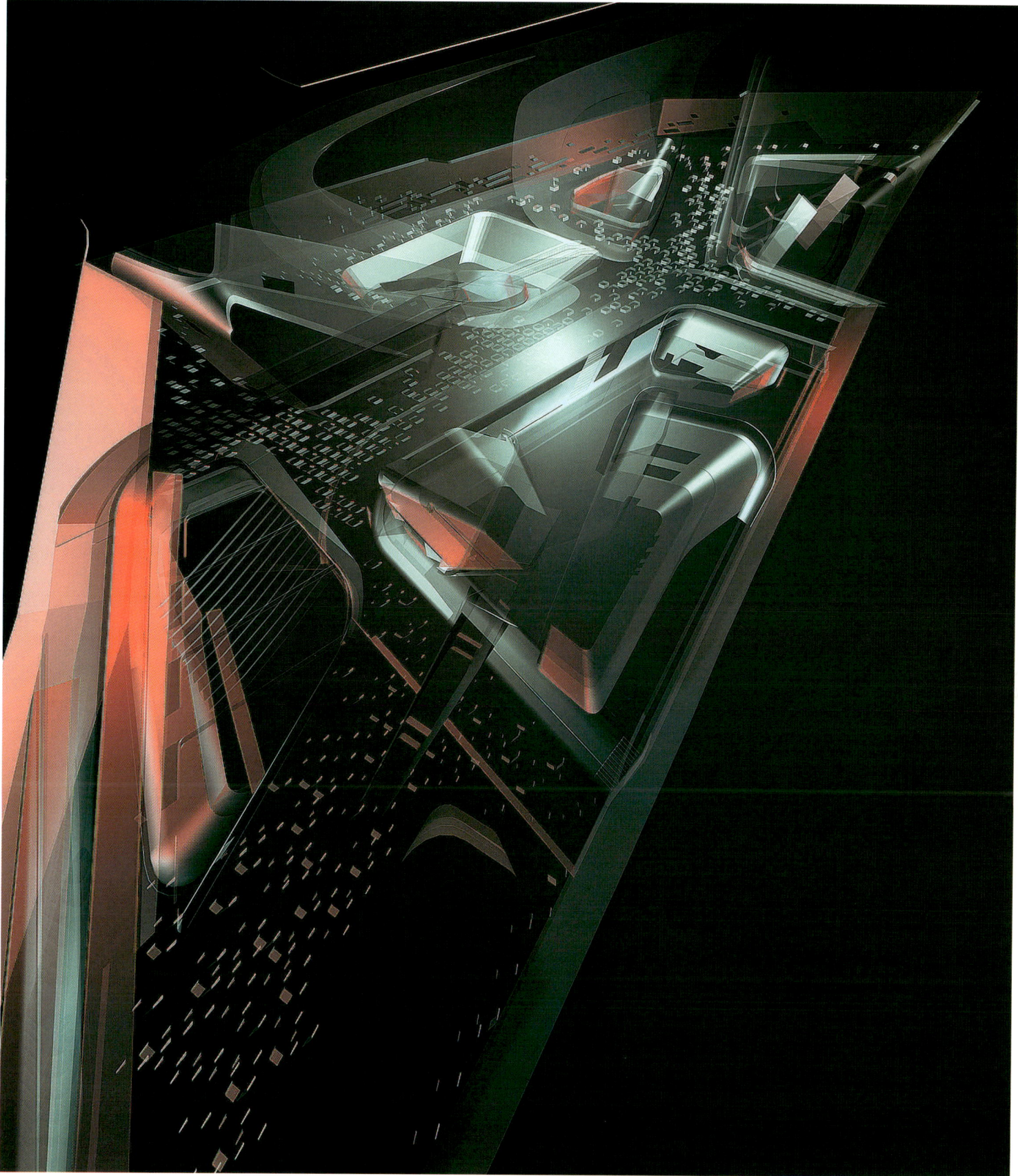

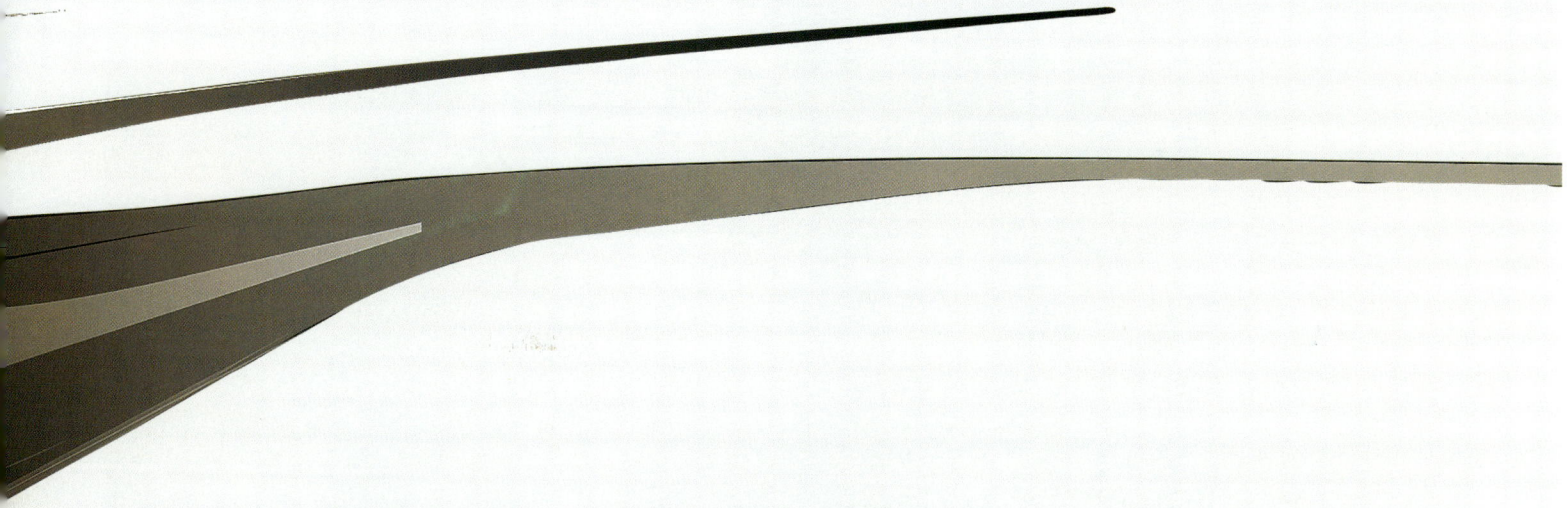

## Central Building – BMW Plant
Leipzig, Germany 2002-2004 (in construction)

**Central Building – BMW Plant**
Leipzig, Germany 2002-2004 (in construction)
The new Central Building for the BMW Plant is intended, in addition to becoming a new representative image for the brand, to be

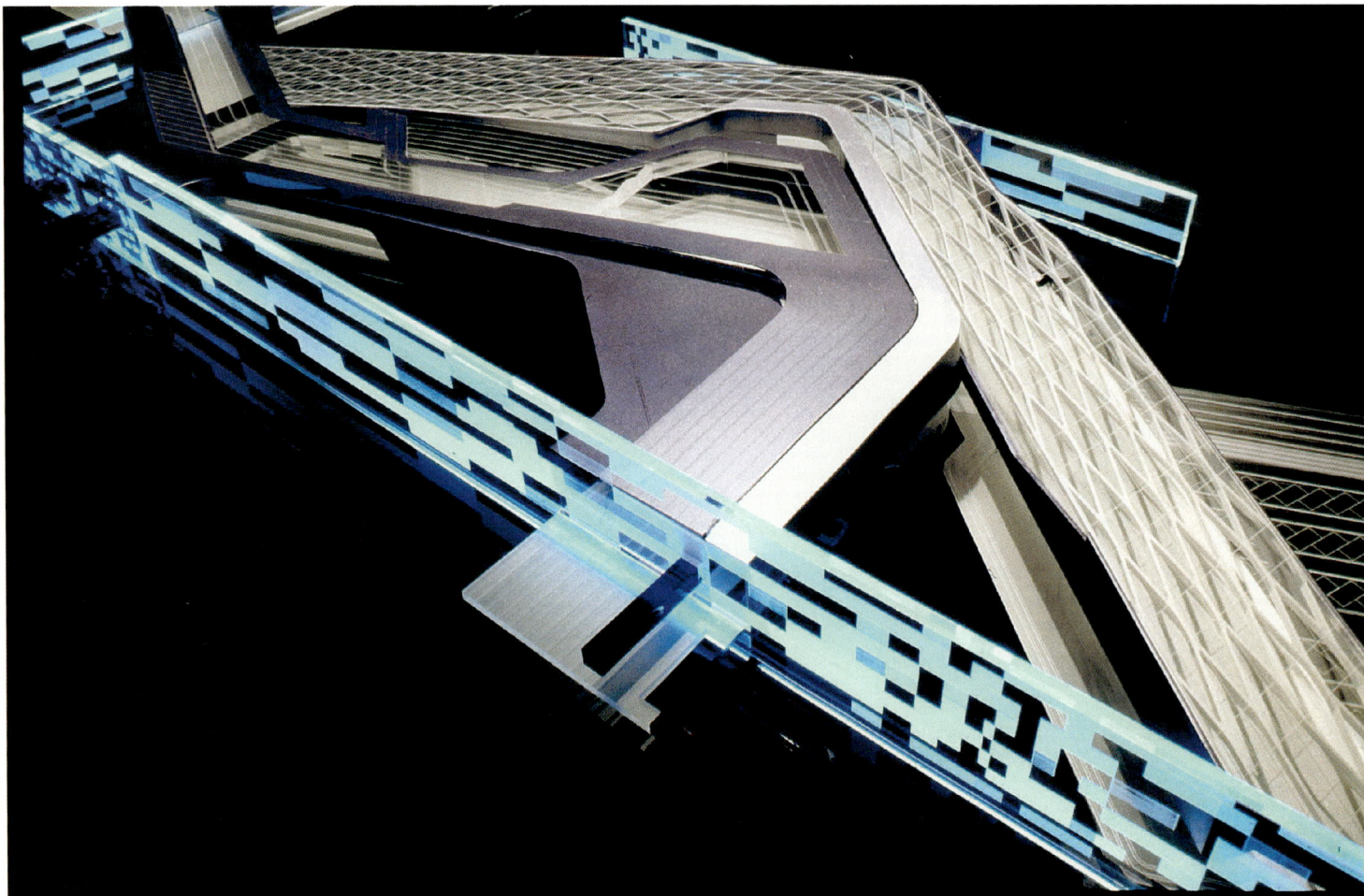

the center or 'intelligence center' of the entire industrial complex. All of the lines of activities of the complex are to be activated and controlled from here. The design strategy takes into account the cycles and itineraries of the workers, the visitors and also the production line that crosses the building. All of the movements that converge in the BMW Central Building cross the zone that includes the three principal segments of production: White in Body, Paint Shop and Assembly.

The organization of the building obeys a sequencing of activities based on noise -- from the front, silent or confined activities, to the rear of the building, the noisier zone. A generous lobby permits deep views into the building. A series of courtyards proportion air and natural light to the heart of the building. The principal organizational strategy consists of a section in the form of a pair of scissors that connects the ground floor with the first floor in one unique surface. Two sequences of platforms – like giant staircases – run from north to south and south to north. This is a system of platforms that allows spaces with different functions to be articulated without any loss of visual communication from one to the other.

The car park has been dealt with as if it were a landscape, like a piece of land-art, creating spectacular dynamism across the location of the parking places that will rotate and create waves of brilliant cars.

# Rafael Moneo

**W**as born in Tudela, Navarra, Spain in 1937. After having graduated from the School of Architecture of Madrid, he collaborated with Sáenz de Oiza (1958-1961) and Jørn Utzon (1961-1962). Since the mid 1960's, he has developed an extensive teaching activity in Madrid, Barcelona, Lauana, Princeton and Harvard. **Moneo** was dean of the design school at Harvard at the beginning of the 1990's.

Since 1970, he has undertaken large-scale commissions such as the Bankinter in Madrid (1976), the City Hall of Logroño (1981), the celebrated Museum of Romanesque Art in Mérida

L'Illa Diagonal

Museo de Arte Moderno

(1986), the headquarters for Previsión Española in Seville (1988), the headquarters of the Bank of Spain in Jaén (1988), San Pablo Airport in Seville (1991), Atocha Station in Madrid (1992), Illa Diagonal in Barcelona (1993). His prizes (including the **Pritzker**), his fame and the international commissions arrived during the 1990's. In this period, **Moneo** built the headquarters of the Pilar and Joan Miró Foundation in Palma (1993), the Davis Museum in Massachussetts (1993) and the Modern Art Museum in Stockholm (1998).

**Rafael Moneo**, more than a designer, is a scholar of architecture. Maybe influenced by his teaching activity, or, per-

haps, as a result of his interest in history, all of his projects are based on a theme of reflection whether it is on the city, topography, classical language or traditional typologies.

In this way, it is often said that **Moneo** is an eclectic architect who, rather than imposing on the setting, integrates into it and adopts many aspects of the surrounding architecture in his works.

However, this eclecticism is not translated into formal caprices: his buildings are rigorously abstract as has been shown by his elegant work in postmodern and deconstructionist styles.

# L'Illa Diagonal
## 1997. Barcelona, Spain.

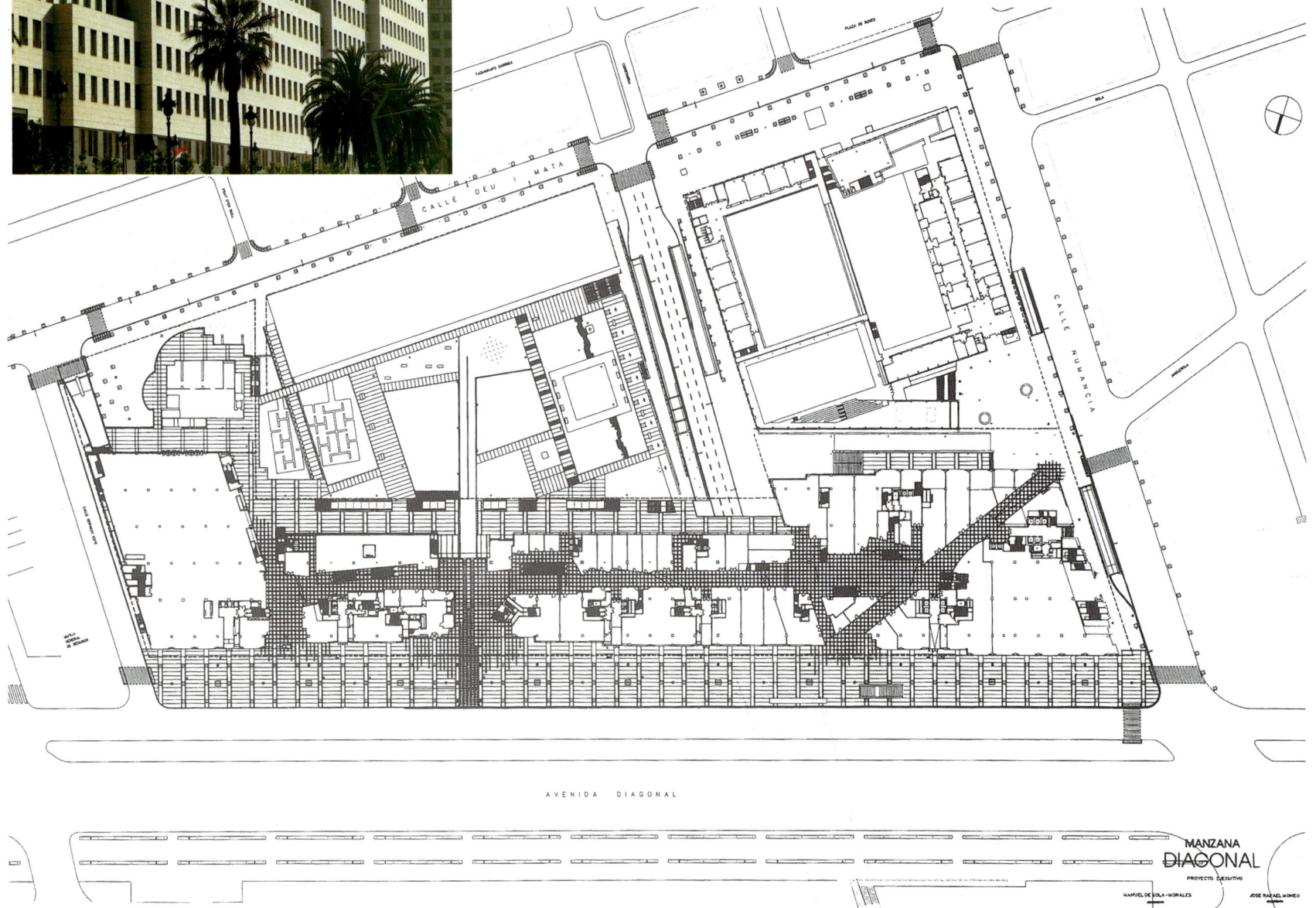

All of the projects that have been undertaken by Moneo are based on a theme of reflection whether it is on the city, topography, classical language or traditional typologies. No two buildings by Moneo are the same. The Spanish architect distrusts stylistic ticks, "I'd like to avoid falling into the ridicule of linguistic equivocation, that feeling we often get when contemplating some

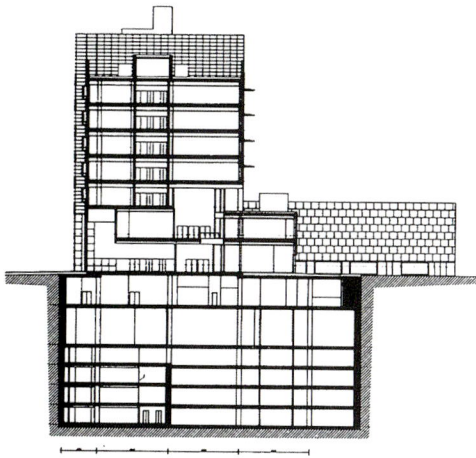
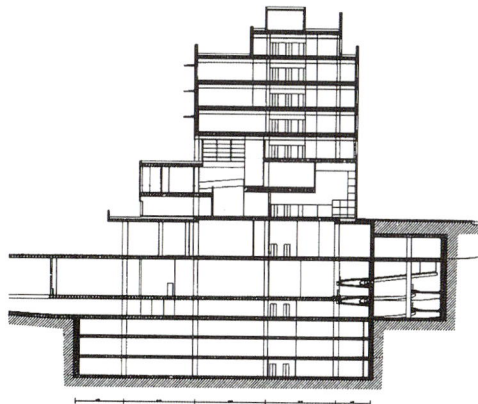
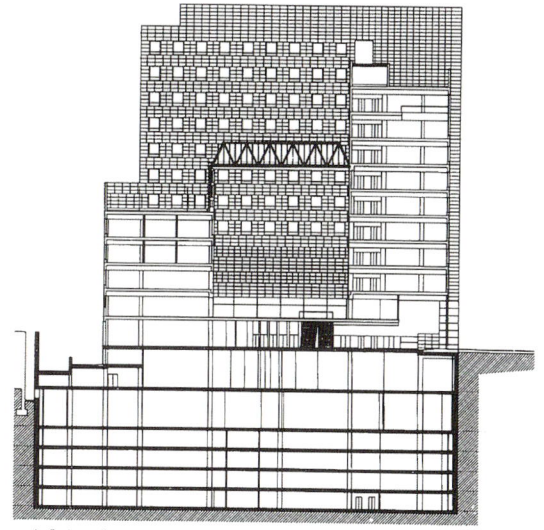

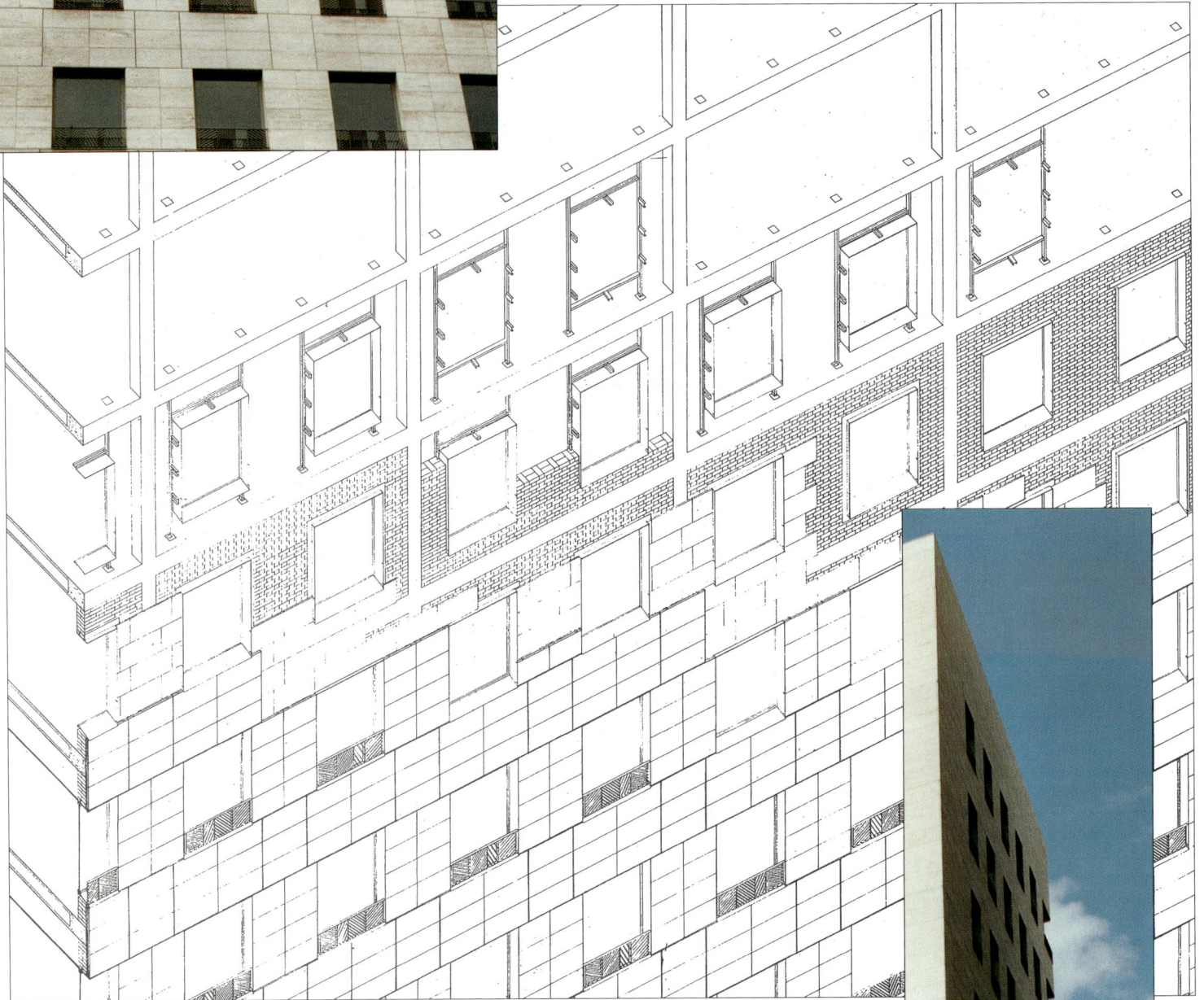

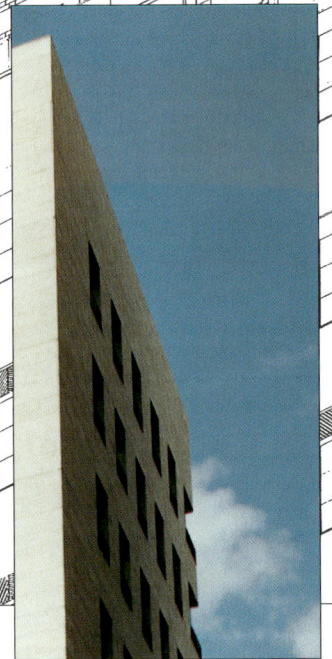

pieces of recent architecture which have been destroyed in an intent to identify paradigms and in which the real problems have been overlooked."

The play on forms presented in this project – in which very diverse uses and activities are integrated – is not destined to produce an architectural image, but an urbanistic one as if it were

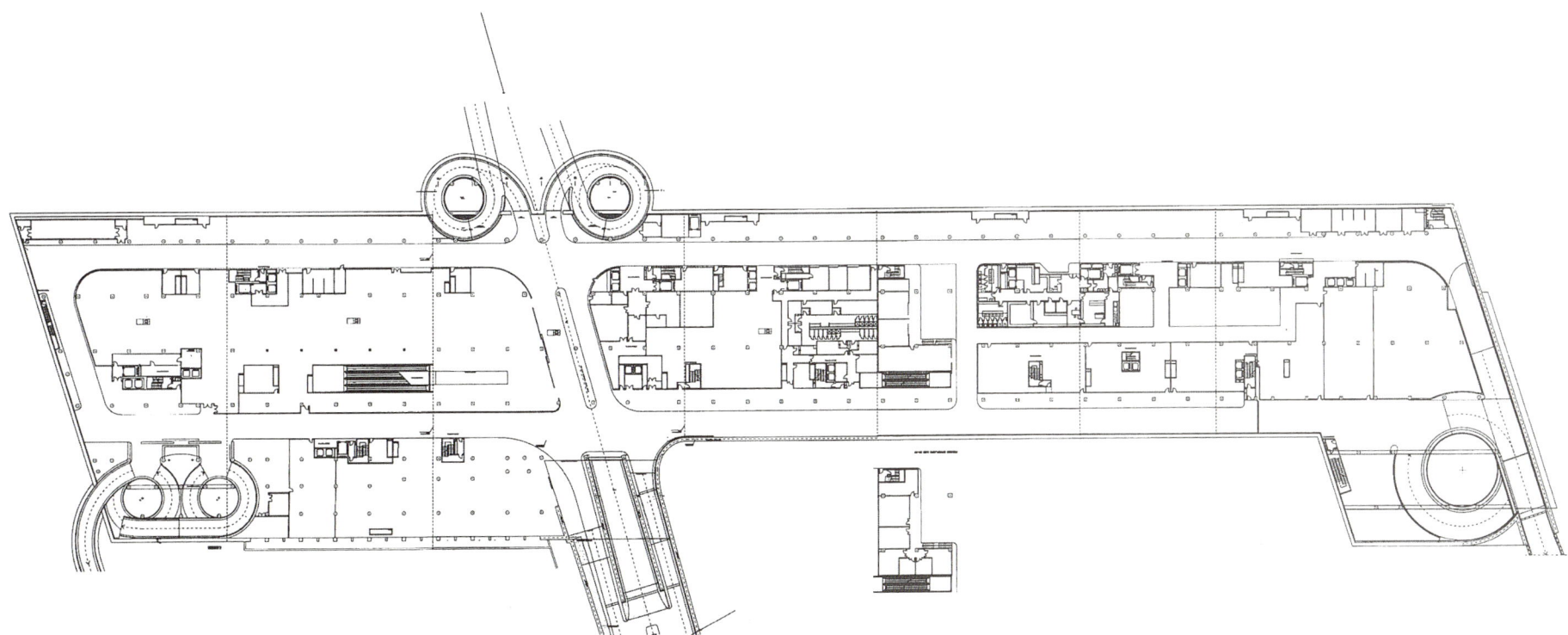

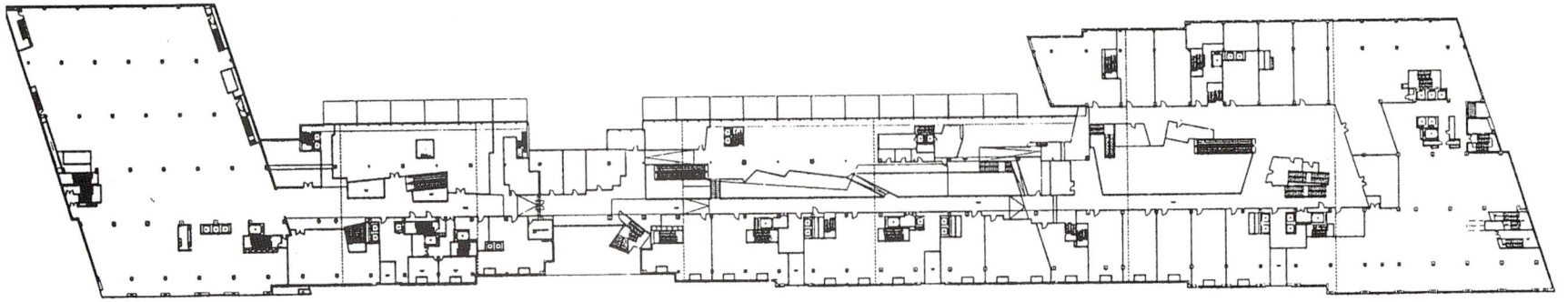

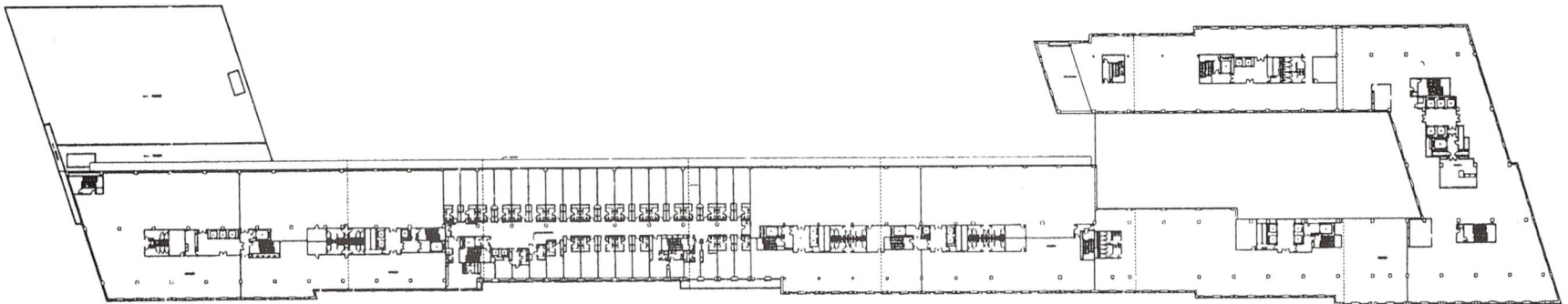

a piece of the city. The façade evokes a group of buildings of different heights and the higher floors step back from the plane of the main façade. The different volumes stand out in the sunlight according to the time of day and the shadows they cast. In this project, both public and private interests have been integrated in such a way that mixed in with the floors of offices and the retail areas, buildings that accommodate cultural activities have been incorporated.

# Museum of Modern Art
## Stockholm, Sweden

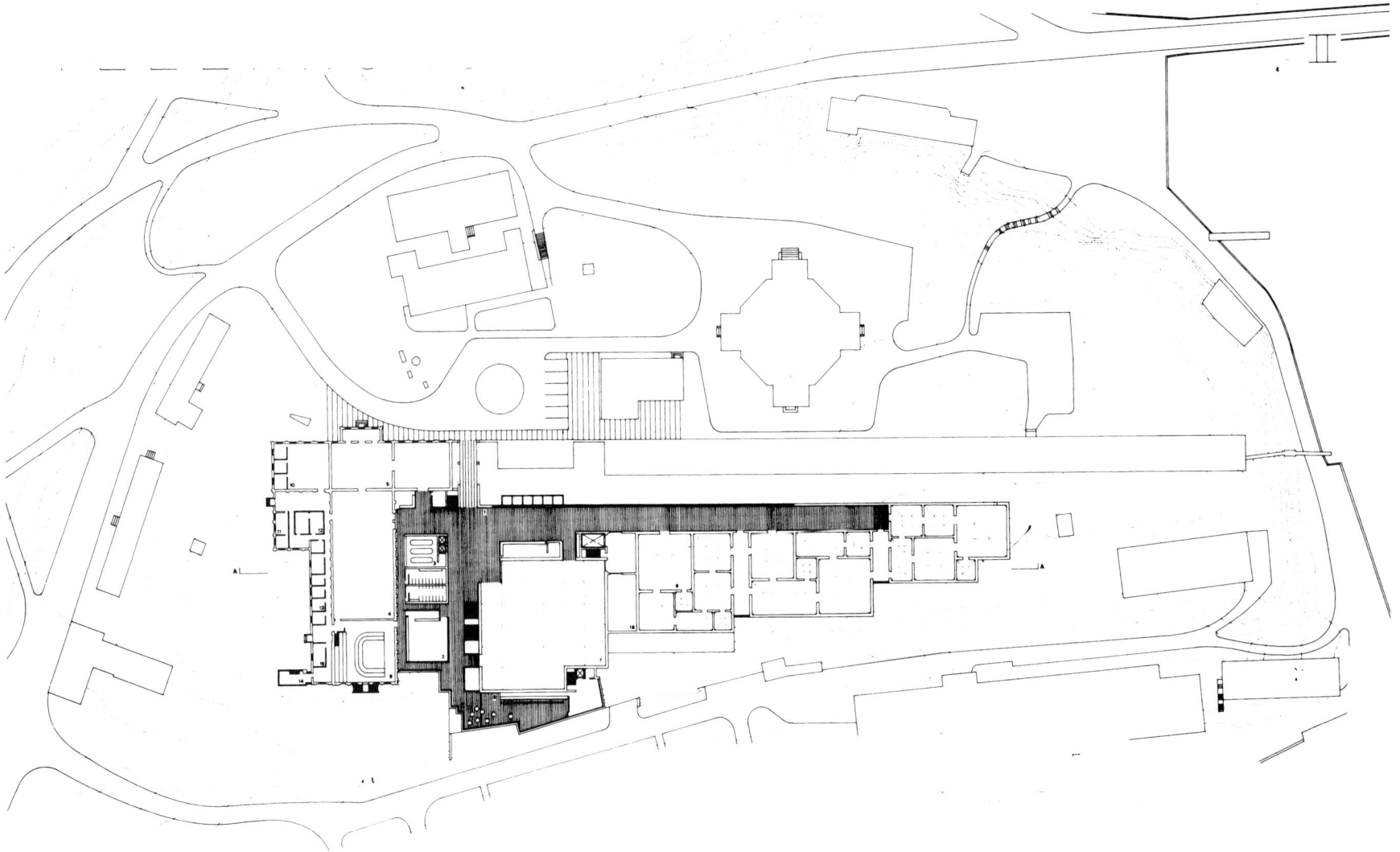

As has often been said, each of **Moneo**'s buildings is unique. The Spanish architect shuns stylistic repetition which he considers to be a trap which a lot of recent architecture has fallen into. **Moneo** considers it to be essential not to lose sight of real needs which often become eclipsed by the obstinacy of identifying paradigms. The project is based on a typological study of exhibition spaces. **Moneo** chose to construct a series of spaces with square floor plans and pyramidal roofs that finish in a cen-

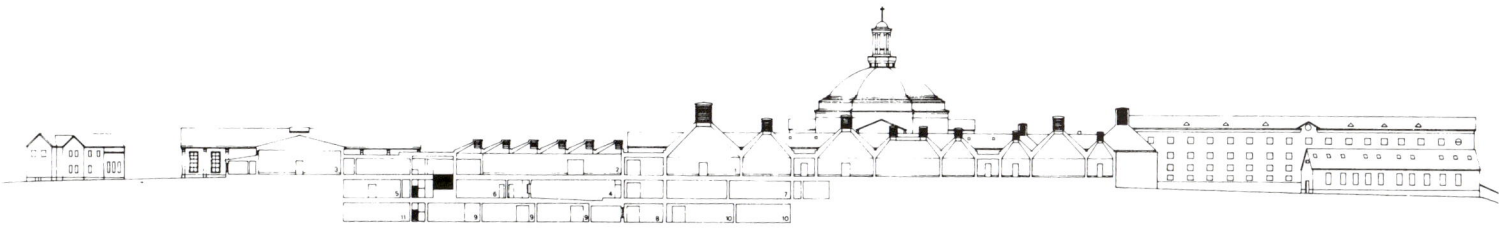

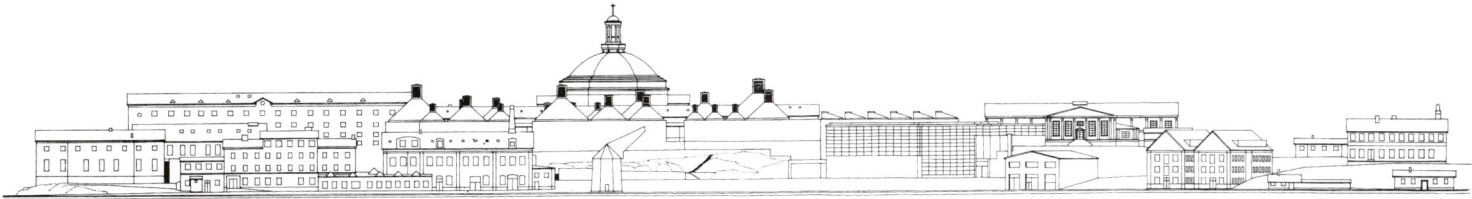

tral skylight. Each space has its own independent roof. Another one of the important elements of the museum is the large glazed terrace of the cafeteria.

The principal volume of the building is set parallel to the street and creates the principal façade of the building while the organization of the rear parts is based on various volumes that step back with respect to the plane established by the façade.

# César
# Pelli

B orn in Argentina in 1926, **César Pelli** graduated in the National University of Tucumán in Argentina. In 1952, he moved to the United States and enrolled in the University of Illinois. He worked in Eero Saarinen's office from 1954 to 1964. In Gruen Associates, he constructed a number of buildings such as the Pacific Design Center of Los Angeles (California, 1975) or the United States Embassy in Tokyo (Japan, 1972-1975). In 1977, he was given the post of dean at Yale University and moved to New Haven (Connecticut) where he set up Pelli and Assocites. He has built an extension for the Museum of Modern Art in New York (1977-1984) and carried out his competition winning project for the World Financial Center (New York, 1981-1987). His work has gone beyond the frontiers of American. In London, he built the Canary Wharf Tower (1965-1991) and he has won international competitions such

Hotel Sea Hawk

Diputación 2002

Bank of America

as the passenger terminal for Kansai Airport (1988). More recently, he has completed the Petronas Twins Towers in Kuala Lumpur (Malaysia, 1991-1997) – the highest towers in the world – and previously to this, he constructed the 30-story tower for the NTT headquarters (Tokyo, Japan, 1995) and the Sea Hawk Hotel & Resort in Fukuoka (Japan, 1995).

Pelli's professional career has basically developed within the field of skyscrapers. As a result, his buildings have significantly modified the skyline of a number of American cities. Pelli defines himself as a pragmatic architect given that he has often had to confront large-scale projects with, on occasions, small budgets. As a consequence, his proposals have become renown for the way in which they faithfully follow the project with no interference from preconceived ideas. In this way, each new response is pre-

sented free of any preceding connections in his work, although some reoccurring themes can be perceived: the use of glass, for example, to produce ambiguities and distortions in the exteriors which is a situation opposed to the order and clarity found in the interiors.

One of his most interesting studies is made up of the spatial relationships through "spinal" circulation as experimented as much in skyscrapers as in projects of a smaller scale and in which each space is interconnected with another of a lesser hierarchy. Within these studies, he elaborated an interesting project that is known as the Long Gallery House (1980) which consisted of a long gallery-passage that related the volumes of the residence. This study was put into practice in Maryland House (1985-1989).

## Hotel Sea Hawk
Fukuoka, Japan

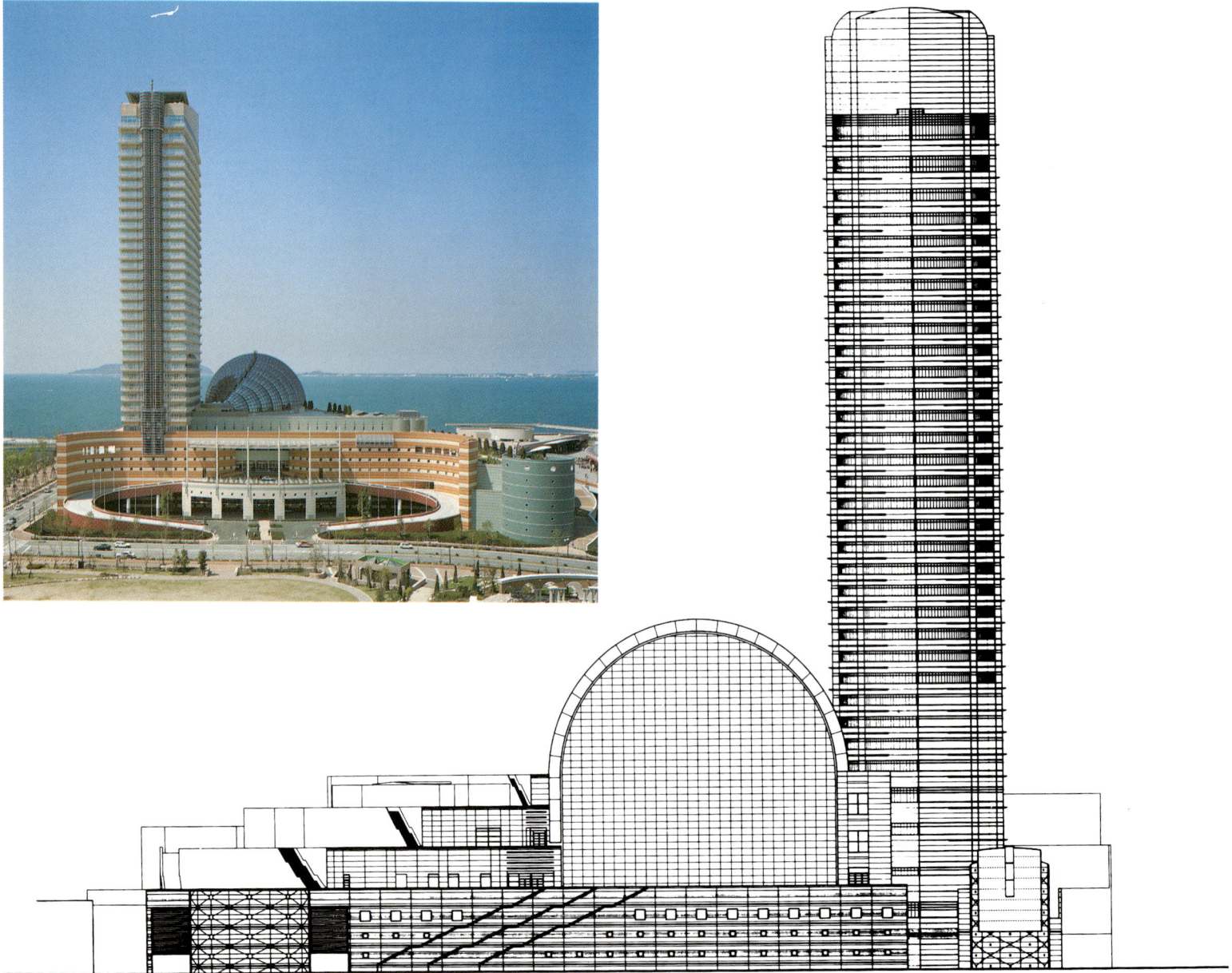

The projects that Pelli has carried out have a distinctive feature in common: the nonexistence of previously conceived ideas. Each project is treated according to site, climate and culture, which is to say according to its surroundings. The volumes of his architectural groups always have a strong and defined design. The materials are used in all of their expressiveness and color and

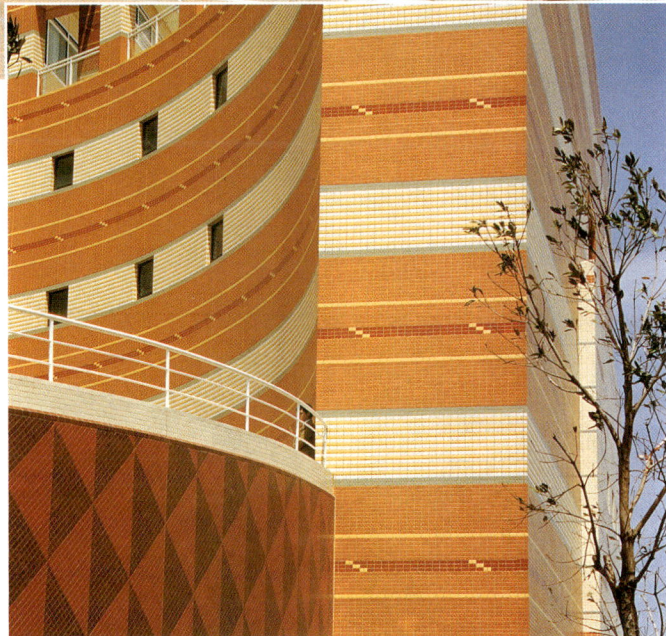

they interrupt the urban spaces with special character and personality. Built on the seashore, visible from the city and as erect as a lighthouse, the design of the hotel creates a composition of sculptural forms in the bay. The curves of the ceiling and of the

walls relate to the elements: water and the wind. It has been made up of different volumes. The walls have been finished in ceramic tiles that form a rich texture of different colors and de-

signs. As opposed to occidental hotels, complementary functions, such as wedding luncheons, luxurious restaurants, bars, meeting rooms and so on are a vital aspect of the hotel.

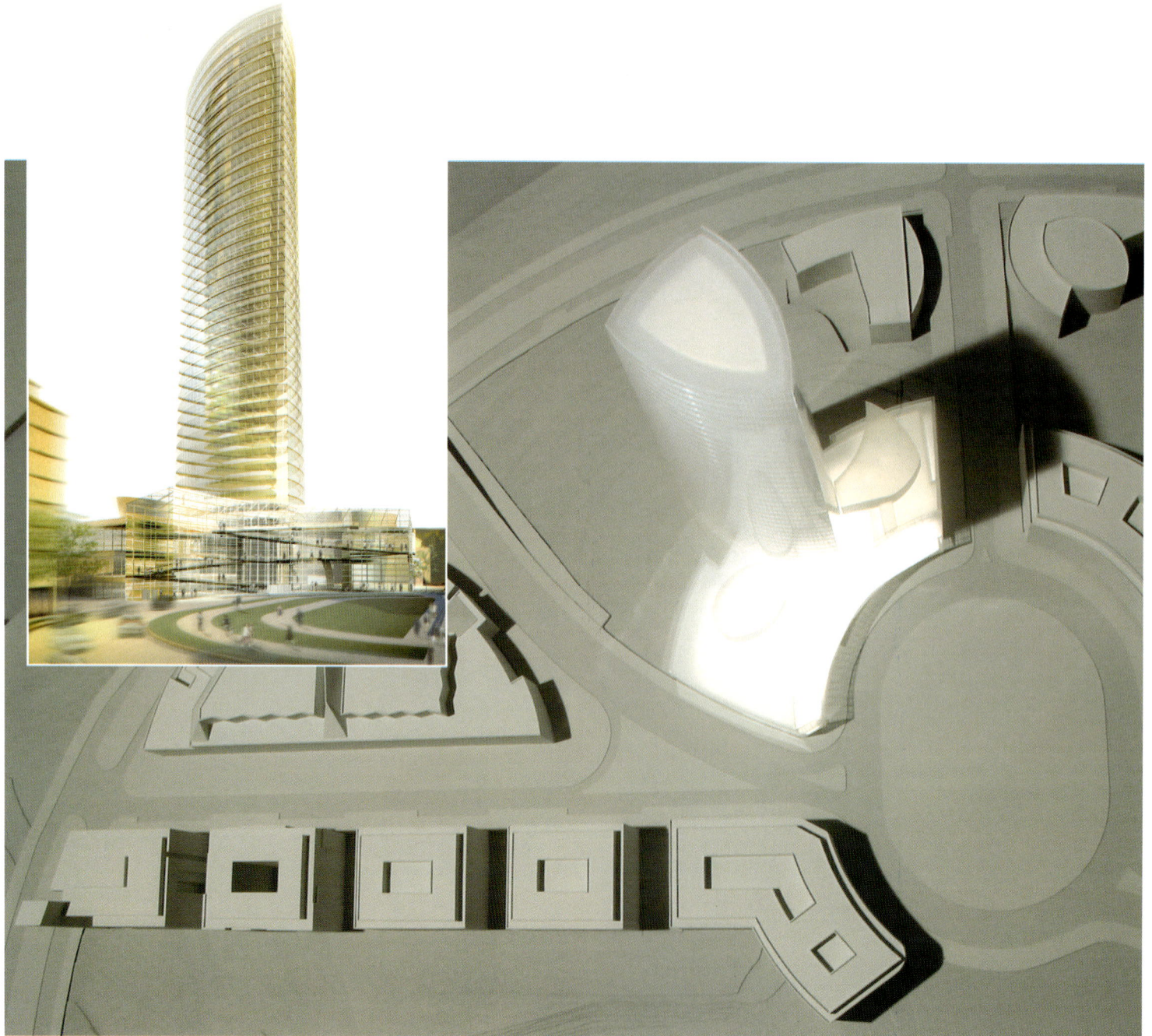

In 1993, the City Council of Bilbao held an international competition for the presentation of ideas for the urban development of the Abandoibarra area. The architect César Pelli won with a General Plan which provides a balance between private and public interests and relates well to the existing city. In addition to being the capital of Vizcaya, it is also the cultural, social and business

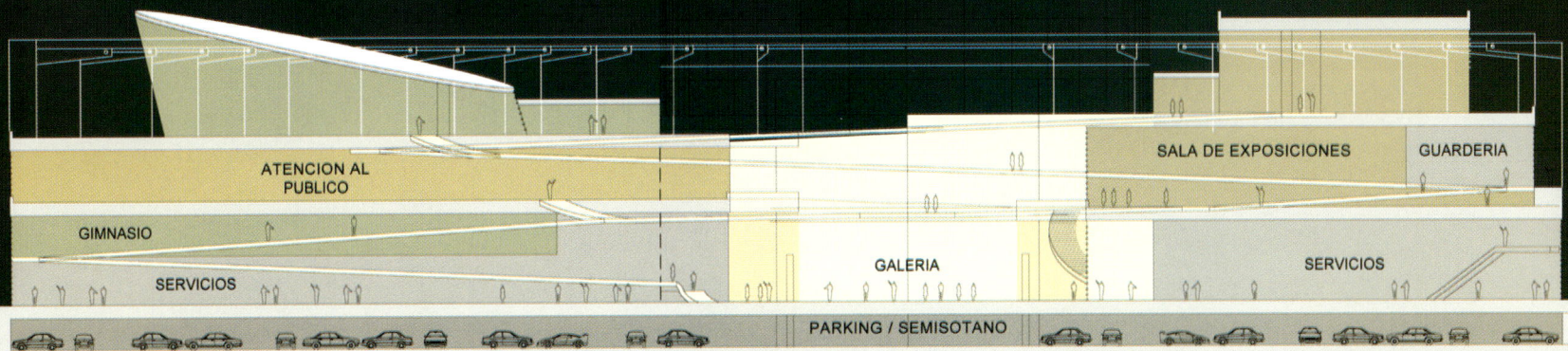

ATENCION AL PUBLICO

GIMNASIO

SERVICIOS

SALA DE EXPOSICIONES GUARDERIA

GALERIA SERVICIOS

PARKING / SEMISOTANO

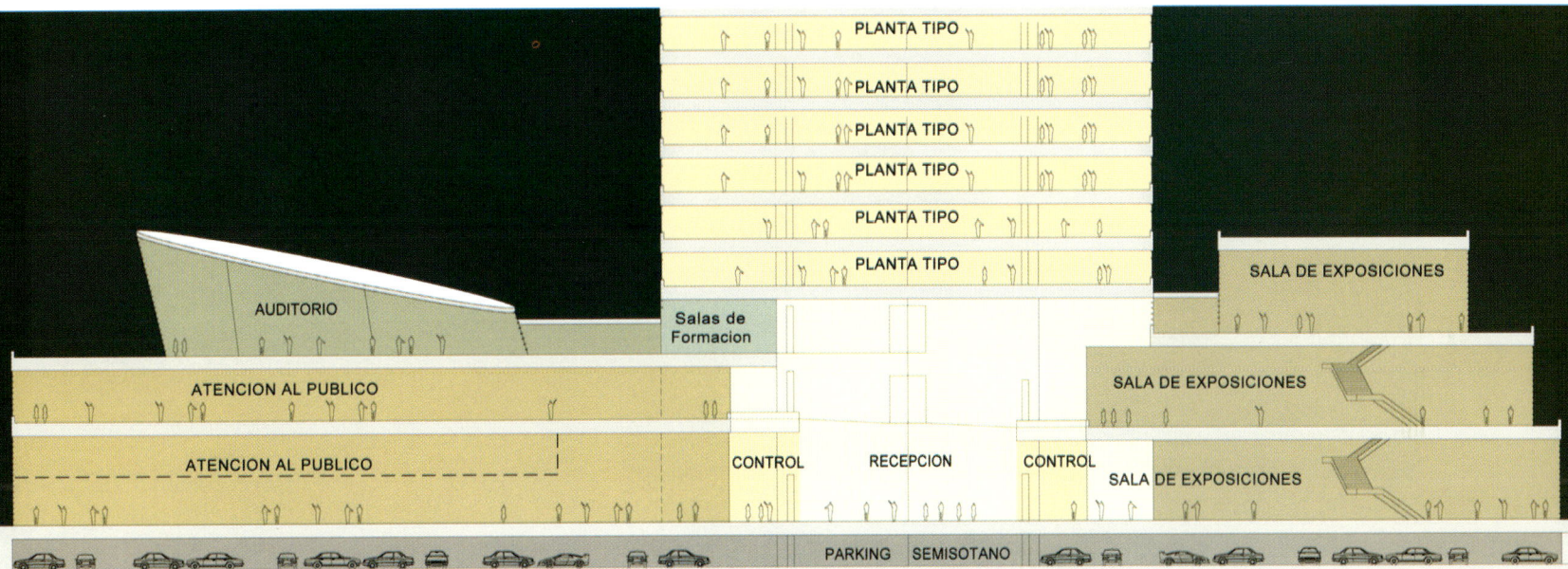

PLANTA TIPO

PLANTA TIPO

PLANTA TIPO

PLANTA TIPO

PLANTA TIPO

PLANTA TIPO

AUDITORIO

Salas de Formacion

SALA DE EXPOSICIONES

ATENCION AL PUBLICO

SALA DE EXPOSICIONES

ATENCION AL PUBLICO

CONTROL RECEPCION CONTROL

SALA DE EXPOSICIONES

PARKING SEMISOTANO

center of the Basque Country. Due to its privileged situation, Abandoibarra will make it possible for the present center of Bilbao to extend toward the river Nervión that will cease to be a barrier to the expansion of the city. In order to recover this space found between the river and the suburban development, the existing urban axes have been prolonged along with the incorporation of new streets that favor open public spaces and pedestrian needs with regard to the use of private vehicles. Totally

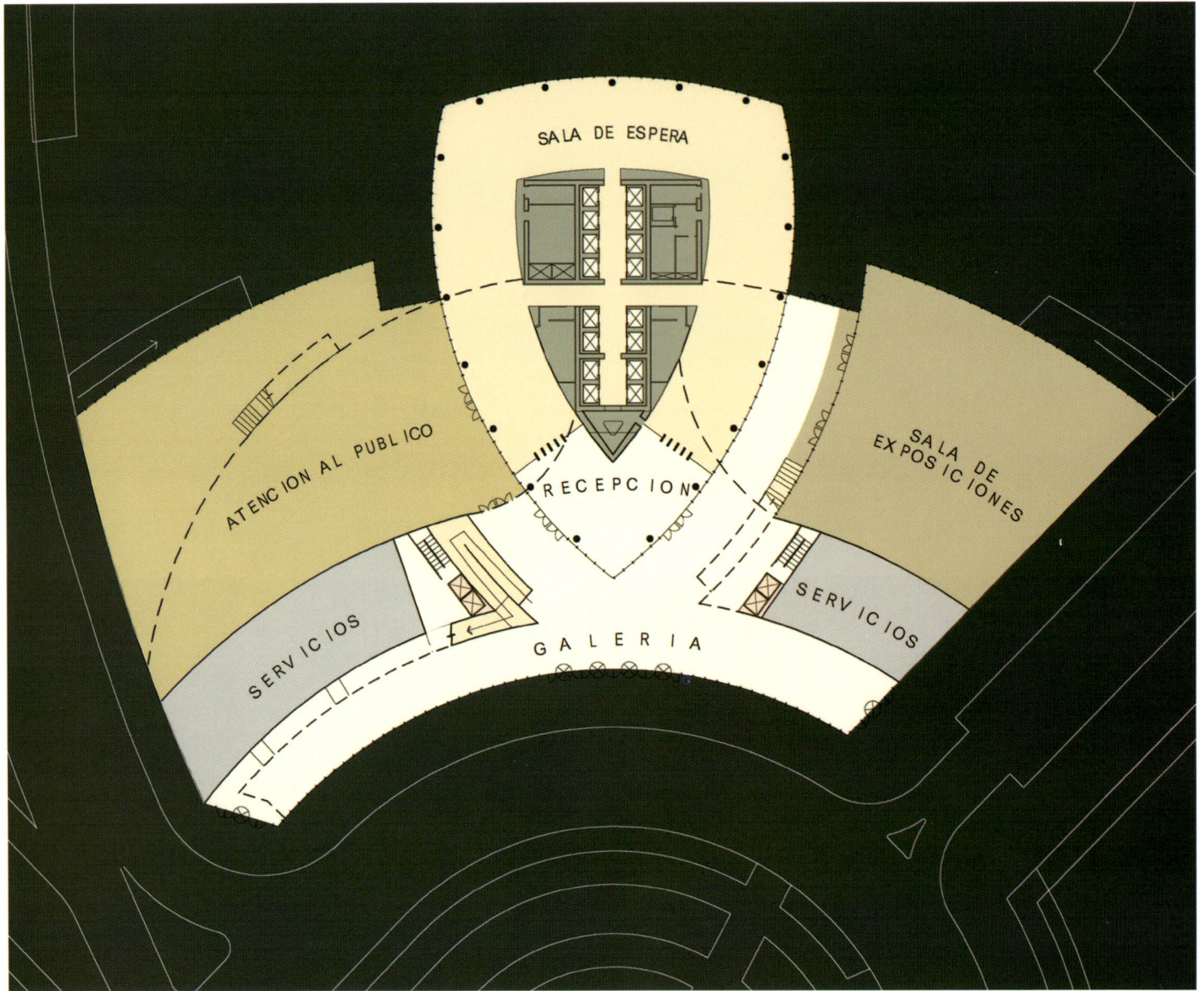

SALA DE ESPERA

ATENCION AL PUBLICO

RECEPCION

SALA DE EXPOSICIONES

SERVICIOS

GALERIA

SERVICIOS

regenerating the one-kilometer space that extends along the riverside between two of the main cultural foci of the city (the Guggenheim Museum and the Palacio Euskalduna de Congresos y de la Música) a new metropolitan center on the banks of the river Nervión will be created. This will constitute a seafront environment consisting of more than 200,000 m2 of green zones and new plots available for the development of offices, the retail center Zubiarte by the North American architect Robert Stern, the

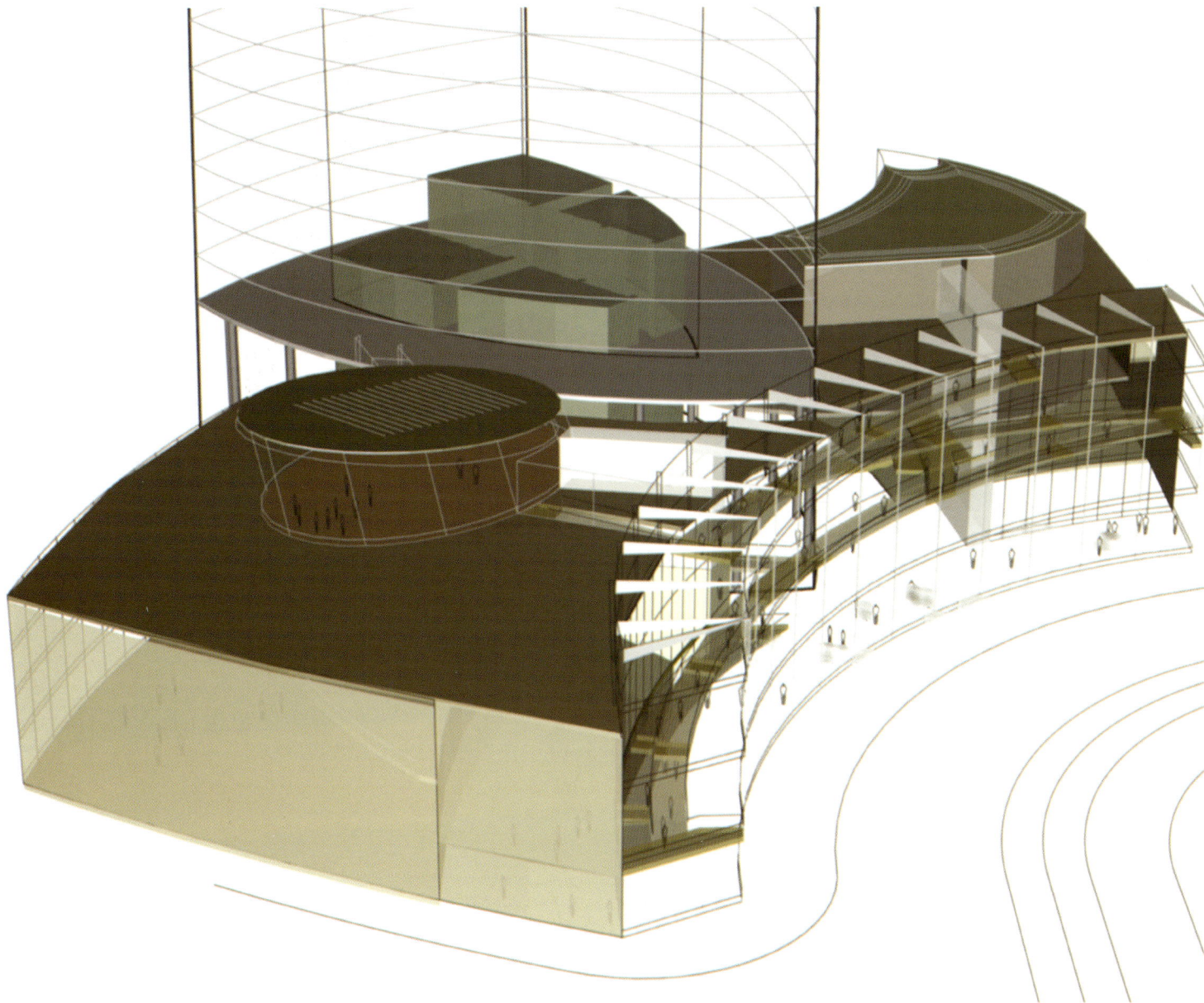

Sheraton Hotel by the Mexican Ricardo Legorreta, university installations and living spaces (of which the first building by the Basque architect Luís Peña Ganchegui is currently under construction). The Torre Diputación 2002 where the new headquarters of the Bizkaiko Foru Aldundia (the local governmental authorities of Bizkaia) will be located will be the main element of the General Plan for Abandoibarra due to its central position and height. It will be Bilbao's highest building and an important land-

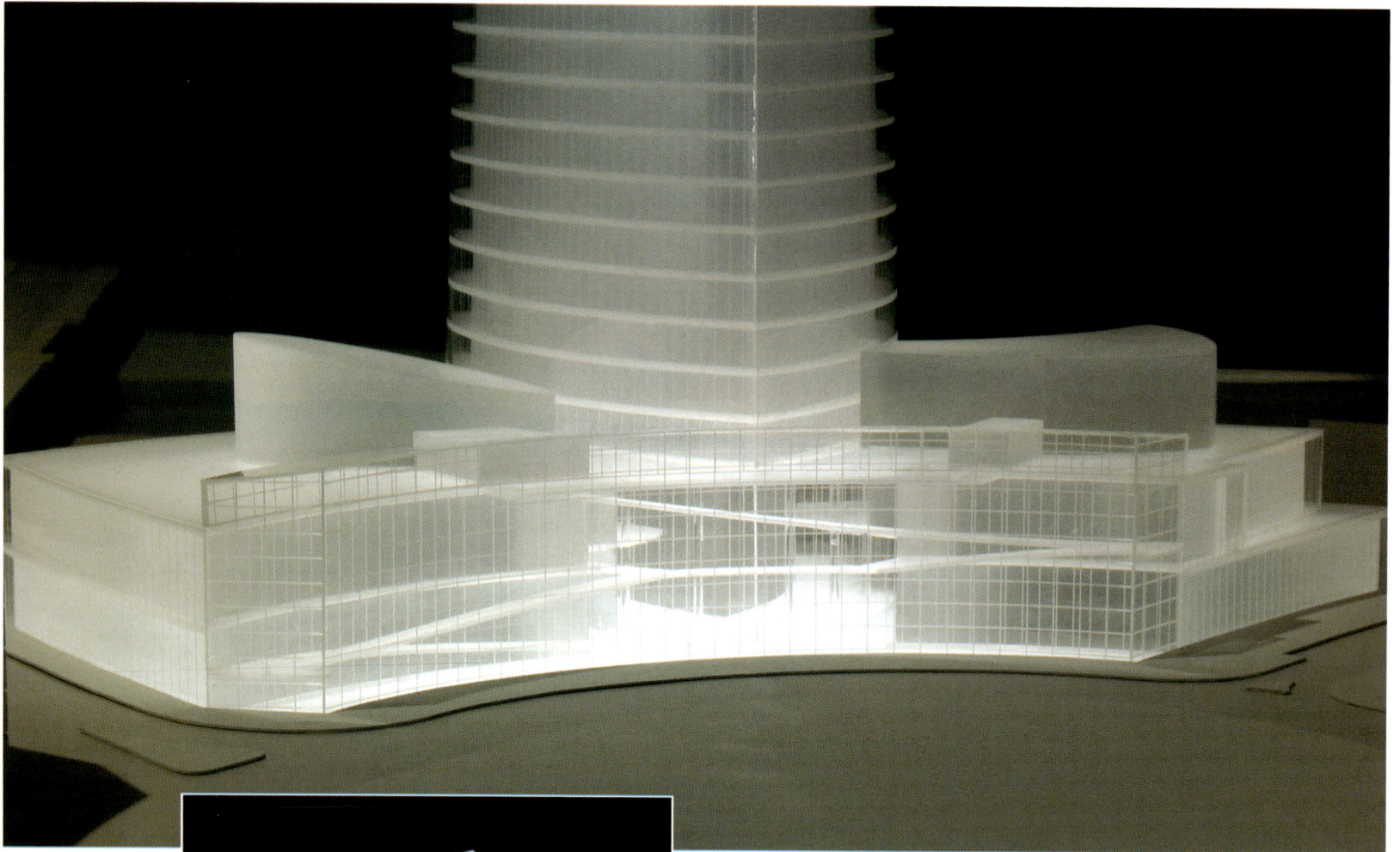

mark as it will be distinguishable from any point of the city. It will be situated in the new Plaza Euskadi where it meets the existing suburban development as a result of the prolongation of the cal-

le Elkano. The building's vocation for public use is manifested by its functional organization. There is to be a base four floors in height that will extend all the way around the plaza. In the interior of this podium, suspended ramps are to be located parallel to the facade which will reinforce the oval form of the plaza and permit the public to circulate vertically in the interior of the building as if it were an extension of the city.

The floor plan of the tower is triangular although its sides are slightly curved. The volume is to be gracefully elevated and will incline progressively as it gains height and evokes a glass obelisk. For the initial project, César Pelli designed a tower with 40 floors which he has had to reduce to 31. However, the architect has not wanted to give up on the initial tower and these floors have been gained virtually with a careful use of perspective. He

has constructed a tower that is, in potential, a great deal higher than it really is and in which if we were to prolong the lines of the arrises, we would be able to imagine how they converged in a point in infinity to form an obelisk. In this way, the architect has conceived a building that will reach the heavens when viewed favorably and this has added sensitivity to his architecture.

# Bank of America
Charlotte (Carolina del Norte, USA)

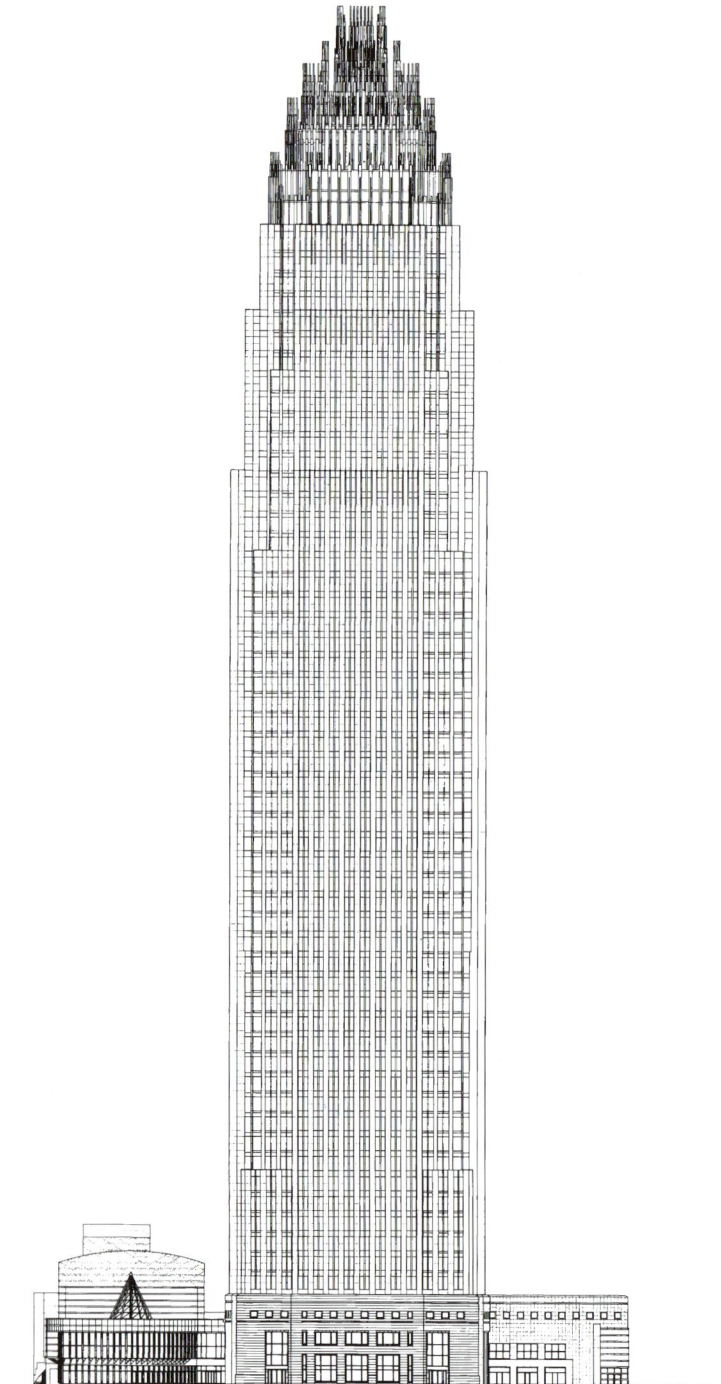

This building that is also known as the NationsBank Corporate Center (given that this is the name of the entity that promoted its construction) in addition to being the corporate headquarters of the Bank of America, concentrates a great diversity of services in its base. It is found in the economic, historic and geographical center of the city of Charlotte where it is a point of reference. Its

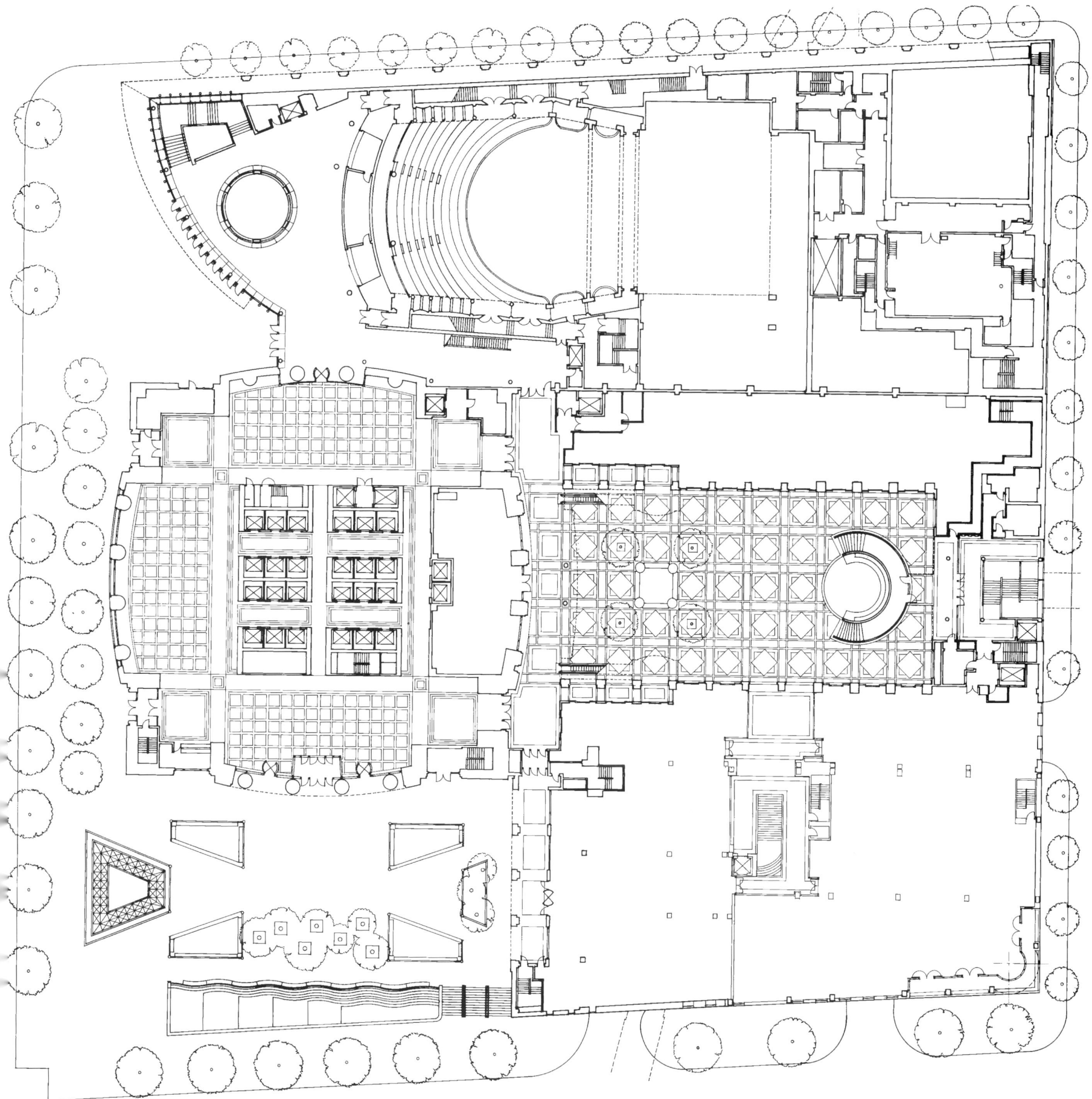

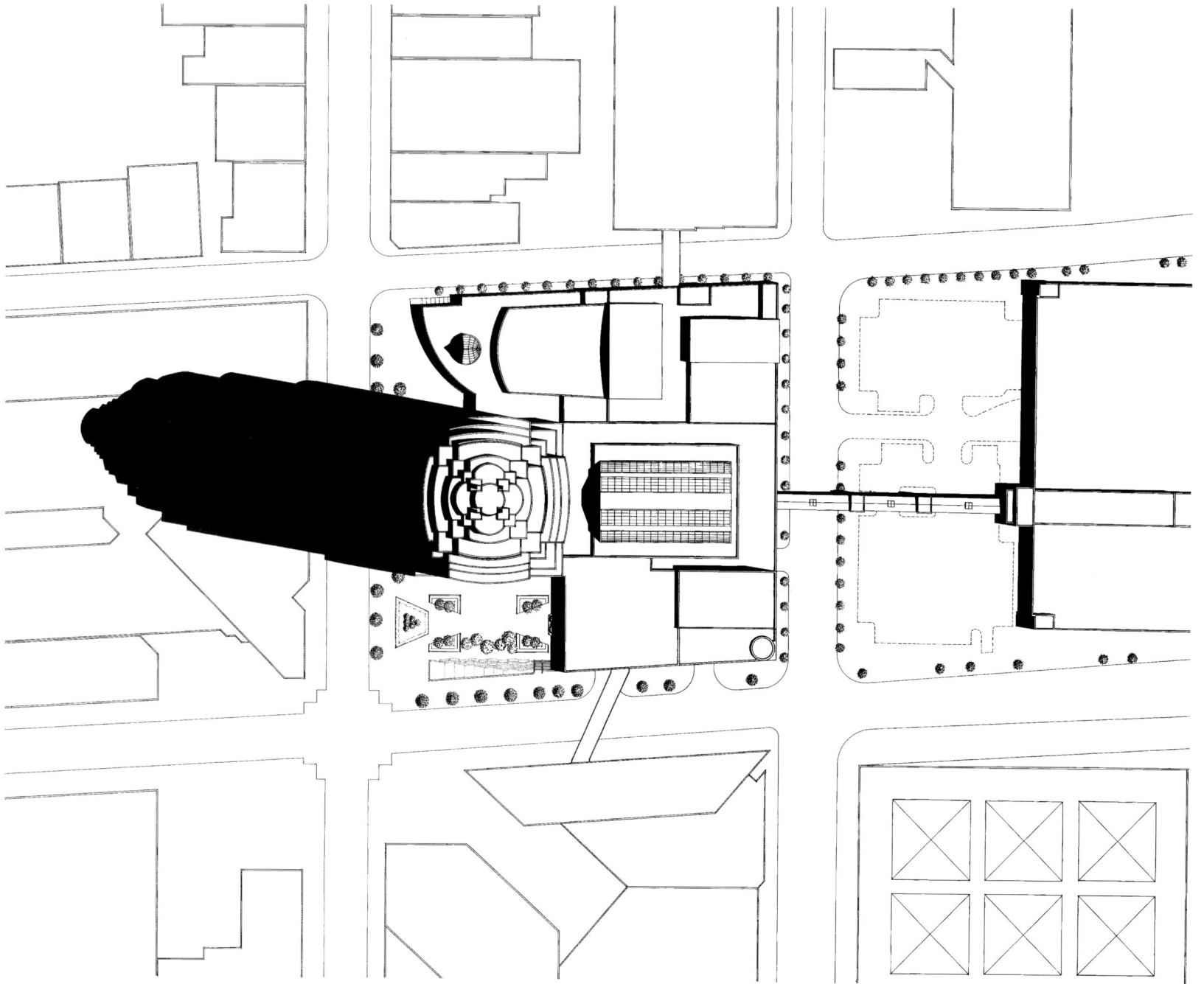

construction responded as much to the economic viability for the developer (maximum height, functional efficacy and cost saving) as to the possibility of revitalizing the urban center of the city culturally and economically. César Pelli understood how to undertake this assignment and came up with a proposal of a functional and architectonic nature that went far beyond the

economic factors and generated a great public complex of which the tower of the Bank of America is the corner stone.

A series of public uses have been integrated into the program for the building. The ground floor occupies the complete block and creates the complex that comprises a hotel, two theaters,

two landscaped gardens and the Founders Hall - a civic and commercial center - in the heart of the tower. Designed as a large atrium covered by a rectangular skylight that organizes the public space around its perimeter and distributes the retail areas, the two halls for the North Carolina Performing Arts Center and the pedestrian entrances to the tower. In an annex on the block behind the complex, there is a public car park connected to the interior of the Founders Hall by means of a walkway that crosses the street. In the same way, two more walkways connect the blocks on each side with the interior of the complex.

The tower also possesses a direct access from the outside that can be reached through a small landscaped garden that highlights the importance of the construction and avoids the necessity for a large independent frontal access. The classical use of volume and the elegance of the tower is enhanced by its crowning that consists of an assembly of aluminum bars that reflects the

light of the sun during the day and emits sparkles when it is subject to nocturnal lighting. The curved lines of the floor plan stand out and define a volume that reminds us of the classical American skyscrapers of the 20's and 30's.

The base, wrapped in dark granite, creates an image of solidity and the trunk ascends vertically in horizontal bands of beige granite interrupted by the holes of the windows that form a square-grid that goes on progressively narrowing following the stepping in of the facade. In contrast to the monolithic character of this section, the upper floors become lighter. The main facades curve slightly and are projected toward the interior as the tower gains in height to culminate with a crown that has earned the nickname of "the queen of the city" from the citizens of

Charlotte. Regarding the image of the building and its architectural conception, **César Pelli** has manifested: "Charlotte is a city that is being redefined. It is almost new. Only a few old buildings exist. So it was a question of writing on a blackboard that was almost clean. The objective was not so much that of referring to a specific context as to building a beautiful tower that would transmit a fitting impression of the NationsBank Corporate Center".

# Shigeru Ban

Was born in Tokyo in 1957. He received his secondary education in the Ochanomizu School of Fine Arts. In this school, he came into contact with specific design problems: "As students we had to create structures with different materials such as wood, paper and bamboo every week. I tended to take in a couple of solutions for each assignment", he explains. Maybe, it was this that aroused his permanent interest in experimenting with structures, materials and construction methods. Shigeru Ban studied architecture at the Southern California Institute of Architecture and later at the Cooper Union of New York. It was during this period that he received most influence from the New York Five, especially from John Hedjuk. After working briefly with Arata Isozaki (1982-83) in Tokyo, he received his title in ar-

Gimnasio Atsushi Imai

PAM Paper Art Museum

Pabellón japonés de la Expo 2000

chitecture from the Cooper Union (1984). The following year, he set up on his own.

Between 1993 and 1995, he was assistant teacher of architecture at the Tama Art University. He also gave classes in the National University of Yokohama and in the University of Nihon. As of 1995, after the devastating earthquake in Kobe, he has been a consultant for the United Nations High Commission for Refugees (UNHCR). After this earthquake, in addition to constructing the Paper Church with the very help of the refugees themselves, he put the prototype of the Paper Shelter into practice: a temporary solution made with cardboard cylinders for those who have become homeless. He has also proposed new paper shelters for the refugees in Rwanda (1995). In this same year, he set up the humanitarian organization, Voluntary Architects Network. At present, Shigeru Ban continues with his commitment to the refugee victims of natural disasters and wars particularly with those affected by the earthquakes in Turkey.

Ban has received numerous prizes among which the Grand Kansai Prize of 1996 from the Japanese Architectural Institute (JAI) and the Prize for the Best Young Architect of Japan in 1997 stand out.

Shigeru Ban has exhibited his work on a number of occasions and his shows dedicated to Emilio Ambasz and Alvar Aalto should also be mentioned. He has also applied his creativity to the fields of graphic and industrial design.

# Atsushi Imai Gymnasium
## Structure in Laminated Wood

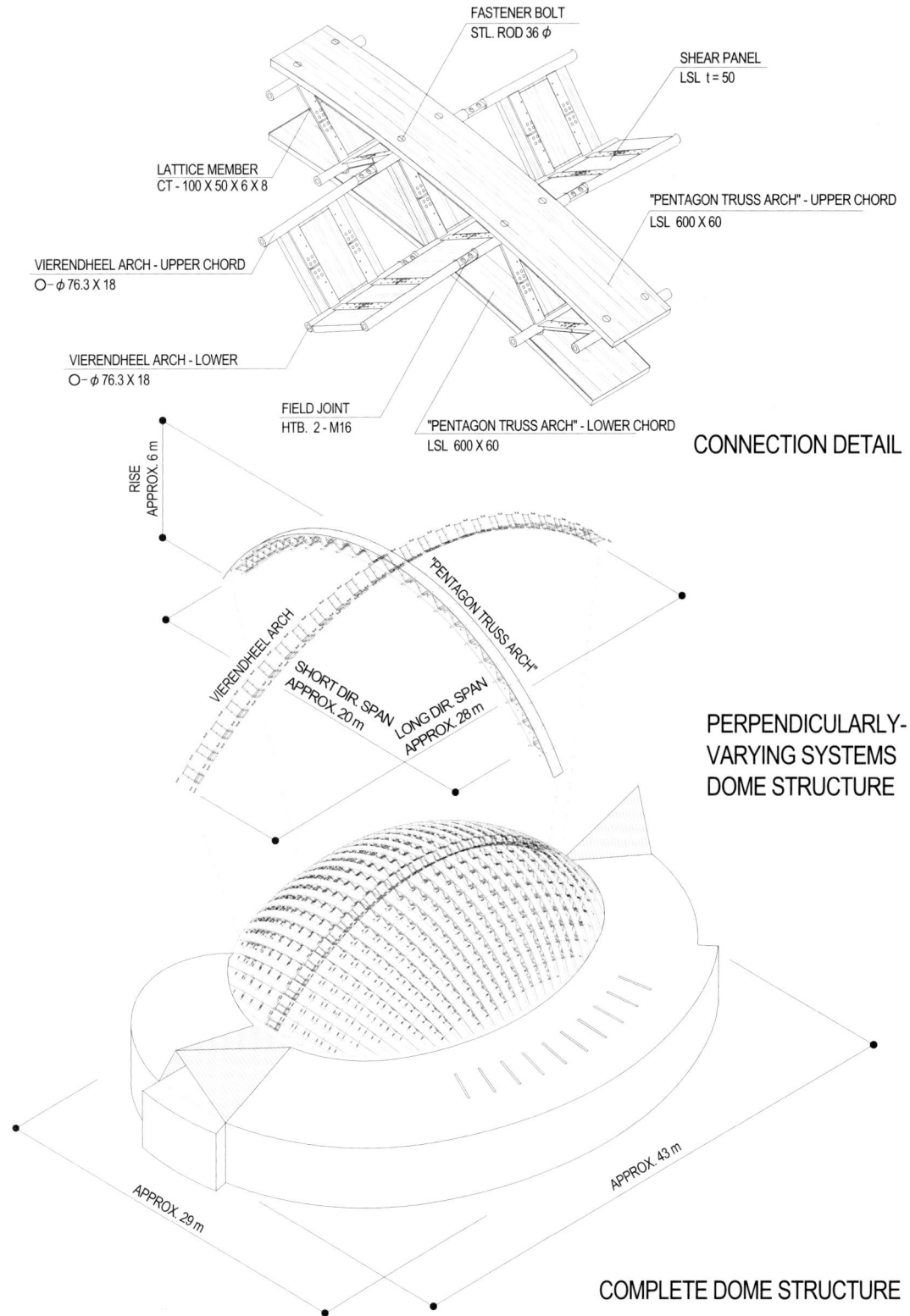

FASTENER BOLT
STL. ROD 36 φ

SHEAR PANEL
LSL  t = 50

LATTICE MEMBER
CT - 100 X 50 X 6 X 8

"PENTAGON TRUSS ARCH" - UPPER CHORD
LSL  600 X 60

VIERENDHEEL ARCH - UPPER CHORD
O – φ 76.3 X 18

VIERENDHEEL ARCH - LOWER
O – φ 76.3 X 18

FIELD JOINT
HTB.  2 - M16

"PENTAGON TRUSS ARCH" - LOWER CHORD
LSL  600 X 60

CONNECTION DETAIL

RISE
APPROX. 6 m

VIERENDHEEL ARCH

"PENTAGON TRUSS ARCH"

SHORT DIR. SPAN
APPROX. 20 m

LONG DIR. SPAN
APPROX. 28 m

PERPENDICULARLY-
VARYING SYSTEMS
DOME STRUCTURE

APPROX. 29 m

APPROX. 43 m

COMPLETE DOME STRUCTURE

The professional career of the Japanese architect Shigeru Ban has been distinguished by his interest in the investigation of new structural concepts for which he uses different materials and forms. When looking at his designs, one is surprised by the in-genuity of some of his ideas: the structures supported by card-board tubes, the houses in which the storage furniture functions as a vertical support, the roofs made of double steel sheets, the cladding-curtain of ivy…

The treatment of the structure is opposed to the high-tech developments of the 1980's and 1990's given that they are not intended to be ostentatious displays of technical resources or to seek ornamentation in the complexity of their constructive detail, but to create spaces that arouse interest through their serenity. In his own words: "I use the structural concept to arrive to a certain type of space or to transform a unfavorable site". For example, in the Furniture Houses (I, II and III), in the 2/5 House, or in the Wall-less House the structure is almost 'invisible' and at the service of being able to achieve 'universal' spaces of a great clarity. In these works, the admiration that **Shigeru Ban** has for the Farnsworth House by Mies van der Rohe can be felt. Ban's architecture is, in some ways, a radical update of traditional Japanese architecture, as much as in the spaces that

he forms as in the materials that he uses. As in traditional Japanese houses, there is, in many of his projects, a physical continuity between the interior and exterior spaces that has been achieved by the use of sliding divisions (transparent or opaque). In the Curtain House, for example, the separation between the interior and the exterior has almost been eliminated and nothing more than a large white curtain which covers the two floors of the building offers visual protection and shelter from the elements. The house can be closed off by sliding glass coverings so that it is habitable in winter. These elements come from the shoji and sudare screens of traditional Japanese architecture. Another example is the 9 Square Grid House. This is a 'universal' square space that can be subdivided into nine parts (rooms) thanks to sliding screens.

In many of his works, he rediscovers materials used in traditional Japanese construction, such as paper. His enthusiasm to experiment with existing materials along with his strong ethical compromise with the conservation of the environment has led him to exploit the possibilities of building with cardboard tubes, a low-cost material which is easily recycled. According to Emilio

Ambasz: "He has converted banal materials into dignified structural elements. In his work, the traditional bamboo house returns in a new way with cardboard tubes". It has been the ef-

forts made by **Shigeru Ban**, along with the structural studies carried out by Gengo Matsui, which have led to the structures of paper tubes being approved by the Ministry of Construction

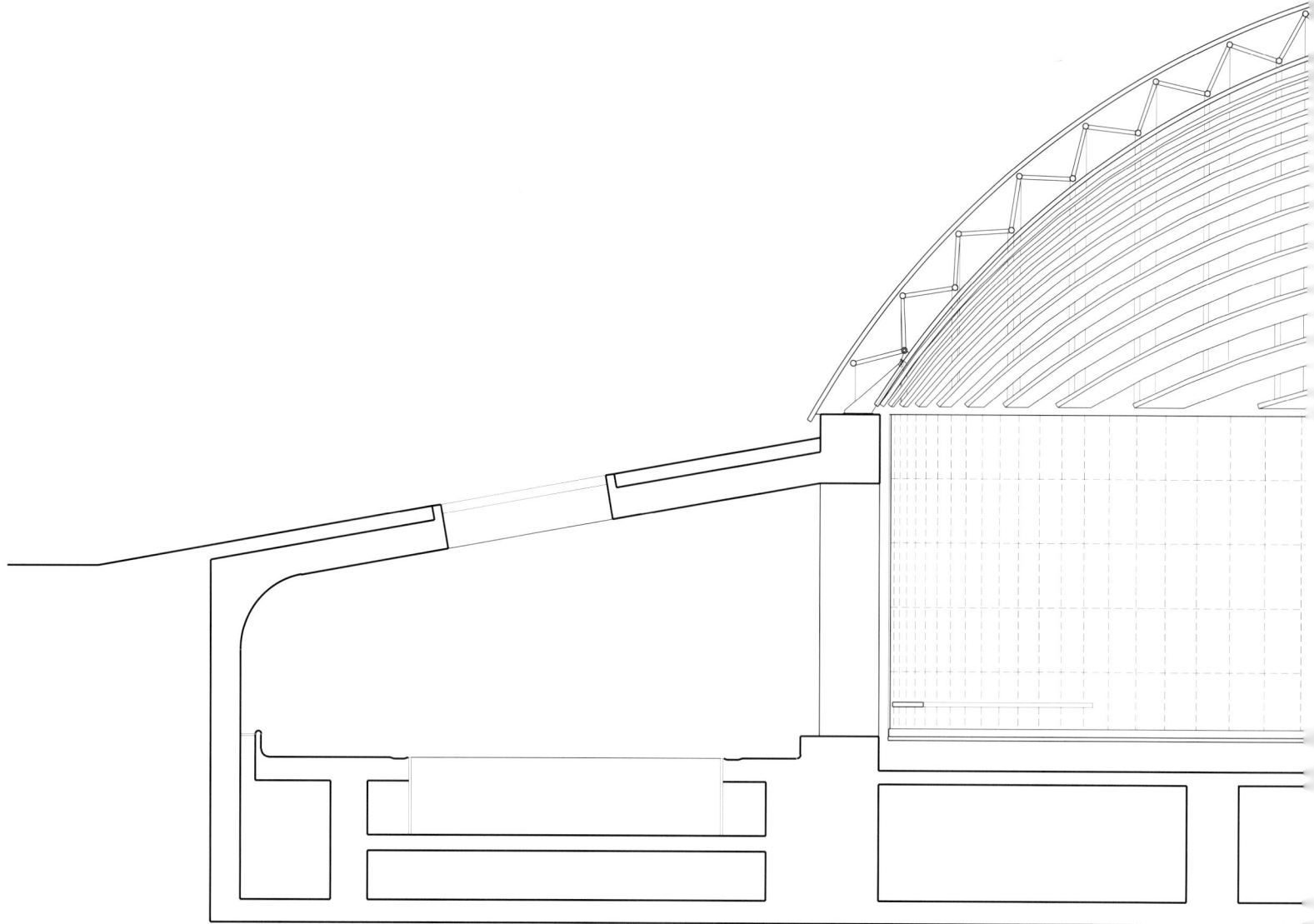

of Japan. "I learnt that everything is possible if the design is credible and one has a desire," states **Ban**. He has used these types of structures on many occasions such as in the Odawara Festival Hall (1990), the MDS Gallery (1994), or the Paper House (1995). He has also investigated into the possibilities offered by other economic elements such as prefabricated concrete pillars, special card frameworks (in the triangular roofing of the Nemunoki Art Museum), or into structures in balsa wood.

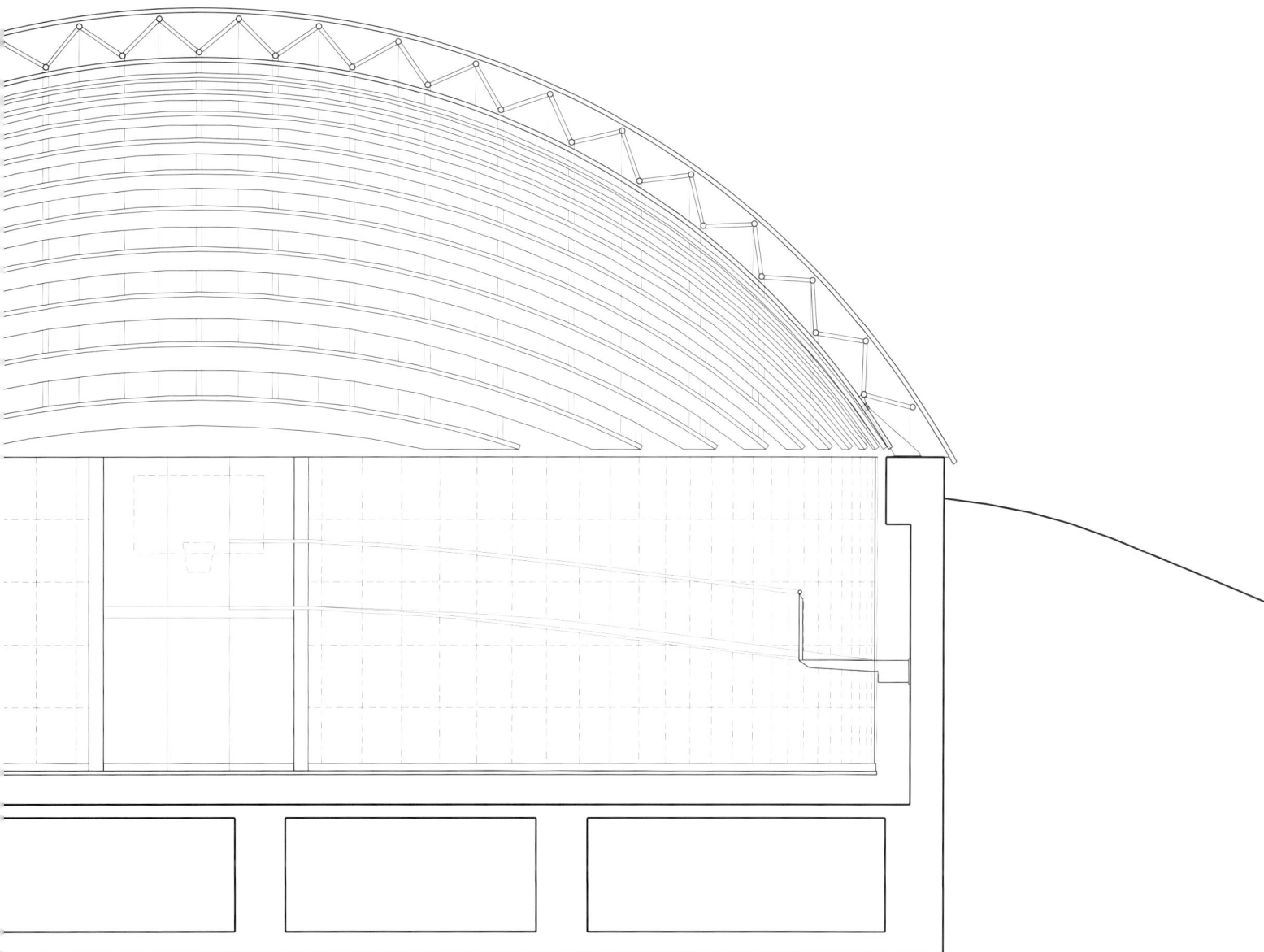

In 1995, the tragedy caused by the Hanshin earthquake in Kobe marked the beginning of an intense collaboration between **Shigeru Ban** and the United Nations High Commission for Refugees (UNHCR). In Kobe, he built, with the help of various volunteers, the Paper Church and also the prototype Paper Shelter to facilitate a roof our their heads as well as some hope for the affected. His commitment to the refugees has continued with the design of various types of shelters for the armed conflicts in

Africa and with a new prototype for the affected by the earthquake in Turkey. **Ban** considers it to be an ethical obligation to propose new architectural models in these cases.

"Sometimes, I have my doubts about the contributions architects make to society (...) The existence of armed conflicts and natural disasters that destroy people's lives and leaves them homeless is on the increase. The way in which architects can serve society, particularly the minorities, will be a decisive factor in forming the character of this age", writes Ban. The architect has managed to unite his professional career, his ethical commitments (his preoccupation for the refugees, his ecological concerns) with his constant investigation into spaces, structures and materials. His view of what it means to be an architect in these agitated times is complete and generous.

### Atsushi Imai Gymnasium
Structure in Laminated Wood

The design, a gymnasium with an indoor swimming pool, uses laminated balsa wood LVL for its structural system. The difficulty of the project resided in the construction of an oval dome 20 x 20 m. This structure was to be able to resist the weight of the snow in winter. To offer a stronger support, the solution consisted

in constructing a special network with elements of laminated wood. In the shorter direction, two parallel arches have been situated to define the curve of the dome. In the perpendicular, longer, direction, the arches have been situated at an inclination in such a way that the whole comes to act as if it were a form lattice. In the same way that paper has acted in a surprising way as a structural element on previous occasions, the LVL type balsa wood has also shown that it can act as a structural element and support much larger spans than originally expected. With this solution, considerably less wood has been needed than had other types of more tradition-laminated woods been used to construct the same dome.

# PAM-Paper Art Museum
Tokio, Japan

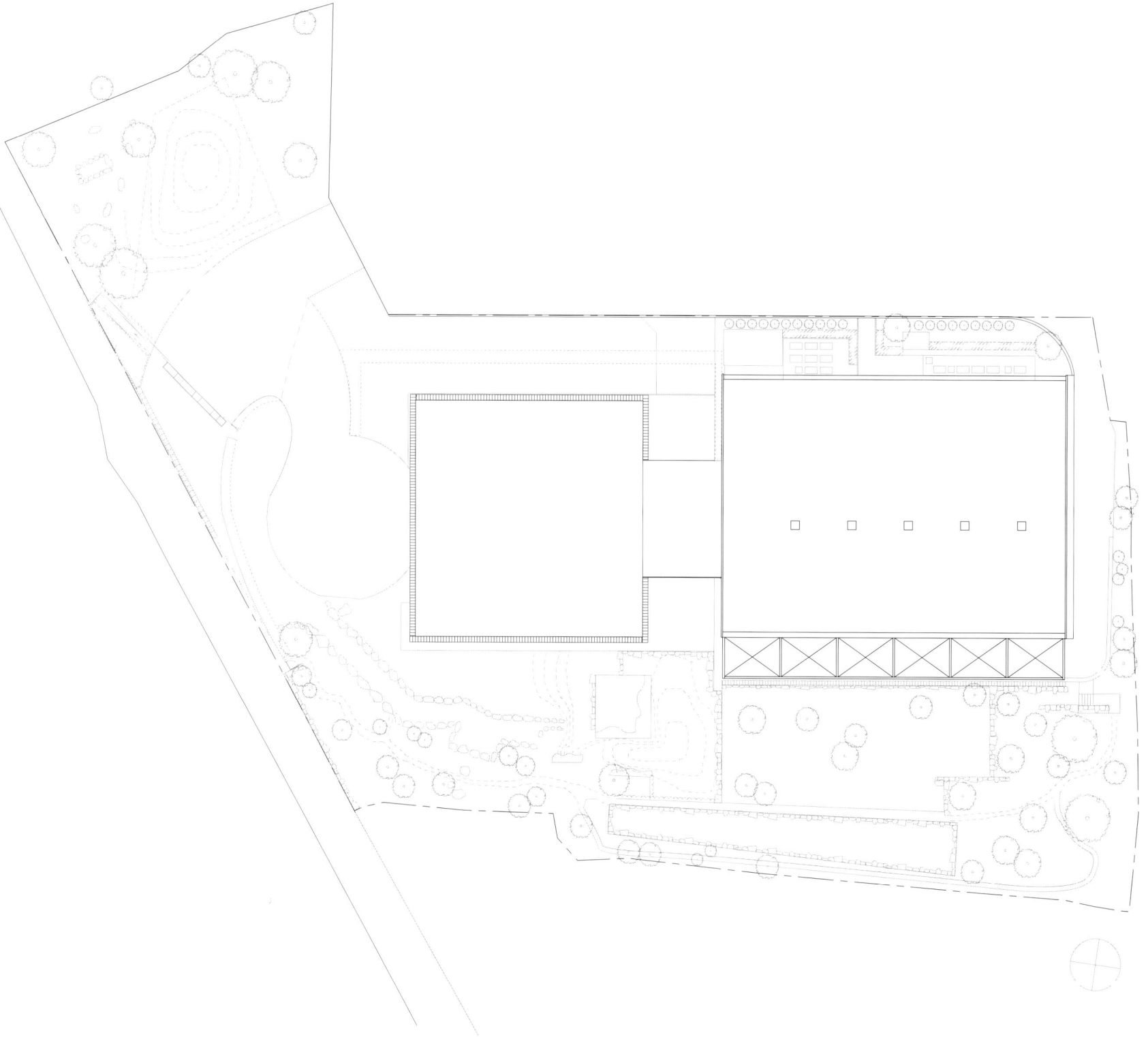

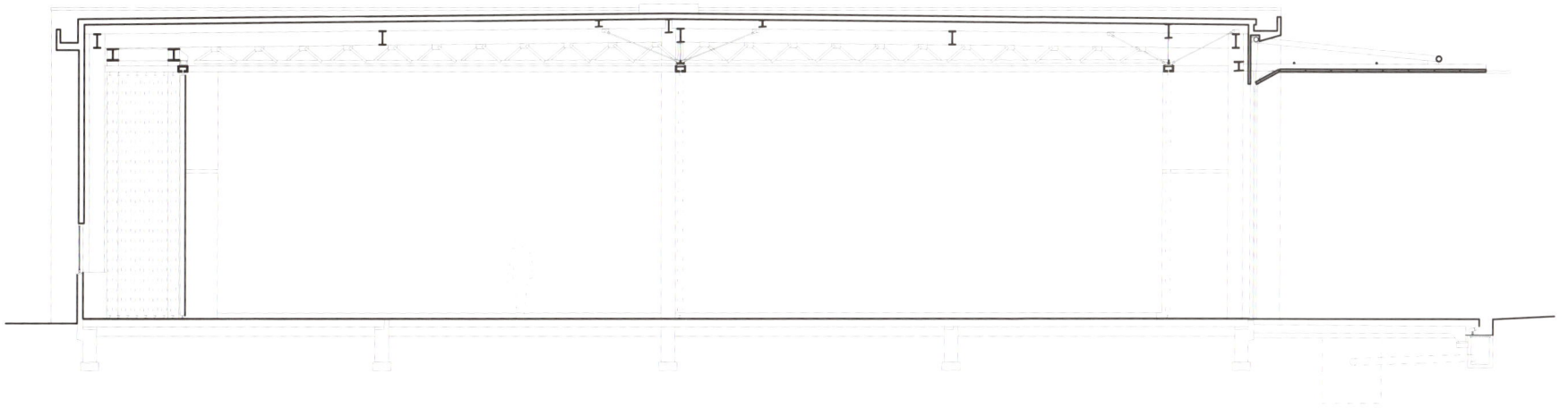

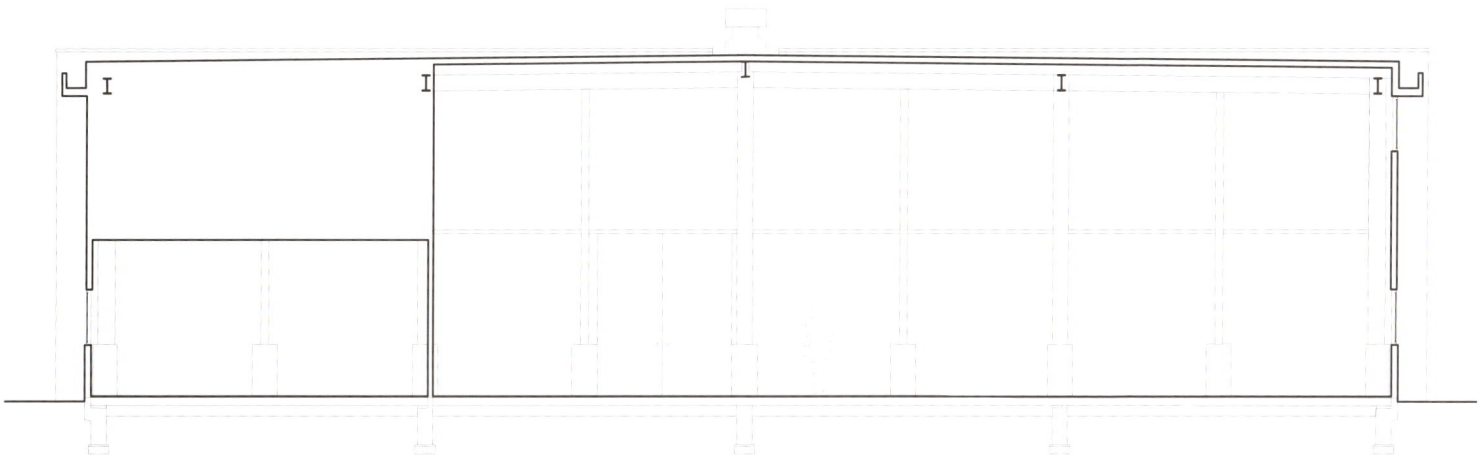

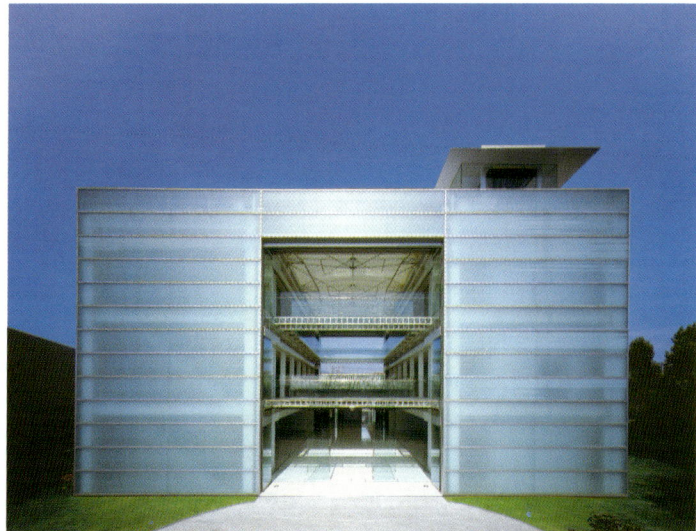

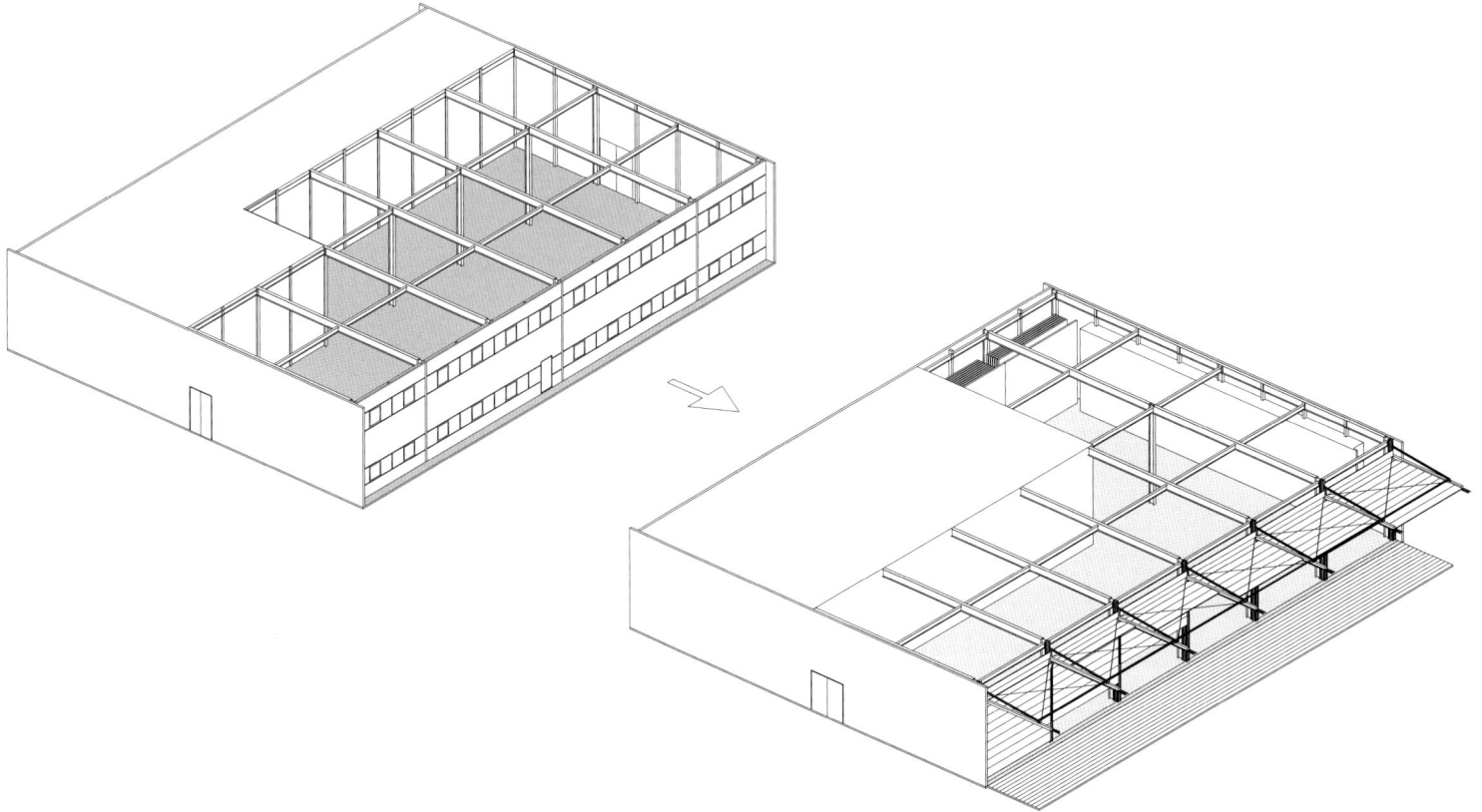

Paper Art Musuem A
Cross Section
Scale: 1:100

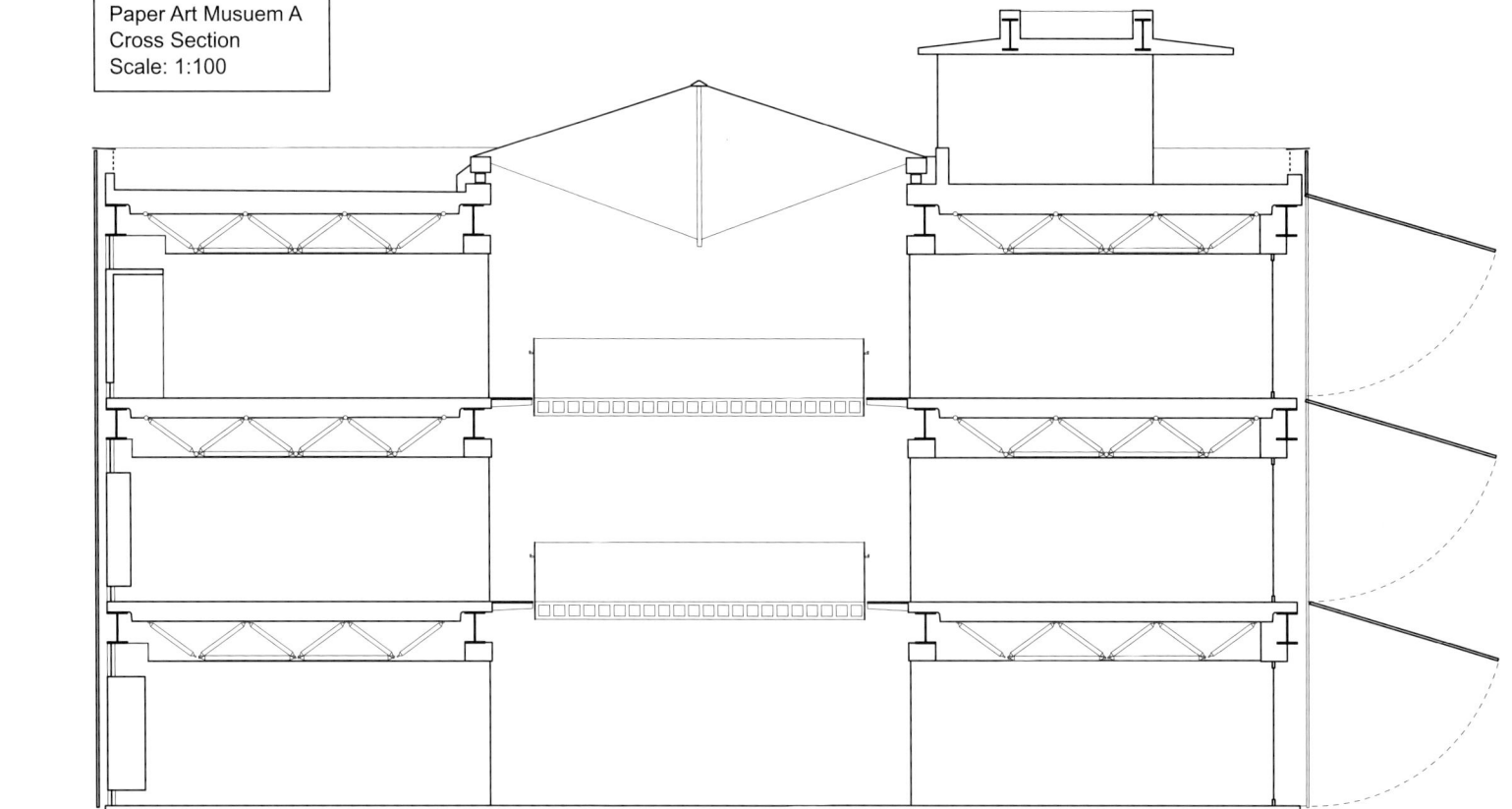

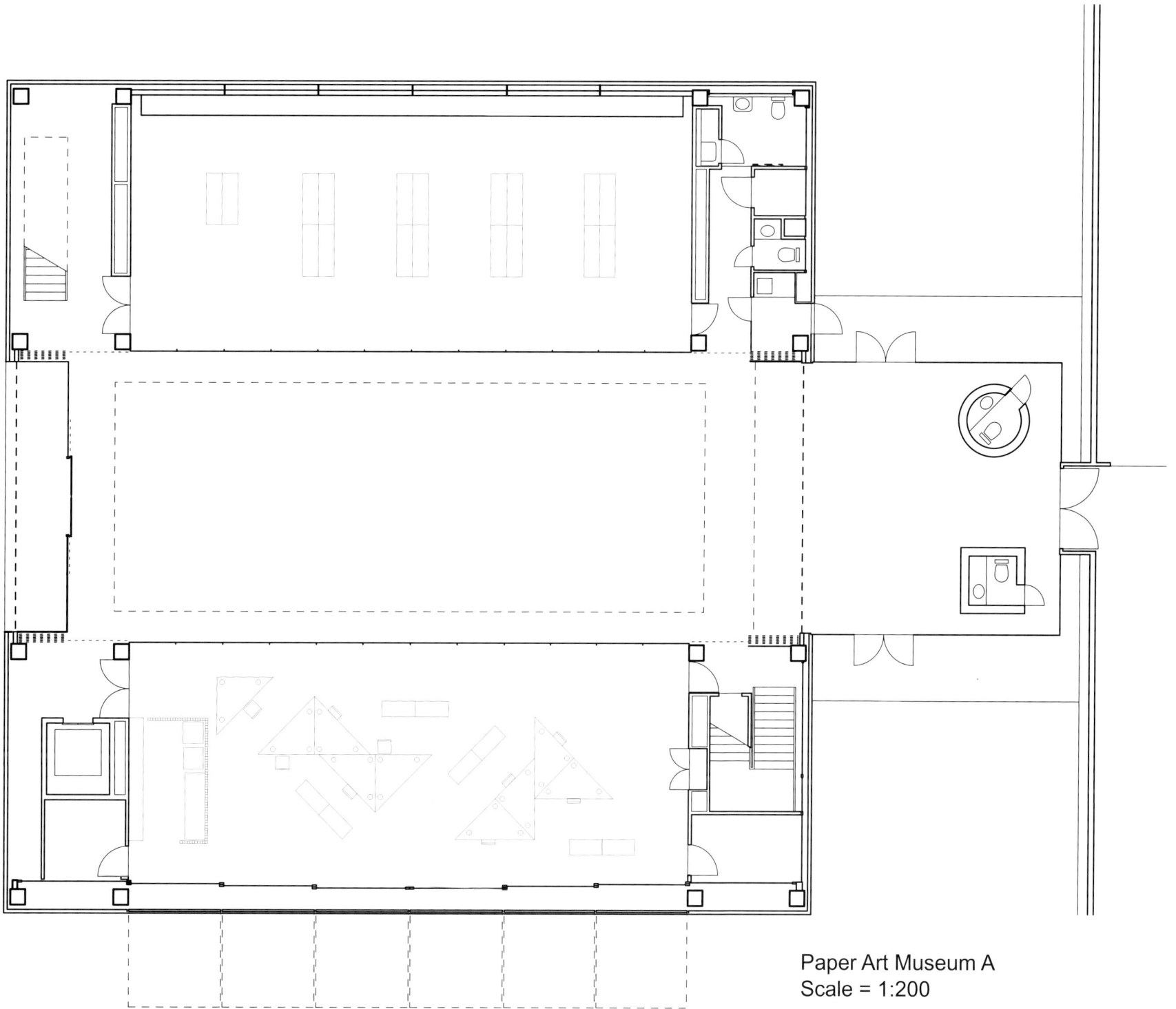

Paper Art Museum A
Scale = 1:200

This project, for a site on the outskirts of Tokyo, is made up of two parts: PAM A, a museum, and PAM B, a contemporary art gallery.

PAM A, the Paper Art Museum, is a private museum that belongs to paper manufacturers. All of the facades are made of reinforced fiberglass. The floor plan of the building is a square di-

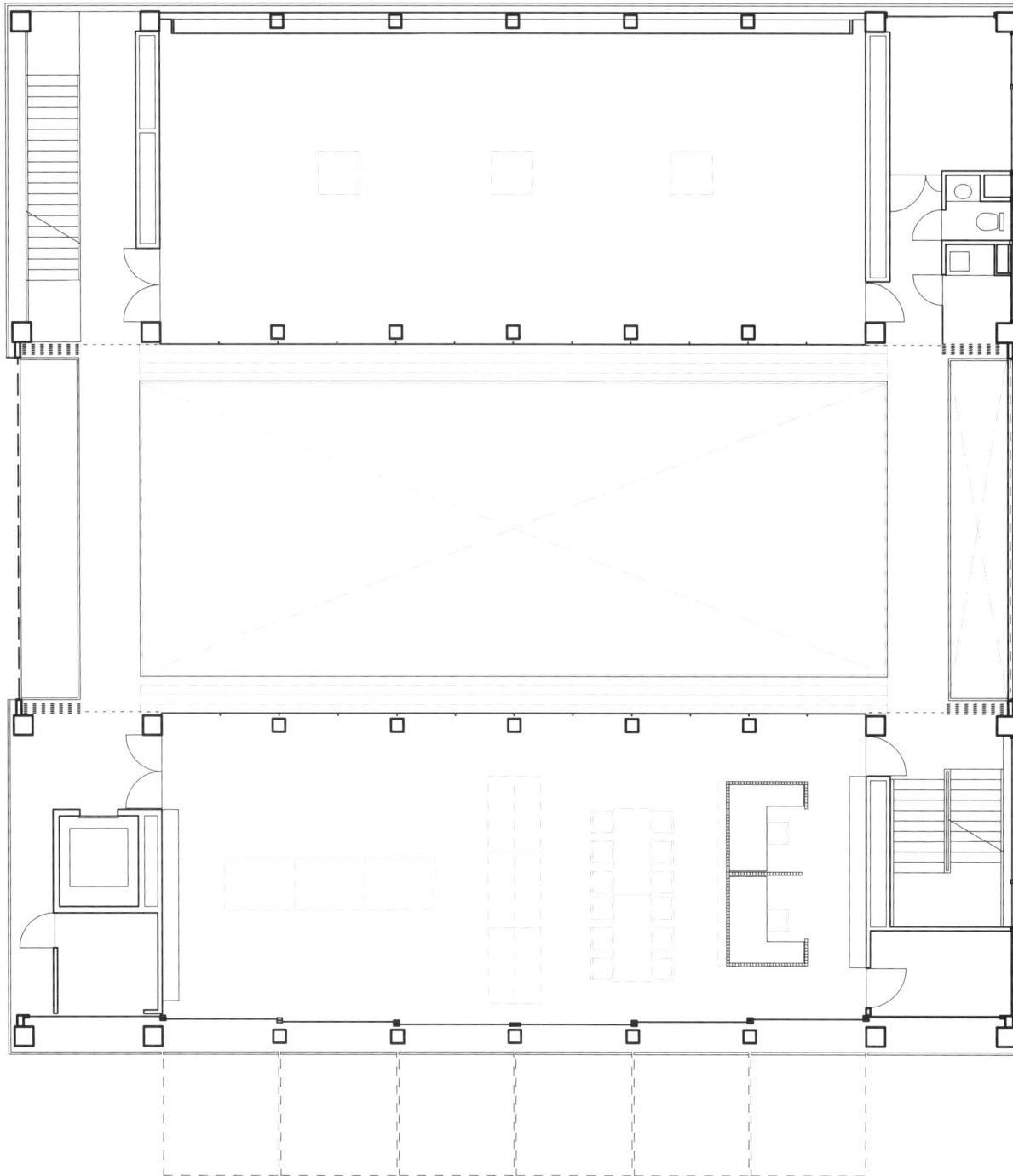

Paper Art Museum
2nd Floor Plan
Scale = 1:200

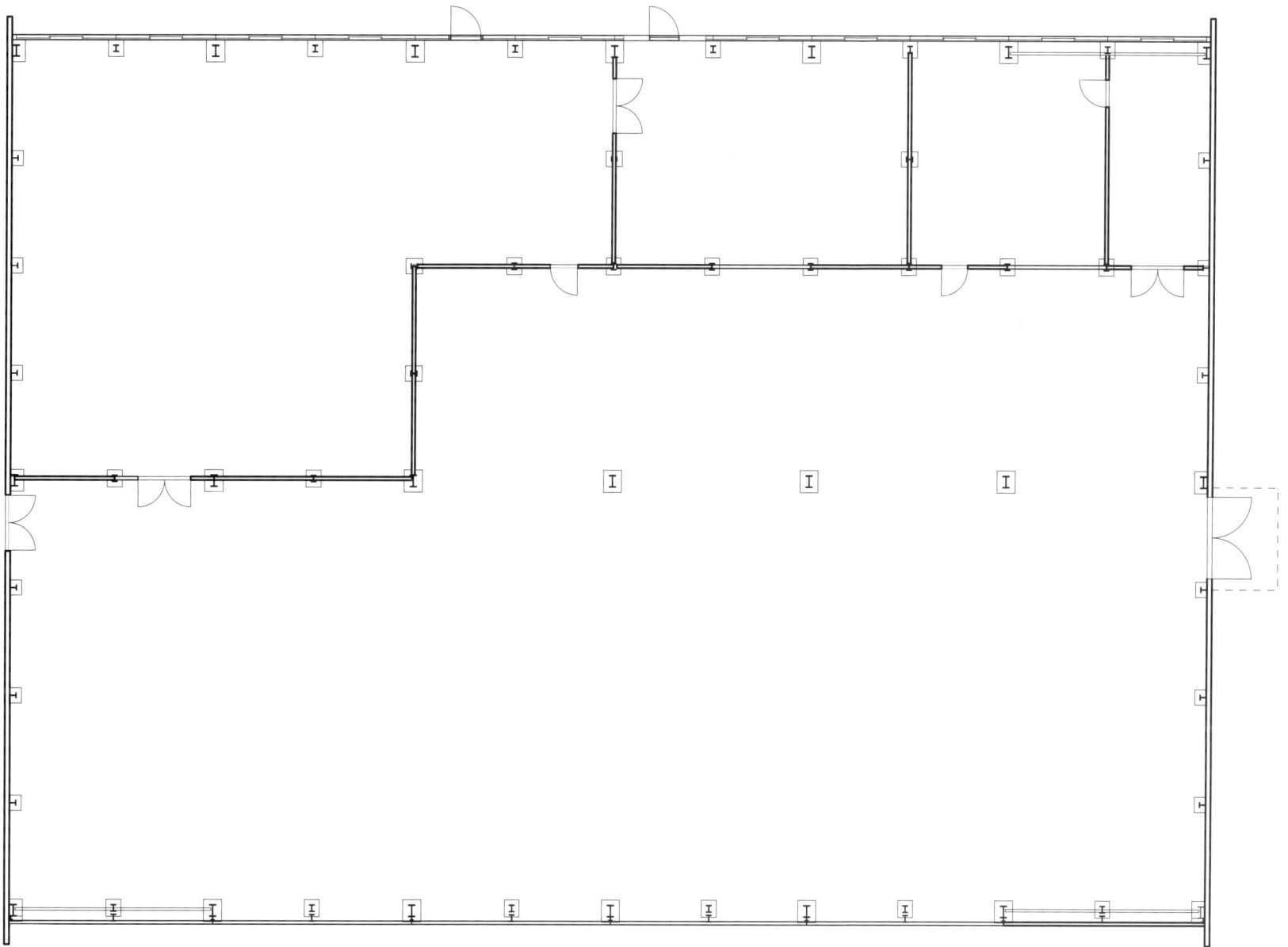

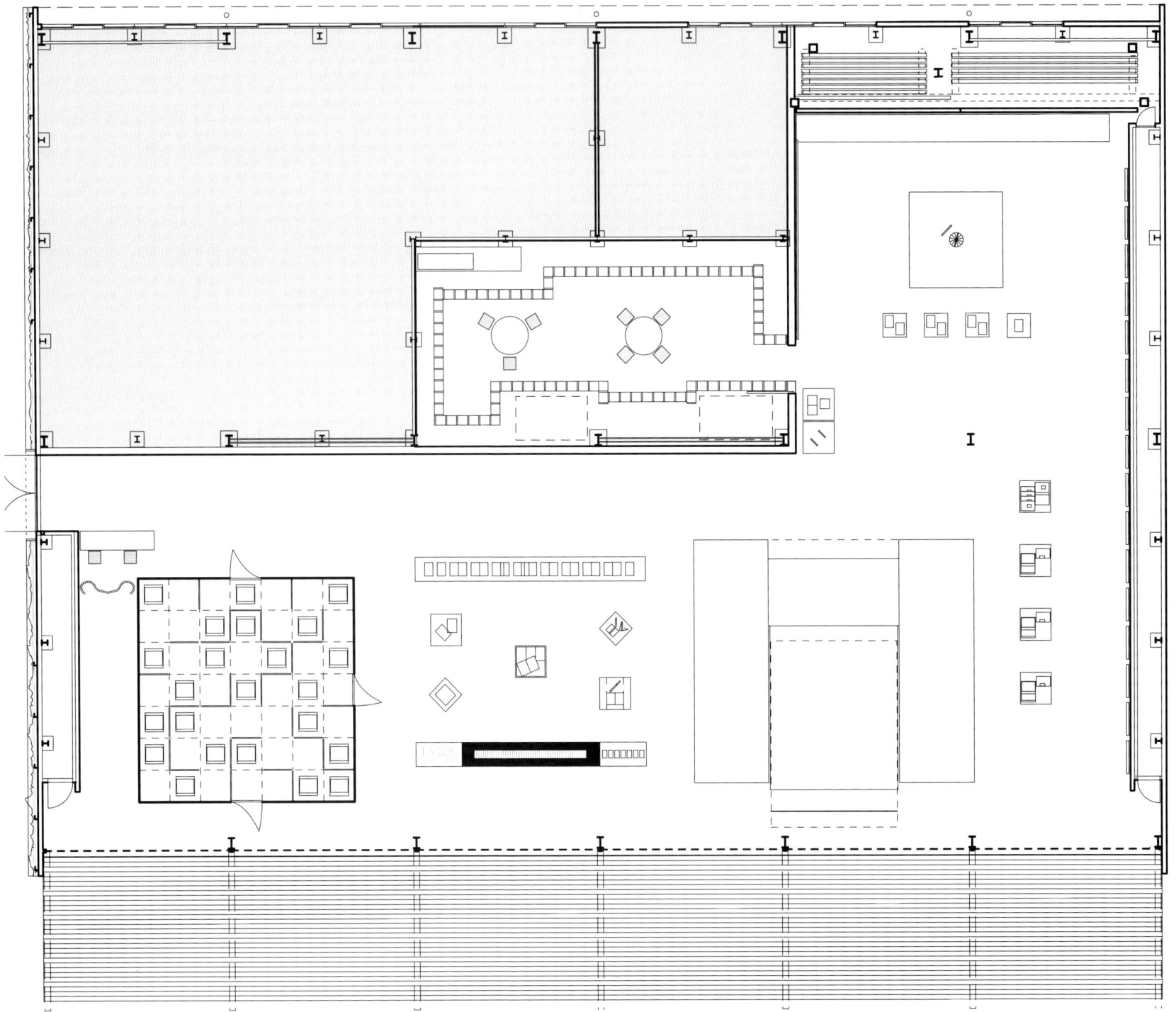

TOP ARCHITECTS OF THE WORLD

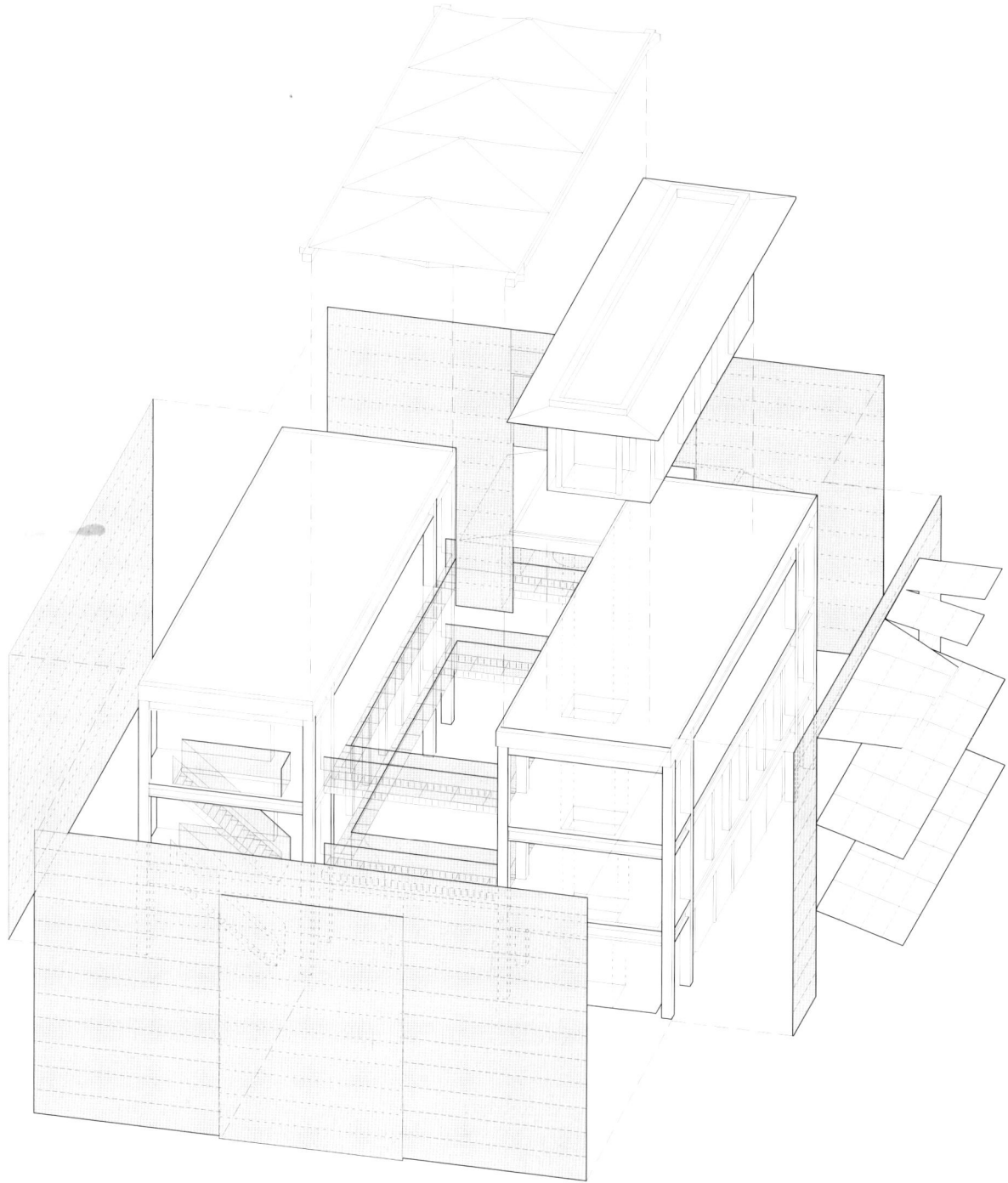

vided up into three rows of which the intermediate is an atrium three floors in height. The possibility of opening and closing the large blinds-canopies, inspired in shoji screens, achieves a spa-

tial continuity between the interior and exterior. PAM B was at first a laboratory and, later, it was converted into a contemporary art gallery. By means of large sliding screens and large translu-

cent doors that become canopies, agreeable spaces with shade have been created in the patio. The main idea behind both buildings has been to recreate, with the use of contemporary materials, spaces for contemporary life while maintaining continuity between the interior and exterior spaces. This is very much in the tradition of Japanese architecture.

## Japanese Pavilion for Expo 2000
### Hanover, Germany

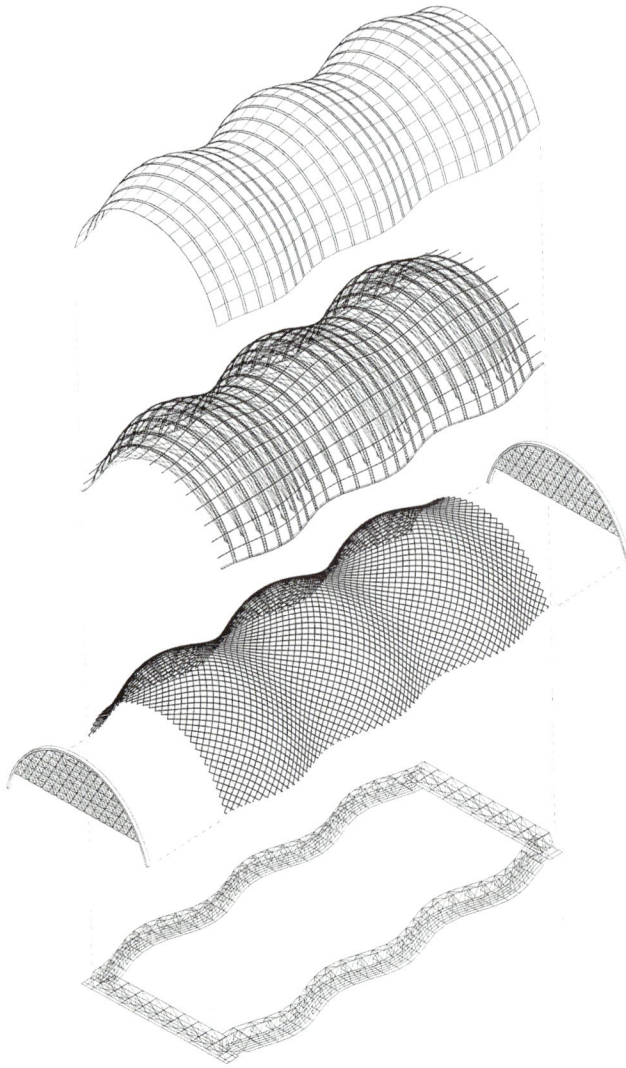

The concept of the Japanese Pavilion for Expo 2000 in Hanover was to be based on sustainability and sensitivity toward environmental concerns, which was the overall theme of the universal exhibition. It was also to address these issues in some way relat-

ed to Japanese traditions. For these reasons, we decided to construct a 'Paper Pavilion' by using the 'cardboard tube structure' techniques. The pavilion suggests a history of construction, demolition and recycling. In architectural design, the construc-

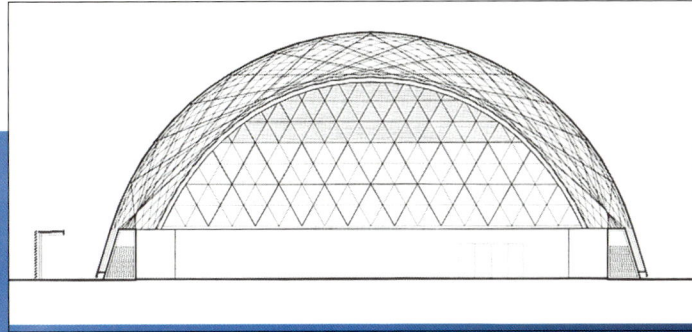

tion of the building normally means the end of the project. However, in this case, the story of the pavilion continues after its elements have been dismantled. Another characteristic of the pavilion is that its design team was made up of professionals of different disciplines from different countries. Although the 'cardboard tube structures' had already been approved by the Ministry of Japan, the large structure had to be developed and tested in order to obtain the necessary permissions in Germany.

TOP ARCHITECTS OF THE WORLD

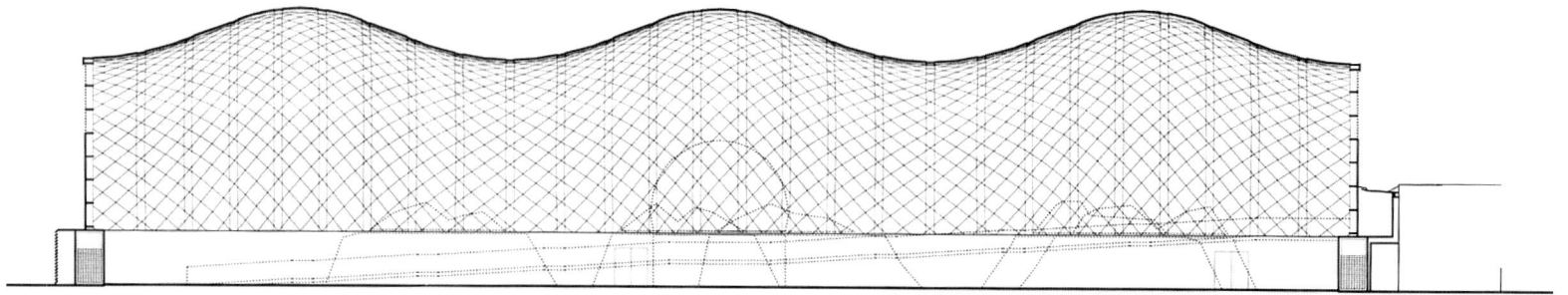

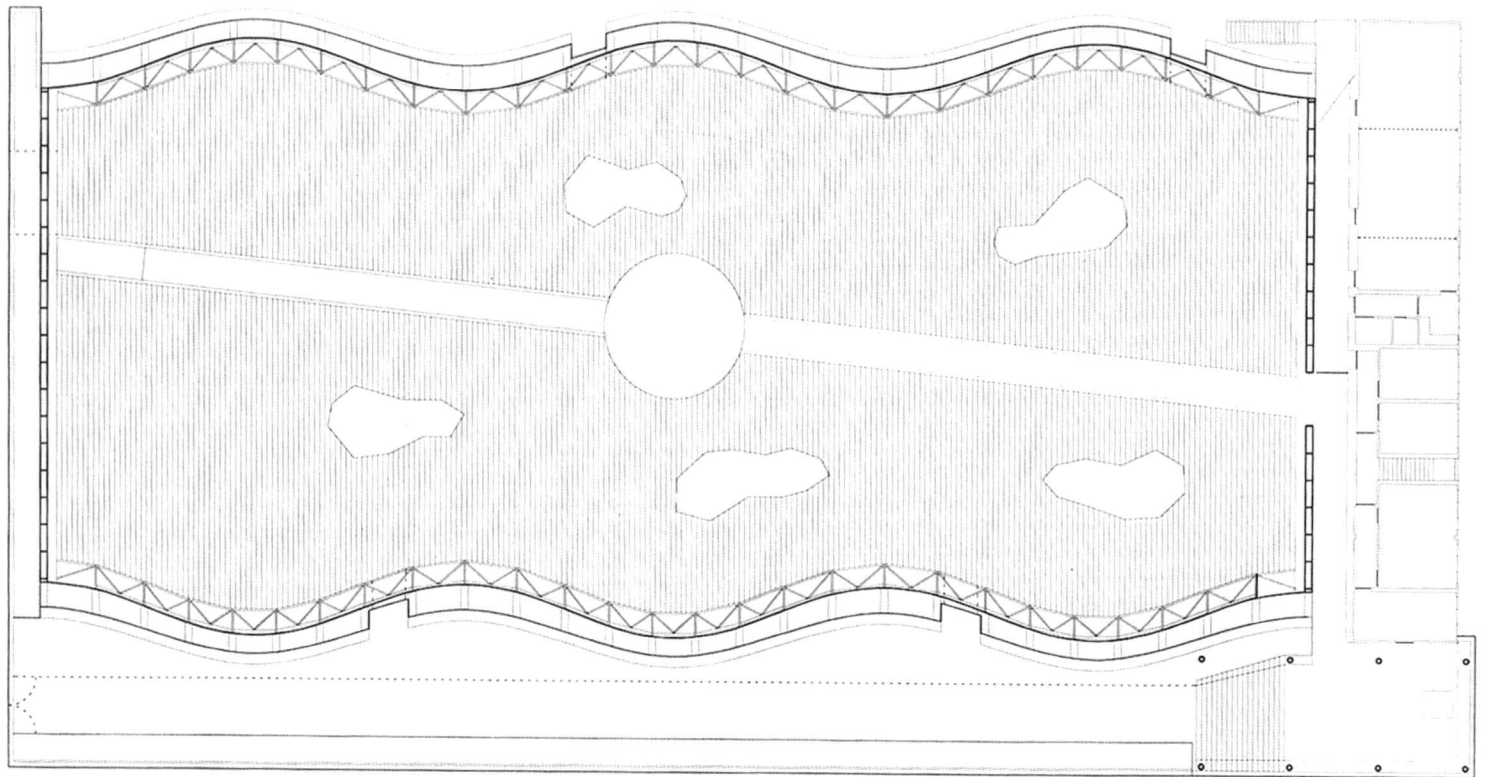

This study was carried out along with Prof. Otto and the British engineering firm Buro Happold. The cardboard tube company that manufactured the tubes was Sonoco Europe, the largest company of this type in the zone. The Japanese Pavilion is the fortunate result of the contribution of various international collaborations and of the combination of ideas and technologies.

# Jean Nouvel

**W**as born in Fumel, Lot et Garonne, France. Although he had wanted to be a painter for a long time, he finally decided for architecture and enrolled in the École des Beaux-Arts of Paris at the top of the list of those to be admitted by means of the access exam. While still a student, he started working with Claude Parent who was, at that time, a partner of the theoretic Paul Virilio. In these two, Nouvel recognizes his true maestros as from that time he started to doubt about the academic doctrines of the École de Beaux-Arts. He experienced the May '68 outburst at first hand, a period that marked his ideas. Before finishing his studies, Claude Parent encouraged him to open his own studio and passed some projects on to him. After having worked in his office for five years, one day Parent told him, "You've learnt enough here, now I'm going to give you a hand to help you continue on your own." In 1972, he received his diploma in architecture. In 1976, along with some of those selected for the first P.A.N. competition, he founded the architectural movement Mars

Main Street-River Hotel Brooklin

Torre Agbar

1976. The following year, he took part in the foundation of the Syndicat de l'Architecture and was one of the organizers of the international competition for the district of les Halles in Paris. During this period, he was commissioned to refurbish a 19th-century Parisian theater, the Gaîté Lyrique and he met the theatrical designer Jacques Le Marquet who came to have a great influence over his later work and particularly over the conception of projecting the perception of his buildings which, in some ways, is close to conjuring. In 1980, he was creator and artistic assessor to the Architectural Biennial in Paris. In the 1980's, he received many more commissions and won various relevant competitions such as that for the Arab World Institute (1981-87) which can be considered his first work of international diffusion and which merited the Aga Khan Prize (1989). He has also received other prizes and honors such as the Silver Medal of the Académie d'Architecture (1983), Chevalier de l'Ordre des Arts et des Lettres (1983), Doctor Honoris Causa from the University of Buenos Aires (1983), Chevalier de la Ordre du Mérite (1987) and the Grand Prix d'Architecture (1987). In the 1990's, he undertook projects of great relevance such as the Opera de Lyon, Equerre d'Argent -- Prize for the best French Building of the Year (1993), the Cartier Foundation of Contemporary Art (1991-94), the Cultural and Congress Center in Lucerna, the Galeries la Fayette in Berlín, or Eurolille among many others. He was awarded the Architectural Record Prize for the Hotel St. James (1990), he is an honorary member of the AIA, Chicago (1993) and of the RIBA(1995), Commandeur dans l'Ordre des Arts et des Lettres (1997) Gold Medal of the Académie d'Architecture (1999). In 2000, he received the Golden Lion in the VII Biennial of Architecture of Venice. The following year, the Praemium Imperiale, the Gold Medal from the RIBA and the Borromini Prize for the Cultural and Congress Center in Lucerna. As of 2002, he has had an Honorary Doctorate from the Royal College of Art in London, a Doctor Honoris Causa from the University of Naples and has been Knight of the Legion of Honor.

Jean Nouvel is one of those architects that does not see architecture as an autonomous discipline, but as an activity intimately related with culture and the possibilities of its times. According to him, "The architect is a receptor, an amplifier and a retransmitter", an individual with a special sensitivity to capture new and unsuspected forms of beauty from within the existing reality. For this reason, he feels that he should always have an open attitude to everything that surrounds him: "Whenever I see something that stays in my imagination, there is always a great possibility that, in a conscious or unconscious way, it will come out somewhere else". In this way, architecture becomes a transformation, like a renewed and amplified expression of effects destined to commotion us. A good example of this is his project for the night club in Nogent-sur-Marne 'The State of Things' (1978). In this proposal, with explicit reference to the world of Godard and Wim Wenders, some zones have been glazed so as to connect the club visually with a tunnel through which a motorway runs.

For Jean Nouvel, each project is specific. The context of the project, as understood in its greatest sense, is never repeated. He strongly rejects academic architecture (whether from the classical or modern school) as a collage of solutions and images that have already been presented: "The way of learning should not be based on copying, but on being able to diagnose a specific situation". The analysis of the context in the totality of its complexity and richness – including geographic, technological, typological, human, cultural and economic elements – is necessary to develop an architectural concept capable of responding to the numerous demands of a project. For Nouvel, finding the concept is finding 'the essence' or the 'deep nature' of this. In this way, the Tour Sans Fin (1989), a proposal for a skyscraper in the Parisian Défense, is conceptually defined as a slender skyscraper that appears to disappear as it gains in height. The Onyx Cultural Center could be described as a 'mysterious black box'. According to Nouvel, the clarity of the concept of a project enables the posterior construction to be given a symbolic and evocative standing.

Jean Nouvel does not project abstract spaces, but rather puts together a series of sensitive scenographic itineraries. His collaboration with the theatrical designer Jacques Le Marquet, companion of many conversations and disputes (the latter confessed that he often had to overcome the temptation of boxing with Nouvel), was without doubt most fruitful for his later architectural production. In his words, "If we analyze a building, we should do so in function of the scenography created by the circulation of those who experience it. The object should be able to provide different scales for each of these sequential experiences. Neither the scale nor the proportion can be understood as abstract and universal relationships". In some way, in Jean Nouvel's projects, there is a desire to direct the emotions of those who pass through his buildings, provoking clear spaces,

dark and mysterious, sudden brilliance, imposing places... Without a doubt, these scenographic tendencies can be recognized in the Opera of Lyon (1986-1993). An evening visit to the Opera is a spectacle in itself: entering through the neoclassical porch (conserved from the old opera house), the dark hall, the discovery of the large volume lacquered in black that seems to float in the enormous void of the foyer, the sensation of vertigo, going into the auditorium... Also in the Palais de Justice in Nantes (1993-2000) with its large dark rectangular spaces we perceive the solemness, the drama and to a certain extent the anguish felt of being on trail. "For me this building is simply a very clear image of an institution that, in itself, is not precisely amusing", says **Nouvel**.

As a manipulator or conjurer of perceptions, Nouvel relies on certain 'tricks': plays on the scale of the spaces, with the differing weights of the volumes, with the evanesce of the materials, with transparencies and reflections, with the deformations, with the penumbra, with the effects of artificial light... Jean Nouvel is not trying to offer a cheap show, but rather interrogation and mystery. In the words of Jean Nouvel, "The tactics of A-dimensionality, the superposition of formal structures and the ambiguity of scaling produce instability in the corporeal nature of a singular object with the intention of connecting it to nonspecific realities". The large roof of the Culture and Congress Center in Lucerna that appears to float on a lake, or the Palais de Justice in Nantes, with its imposing common spaces are good examples of these plays on scale and proportion.

In the architecture of **Nouvel**, it is also habitual to find an apparent lightweightedness in his buildings which sometimes have an ambiguous aspect and seem to be almost immaterial. In order to achieve this effect, he tends to count on the gradual transparency of materials, such as the planes of the glazed facade of the Cartier Fundation (1991-1994) which are prolonged over and along the sides of the building; Praga-Zlaty Andel building (2000) with the screen print of a fallen angel, the angel from the film 'The Sky over Berlin'; or the project for the Tour Sans Fin (1989) that changes its skin as it rises: granite in the base, gray stone further up, screen printed glass that gradually makes it transparent... Also, the Torre Agbar (1999) is a display of, "These images in which we don't know where things start or finish; in which we don't know where the matter is or where its limits are". Although from a structural point of view the tower is very different in its lower part, it has a unitary aspect from the outside. The Torre Agbar is intended to vibrate with the undetermined brilliance and multiple reflections from the sheets of glass that make up its facade. The housing 'Gasometers' in Vienna (2001), with its communal spaces in silvery brilliance, are also exercises in how reflections can do away with our spatial perception.

Another way in which **Jean Nouvel** shows his opposition to a Cartesian concept of space is in his spatial deformation.

The Galeries Lafayette in Berlin (1996), with their cones that run through and transform the floors of the retail center are a good example of this. Another example are the deformations in the Quai Branly Museum (1999). This is a museum dedicated to primitive cultures which, in its undefined aspect, is intended to softly welcome without the arrogance of western civilization, objects from ancestral cultures.

The architecture of **Jean Nouvel**, in its scenographic conception in the widest sense of the word, pays intense attention to the effects of light, as much as to natural as to artificial as well as to the shadows it produces: "Light only exists in virtue of shade. It is a sensation that interests me a lot and that is sometimes perceived as a disturbing thing in the complete sense of the term". The penumbra and sudden contrasts in light manage to create mystery and undefined deepnesses in some of his architectural works such as the Cultural and Congress Center in Lucerna, the Opera de Lyon or the Palais de Justice in Nantes.

**Jean Nouvel** uses everything within reach in order to provoke the desired emotions which tend to be those that connect with the contemporary world's latent poesy. "I believe that the specificity of architecture consists in being able to concentrate the cultural values of a particular time and place in a durable and inhabitable form", states the architect.

## Main Street Peer - River Hotel Brooklyn

Brooklyn, New York USA 1999-?

The River Hotel in Brooklyn is the looking glass of Manhattan, a place where you can enjoy its images and splendor. The panoramic views open up to a maximum; the windows are so large and transparent that we ask ourselves if they really exist; the images are stretched and duplicated in the mirrors; there is an on going play between the real and the virtual.

On one side, the rooms have been conceived along the lines of theatre boxes over the Brooklyn Bridge and the city's skyline and on the other, over the Manhattan and Williamsbourg bridges. The strength of the foregrounds, made up of bridges, contrasts with the precision and delicacy of the silhouettes in the back-

ground: the Statue of Liberty, the Empire State Building as well as all of the other skyscrapers situated beyond the shores of South Street. Other rooms exploit the lower views of Manhattan Bridge. In reality, the River Hotel is a bridge between bridges: a place from where you can observe the bridges as if you were on a boat.

The building obeys the strict logic of the quays of New York and the rectangular urban network that extends to the water's edge. Its front extends over the river as if it wanted to reach the opposing shore: the symbolic gesture of a 'wharf' that belongs as much to Manhattan as to Brooklyn.

Along the walkway in the western part of the hotel foyer, there is a window that is more than 100 meters long overlooking the opposite shore. Even the multi-screen cinema assert their claim to their situation: the screens can be raised so that the skyline and bridges can be seen. The gymnasium, situated directly over the water, unfolds below the Manhattan Bridge and behind a 20-meter-high glass wall.

Stores occupy the quays along the pathway that follows the shore of the river. In this way, a small part of Brooklyn next to the bridge, as a result of overlooking the opposite shore, can become part of Manhattan.

# Torre Agbar
## Barcelona, Spain (1999-2004)

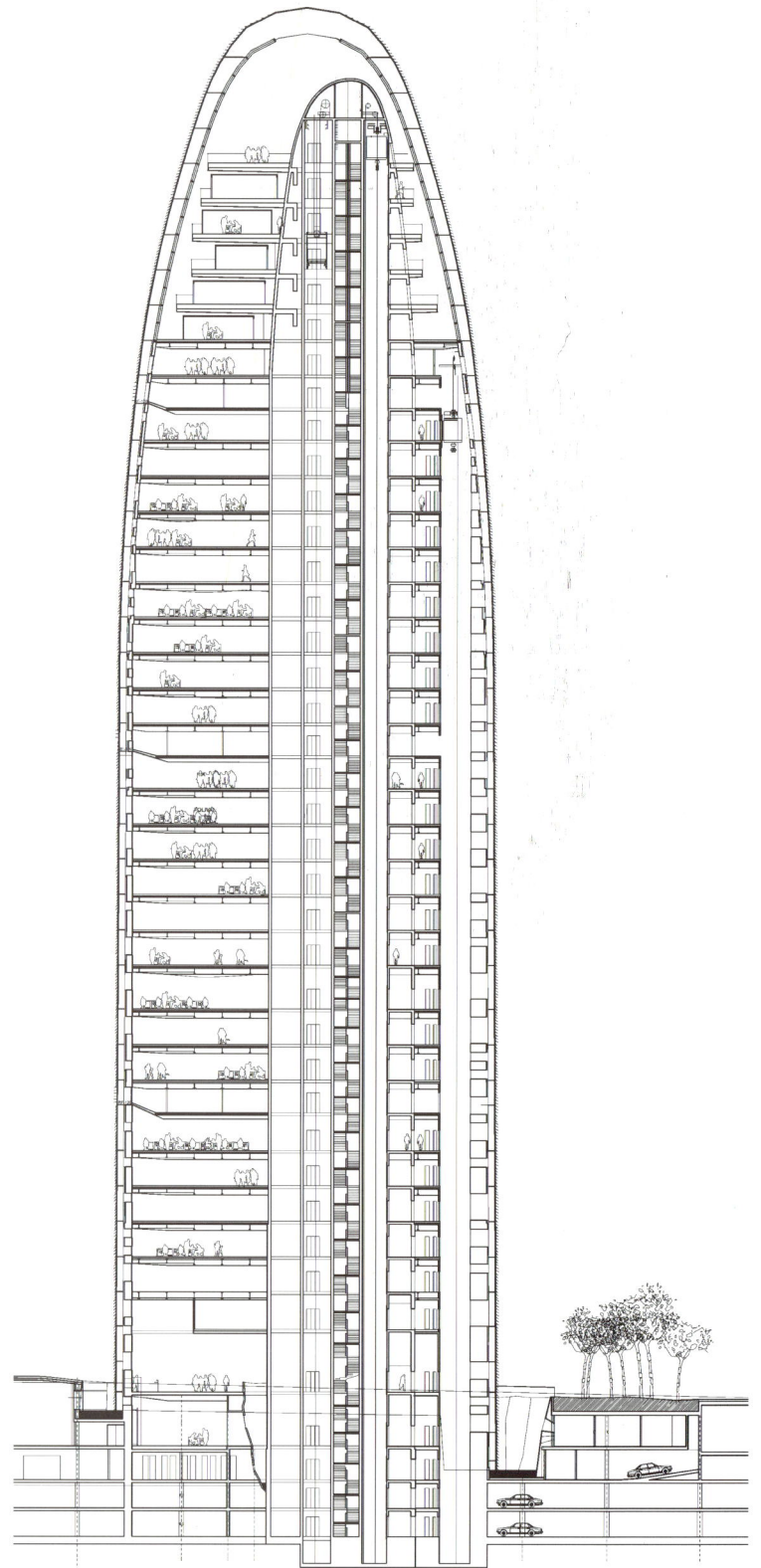

It is not a tower, a skyscraper in the North American sense of the word; it is a unique, singular, emergence amidst a generally calm city. However, it has nothing to do with a sharp or nervous vertical such as the belfry needles that tend to accentuate horizontal cities.

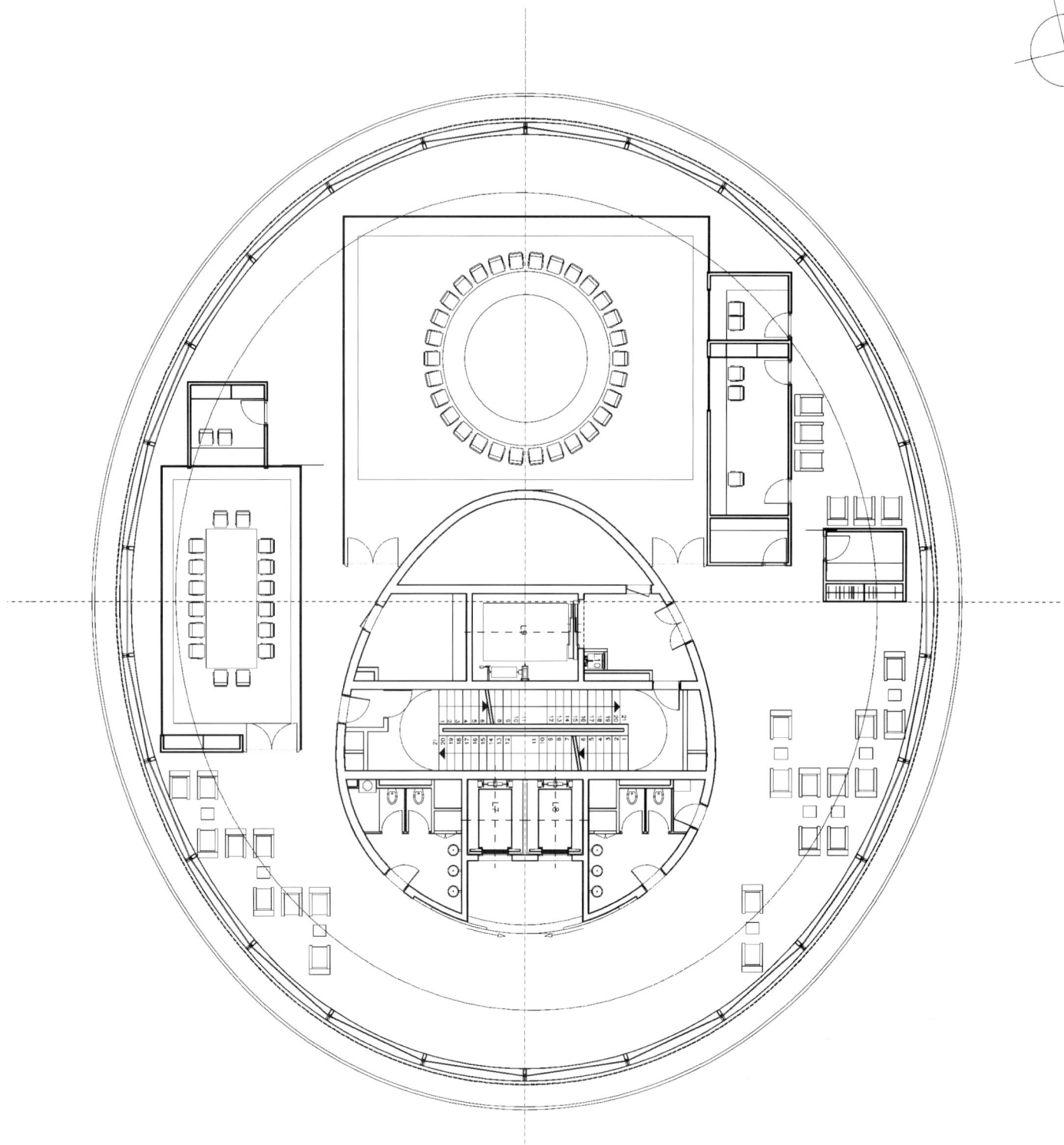

No. It is more of a question of a fluid mass that has perforated the ground, a permanent high-pressured geyser.

The surface of the building evokes water: a smooth continuous texture, but which is also vibrant and transparent and the mat-ter of which is read in its colorful uncertain and luminous depths.

This architecture comes from the earth although it does not have the weight of stone. It could even be a distant echo of tho-

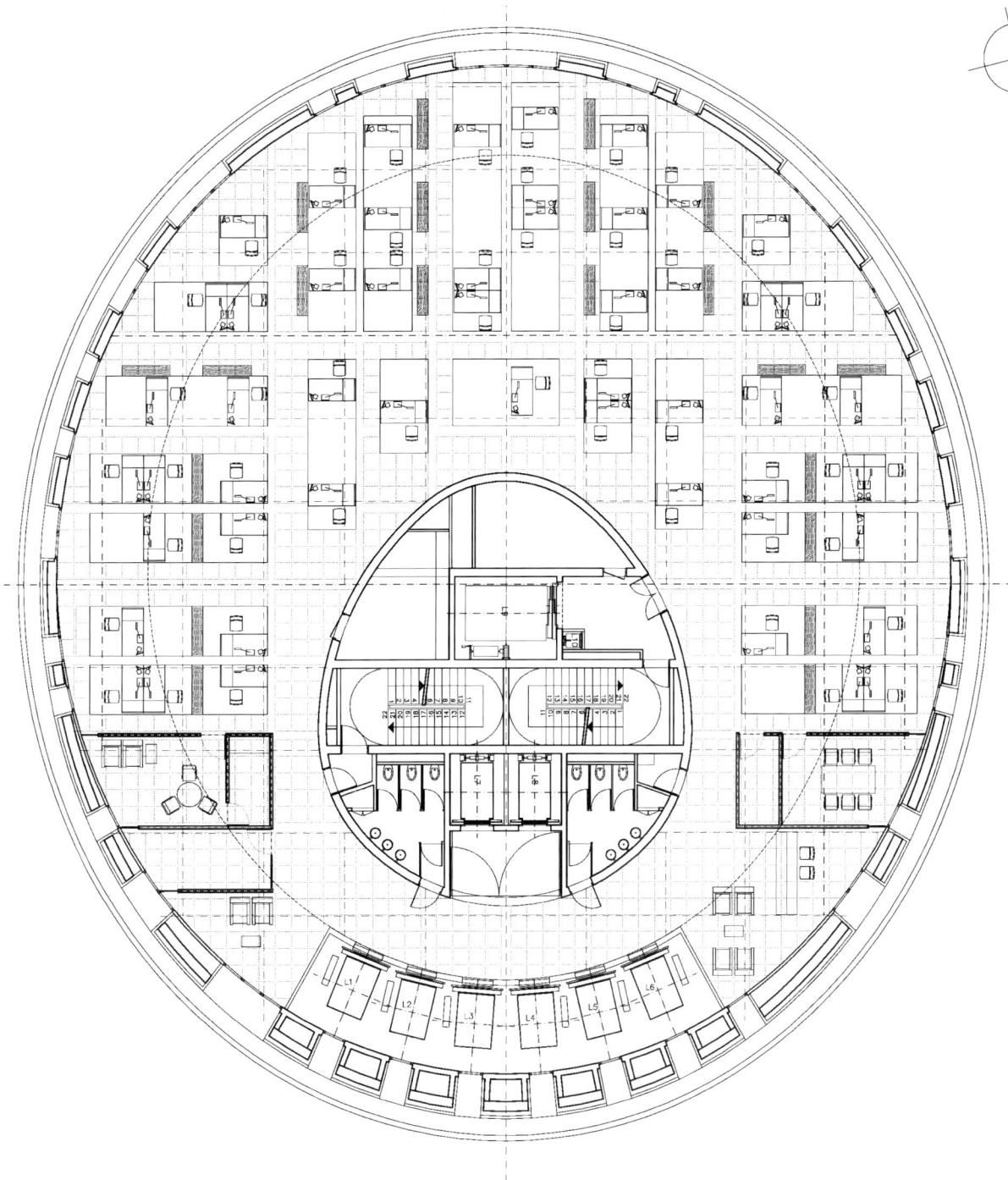

se ancient formal Catalan obsessions induced by the mysteries of the mountains of Montserrat. The light and the uncertainties of the material make the Torre Agbar vibrate in the profile of Barcelona. Illusionism at a distance, as much during the day as during the night. It is a precise landmark at the entrance to the new Diagonal from the Plaça de Les Glòries Catalanes. This singular object has become a new symbol of the international metropolis and one of its foremost ambassadors.

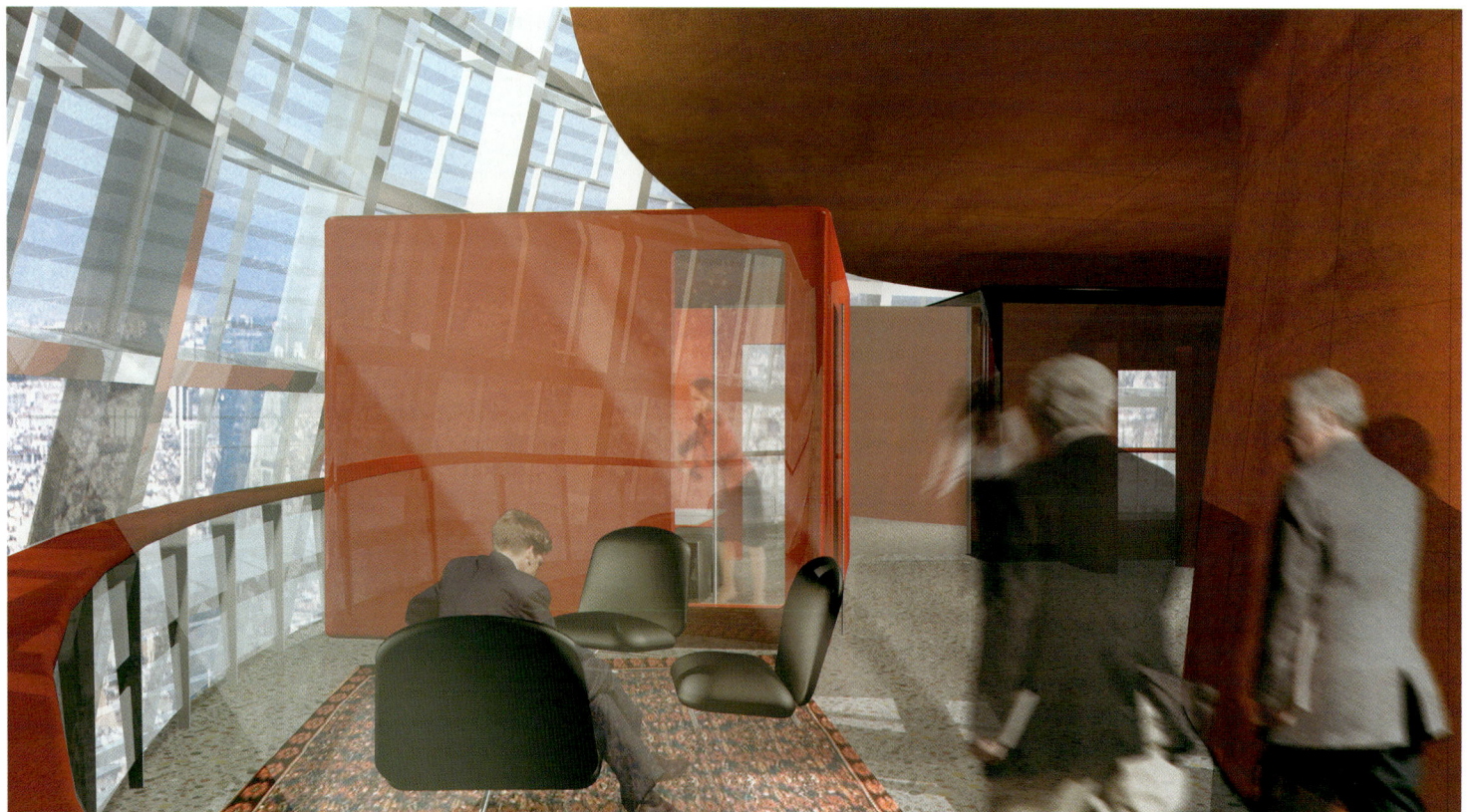

TOP ARCHITECTS OF THE WORLD

# Ben
# Van Berkel

**W**as born in Utrecht in 1957. He studied architecture at the Rietveld academy in Amsterdam and at the Architectural Association in London, receiving the AA Diploma with honors in 1987. After having worked in various architectural offices in Europe, he set up his own architectural practice along with Caroline Bos, art historian, in 1988.

His studio does not only stand out for its buildings and proposals for urban development and infrastructures, but also for the union of an architect with an art historian that has attracted great interest in theoretical and teaching circles.

Mercedes Benz Museum

National Museum of Twenthe

Among the projects that stand out are the new wing to the Rijksmuseum, the electric substation REMU, the Erasmus Bridge in Rotterdam, the retail center Vroom & Dreesman, the new museum in Nijmegen and the plan for urban development in the city of Arnhem.

He has participated in various international competitions in cities such as Paris and Berlin.

In the theoretical field, **Ben van Berkel** has been a teacher at Columbia University (1994), in Princeton University (2000) and invited critic at Harvard. From 1996 to 1999 he di-

rected the Urban Studio, Unit 4, at the Architectural Association in London. The Urban Studio was centered on the development of new organizational structures in architecture and urban development. **Berkel** has also participated in conferences and exhibitions such as Architecture and Utopia, das "*Schlob*", or the Venice Biennial (1991-93). In 1998, **Ben van Berkel** and Caroline Bos set up UN Studio (United Network Studio) which encourages collaboration among professionals from the fields of architecture, graphic design, engineering, construction, photography and so on.

**UN Studio**, United Net Studio, founded by the architect **Ben van Berkel** and the art historian Caroline Bos, stands out for its desire to cross established frontiers without falling into any rigidly defined category in either terms of its architecture or in terms of its working methods. **UN Studio** is an organization of professionals in architecture, urban development and infrastructure which has the intention of seeking new ways of more strategic, efficient and creative collaboration among architects, graphic designers, engineers, constructors and service companies.

The studio diminishes the barriers between the different disciplines in its concern as much as for the design of public buildings and homes as for bridges, tunnels and electric substations. Its constructions manifest its interest in finding new organizational and structural forms that can make more extensive and freer uses possible: "There are certain themes that I am very interested in such as the concept of organization – the way in which a building is structured– and the geometry –let's call it how it is used– not in the conventional sense of function, but in the sense of creating a space for mixed-use and, thus, extending its possibilities". This search for non-coercive structures is also manifested in the Studio's proposals for urban development.

In the words of **Ben van Berkel**: "I am more interested in dispersed structures –those which lead to open–, more evolutionary systems in the sense of static urban structures which constitute open energy systems and which incorporate economic, social and political information".

In the development of these open organizational systems, the architect must analyze the so-called "vague essence" –those

forces, behavioral patterns and undetermined dynamic relationships which affect the project–. So that the possibilities of these forces can be integrated into the project, a process of abstraction and systematization of these forces is developed by means of diagrams. On occasions, these diagrams are produced with the aid of the new technologies which promotes the use of computers as design instruments rather than simply as tools with which to draw: "Everybody uses a computer, but without using it as tool for thinking". The lack of hierarchies of these forces in the computer representations motivate new unexpected fluid relationships: "What most interests me about computing techniques is this undulating process".

An idea that appears in many of his projects is that of a never-ending path, a search for fluid spaces that possess differentiated qualities and allow for mixed-uses without becoming isolated or requiring the raising of barriers among themselves. An outstanding example is the Moebius house which, with a scheme based on the Moebius strip, transfers the twenty-four-hour cycle of sleep, work and life to the interior.

The intention in this family residence has been to transmit the idea of a stroll in the country in its interiors and to avoid partitioning off spaces as in traditional homes.

**Ben van Berkel** defines his design process as a process of transformative hybridizations in the sense that he develops the aesthetic, functional, structural and technological factors at the same time or in the same action. To clarify this, he refuses to accept any form of categorization.

He rejects a "bricolage" in which independently developed sculptural forms are added after the completion of the program, or a design process that calls in a structural engineer at the last moment to resolve aspects of a building's stability. In his own words: "Technical consultants have been getting more and more involved in the earlier phases of the project. Rather than waiting for them to contribute their knowledge at a determined point towards the end of the design process, their influence affects the project from the outset".

His way of working always integrates the concept of time (clockwise planning). In this way, he intends to foresee the activities and movements of the users. According to **Ben van Berkel,** the architect should act more and more as a "public scientist" and understand the factors that lead to a building having the desired ambience in the future. **UN Studio** seeks a synergy among these elements so as to fill its buildings with life.

The careers of **Ben van Berkel** and his partner Caroline Bos have been marked by the rich and broad view of cultural, social and technical implications that they have and that characterize architects of this new century.

# INTERVIEW

ATRIUM - A quicker way and a longer way to go down to the ground floor?

BVB- Yes. The Mercedes Benz Museum has many features. It has also iconographic landscape qualities, it will occupy a distinct place against the Stuttgart horitzon.

ATRIUM -Something I think is very interesting is that you try to work as well with forces that could be called "indeterminate" or not fixed. What can you tell me about your working methods?

BVB- I don´t believe very much in top down strategies, I´m very much more interested in a bottom up philosophy…I can study infraestructural movement, the amount of people coming to the location. I´m looking very much to user groups, also to accessibility and publicness. I´m very much interested in the phenomena of planning in time, I call it clockwise planning.

ATRIUM -I can see you are very interested in studing the users…

BVB- My philosophy is that if you have no people, you have no shop. You can have a beautiful shop, but if you have no people, it´s worthless. So you need this sinergy between public forces and what they need. In planning, I´m thinking a lot what kind of location needs a evening program, or what kind of location needs a morning program in order to create a better distributions of people. Certain locations were planned to be lively but then they never were. It 's about planning in time. This needs careful studies we are developing with specialists all over the world. It's not really urban planning, it´s more like a deep study of urban forces and how you can deal with them.

ATRIUM -Collaboration with other proffessionals, engineers etc…, at almost all the stages of the project and construction is a fact you apparently like to underline. Ignasi de Solà-Morales, paraphrasing Walter Benjamín in " The architectural work of art in the times of technical reproductibility" compared the actual work of the architects, with that of the cinema director or editor, that must unite the fragments and collaborations of people with very different interests. What is your actual perspective of this matter?

BVB- I´m interested in colaborators simply because I believe the world now is not interested in a master architect. No one cares about the "baumeister" figure anymore, so I think the time of the superheroe architect is over. The clients and the world around us demand forms of complex collaboration. The client before could be someone rich, that could trust the architect to realise a project. You don´t see this kind of client anymore.

ATRIUM - Is it more a multiple client now?

BVB- Yes, exactly, and a lot of specialists also around them. The client is much more professional that for example ten years before, they have their own financial people, infraestructure people,…etc. In this reality it is necessary to develop new concepts of control. I think a lot of architects are loosing control of their works. They have not been aware of the growing professionalism in the clients side. I

have been looking a lot to car and fashion industry, and I learned a lot from analysing how they produce their projects.

Sometimes even artists are quite clever at this. So I learned the system to colaborate, it's the duty of today.

ATRIUM - Are you still collaborating in United Architects?

BVB- Yes, it's very interesting, we have a good model that is having a history, like Team 10 model, or a CIAM, like a Group 8. We have theorethical and academic influence in each other, we support each other, we fight sometimes. It is very good.

ATRIUM - What can you tell me about UN Studio's work and the will of "the deliberate and complete negation of any categorization"? For me it is very interesting how you manage to achieve interesting architectural projects in areas in witch architects normally don´t have a role, like electrical subestations and tunnels for example.

BVB- I been long time very interested in engineering and in product design. I´m interested in let´s say the overall cultural aspect of the discipline of the architect. For this reason, I don´t want to be paradoxical or ambiguous about it. Or even ironic. The way I´m looking at the proffession is unhumorous, and very straight forward. I think we should widen what are our tools.

As if you look at the story of architecture, we have always been together with politicians, artists, writers. There is a scientific precise aspect of the profession together with a light-hearted part of it, both need to go together.

ATRIUM - Unhumurous?

BVB-It is something I take extremely serious, to understand what is your profession. I think it may sound very conservative, maybe. To be in a full front. Not a lot of people say that aloud. I´m very happy to say aloud not to make fun of the profession.

ATRIUM -Many architects keep searching for a "architectural concept" that seems to be somewhere in the gap between an idea and a physical description.

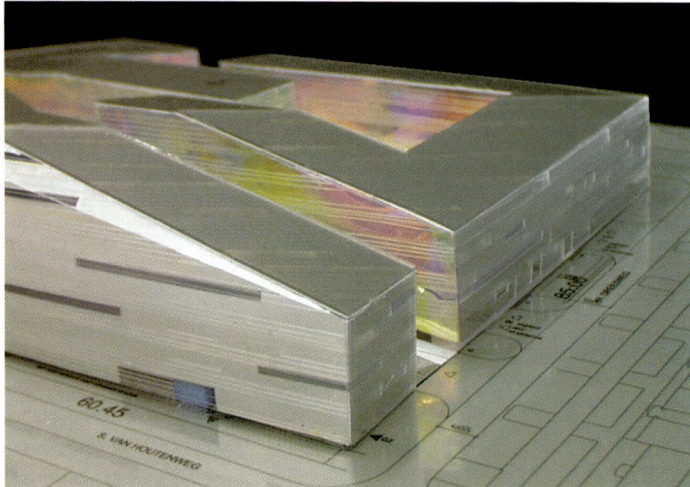

ATRIUM -Observing the work of many contemporary architects there is something that could be called "architectures of the movement". Yourselves, Zaha Hadid, FOA, Asymptote, seem to want to provoke or at least to follow with architecture the movement of visitors inside the buildings. This seems to be very efective in museums, comercial areas and anything related to transportation. In my studies I had a teacher (a fan of the modern movement and Mies Van der Rohe) who criticized this type of architectures saying "people are free to walk how they want to". What can I answer him the next time?

BVB- Mies would go for the open space and the optimum flexibility, but maybe it is not the best plan to live on. Hiding is as important as to be visible. So I don't believe it is so important to be so extremely flexible with movement (Mies Van der Rohe is one of the most over-estimated architects of the last century). I think that you can sometimes be very precise, and make a wall guide you. This is my philosophy of that it doesn't matter anymore if you are going for the box or the blob. The discussion is more how you deal with an infraestructural condition. If you have an infraestructural organization then you can work with surfaces that guide and orient you. The transformative aspect today is very important.

Why is it that a "architectural concept" or a "figment" is still useful? (What is a figment? this concept appears quite often in your latest texts)

BVB- Figment is one of the latest theorical ideas I am interested in. Sometimes it's important to predict what you would like to make. I never look at one only side when I'm looking at the future of a project, with an idea or with a diagram. I like to see the diagram not as a pure abstract system alone. A figment, is a construct, like a mythologycal figure.

ATRIUM - Something between an idea and an object?
BVB- Yes, almost like a ghost.

ATRIUM - In many of the contemporary architects I view a rejection for linguistic narratives...
BVB- Yes, everyone is interested in the real thing, the material. The narrative was more in the 70s and 80s. The good thing about the figments is that they are having both, the narrative and the abstract system combined. Sometimes you can see things once you look back and remember —an after image—. For me this is more evocative and stimulating than a pure icon, a more hybrid and rich concept.

ATRIUM - About your architecture, does it have the ambition to be contemporary in the sense of following the beat of its time, or is it in some way timeless?
BVB- Of course I'm interested in ths time, I'm looking at everything, I'm reading... But, I'm not so interested anymore in being the most contemporary architect, because I think the danger is that you become superficial, quickly finished. I'm interested in looking for something new, but then letting it grow naturally, let it become deeper. Sometimes I like to step back and think, and do other things (paint, photograph) and then come back

ATRIUM - I think your partner Caroline Bos studied history of art. How do you relate your interest in art with your architectural work?
BVB-When Caroline studied history of art, I was getting more and more interested in her studies. For example Venetian painters, like Tintoretto, never set up a geometry before they did the painting. In a way they experimented. We are both very interested in art, in people like Clemente, Bacon, the writtings of Dali (not his paintings). The Staedelschule of Frankfurt, where I teach now, is very interesting in this sense, for its mix of disciplines (architecture, art, cinema).

ATRIUM - In what way do you integrate your interest in history of art in your work?
BVB- For instance Caroline is a very bright writter, a very sharp critic. She is also important part of the design process. She is very involved in the selection of why we do things and how we can make them better. It's really necessary to know to clear up your thoughts.

ATRIUM - About being an architect, what do you like better from your profession and what do you like worse?
BVB- What I used to like less was the feeling of being overwhelmed by production. But in the last years I found a very interesting system to develop my ideas in architecture. Observing other types of enterprises I created much more space and time to develop them. With a clever infrastructure, with very clear and quick communications, you don't have to spend so much time in management anymore. I can release maybe 55% of my time in design, while in the beginning I could only spend maybe 25% in it.

ATRIUM - How do you organize your collaborations?
BVB-Very simple system. Normally I try to be here the first 3 days of the week. People in the office can book my time then. I'm trying

to travel less. Having a good system keeps me quite calm. The organization of the office is very important for me, I have spent a lot of years designing the system of the office. In fact , opposed to the idea of the artist´s messy place, I believe that if you can´t design a good office, it is difficult you are able to design a good building.

ATRIUM - And what do you like best?
BVB- We have a house in the Canary Islands, I like to spend time there. There I photograph, I paint and enjoy being there.

ATRIUM -Do you think there has been an evolution from the beginning of your work until now, in your thoughts and in your projects?
BVB-Of course you learn and you develop. I have been always very fascinated by the phenomenom of geometry. Actually, I'm very interested in geometries with capacity of endlessness, no dead-ends.

ATRIUM -What do you think is the effect of new technologies in architecture? In what ways do you use informatic programs as a tool of design? I read you said- "many people use the computer to draw, but they don´t use it to think"
BVB- The use of the computer can be extended by programming. We program a lot.

ATRIUM - So it´s not really so much drawing with the CAD, but making programs for your needs?
BVB- For example now, in the project of the Mercedes Benz, we have a program that can make changes in several drawings at a time, immediately, it's kind of a recalculation program. We have programs that include in them many different kinds of informations, to achieve global solutions of several problems at a time. We call this A-dimensional design. It is very important to be critical when you are dealing with this complex systems in the computer

ATRIUM - Which are your strategies to obtain the trust of your clients?
BVB- New techniques, that is my secret. Showing you are in the edge of the design and construction industry. I don´t bother my clients with my interests in art and culture. I only tell them about my tools, and normally they are really interested. I think they feel it like a sign of being efficient.

ATRIUM - Which is the actual role of the architects in the evolution of cities?
BVB- The most important in the future for a planner is that he doesn´t think anymore in the phenomenom of expansion. I think it 's more important to think about intensities and about better qualities of intensities, in how we may live.

ATRIUM - Cities like Barcelona, Madrid or Florence seem actually more interested in acquiring buildings with a brand than in urban planning. What do you think about this situation?
BVB- I'm now interested in what I call deep planning. Planning according to liveliness, time, knowing how people move, problems of

congestion… In finding out how can we make the city work a little bit better. Looking at the social movement, not for political ideas, but more like a public scientist. The future architect is only having a future if he is thinking like a public scientist. Design is good, but it is not enough.

ATRIUM - What do you think of Amsterdam, the city where you live?
BVB- I love Amsterdam, it is the best city in Europe. It is not a metropole, but it is highly cosmopolitan and international (sometimes you feel a little far from Europe). And the quality of life is very high.

ATRIUM - What changes do you observe, or wish to observe in actual architecture? In housing?
BVB- The problem with housing is that we should really think of new concepts, new organizations, not only superficial variations. The cultutre of living somewhere today is more having to do with change. We will have much more eldery people. New forms of living have to determine new forms of designing ideas for housing ■

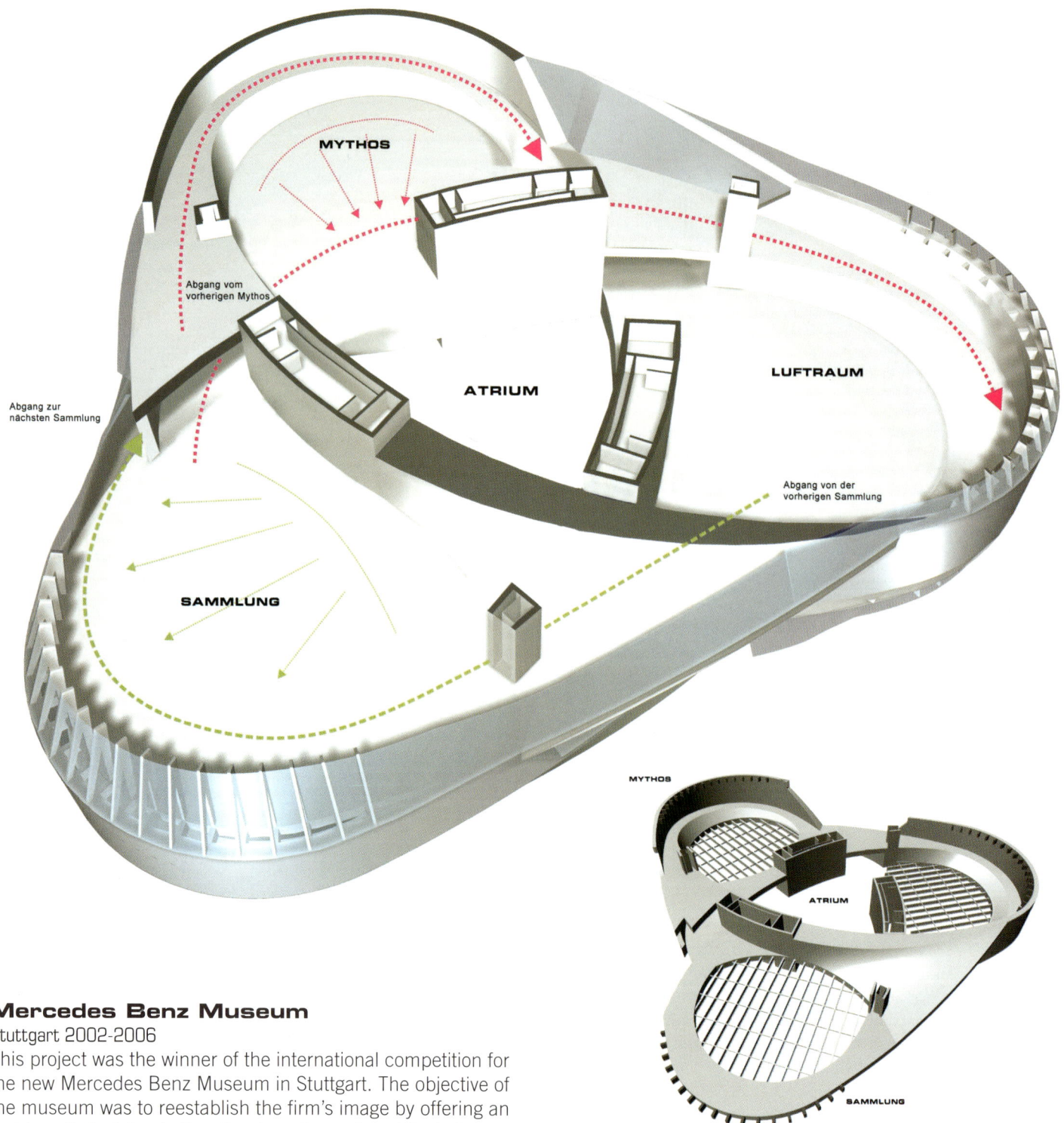

MYTHOS

Abgang vom
vorherigen Mythos

Abgang zur
nächsten Sammlung

ATRIUM

LUFTRAUM

Abgang von der
vorherigen Sammlung

SAMMLUNG

MYTHOS

ATRIUM

SAMMLUNG

## Mercedes Benz Museum

Stuttgart 2002-2006

This project was the winner of the international competition for
the new Mercedes Benz Museum in Stuttgart. The objective of
the museum was to reestablish the firm's image by offering an
emblematic building in the city where the make originated.

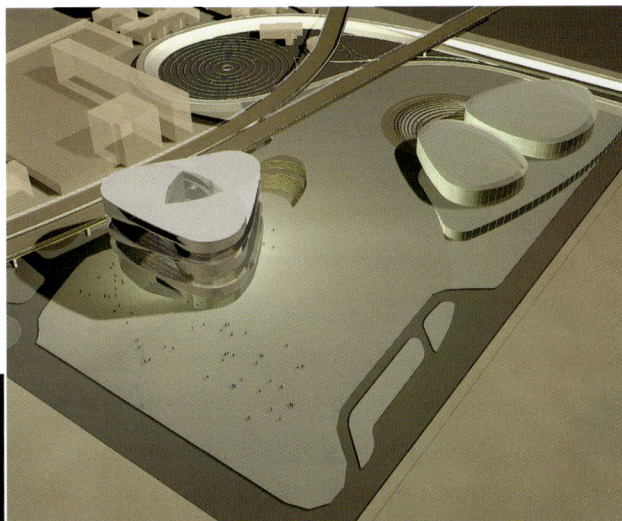

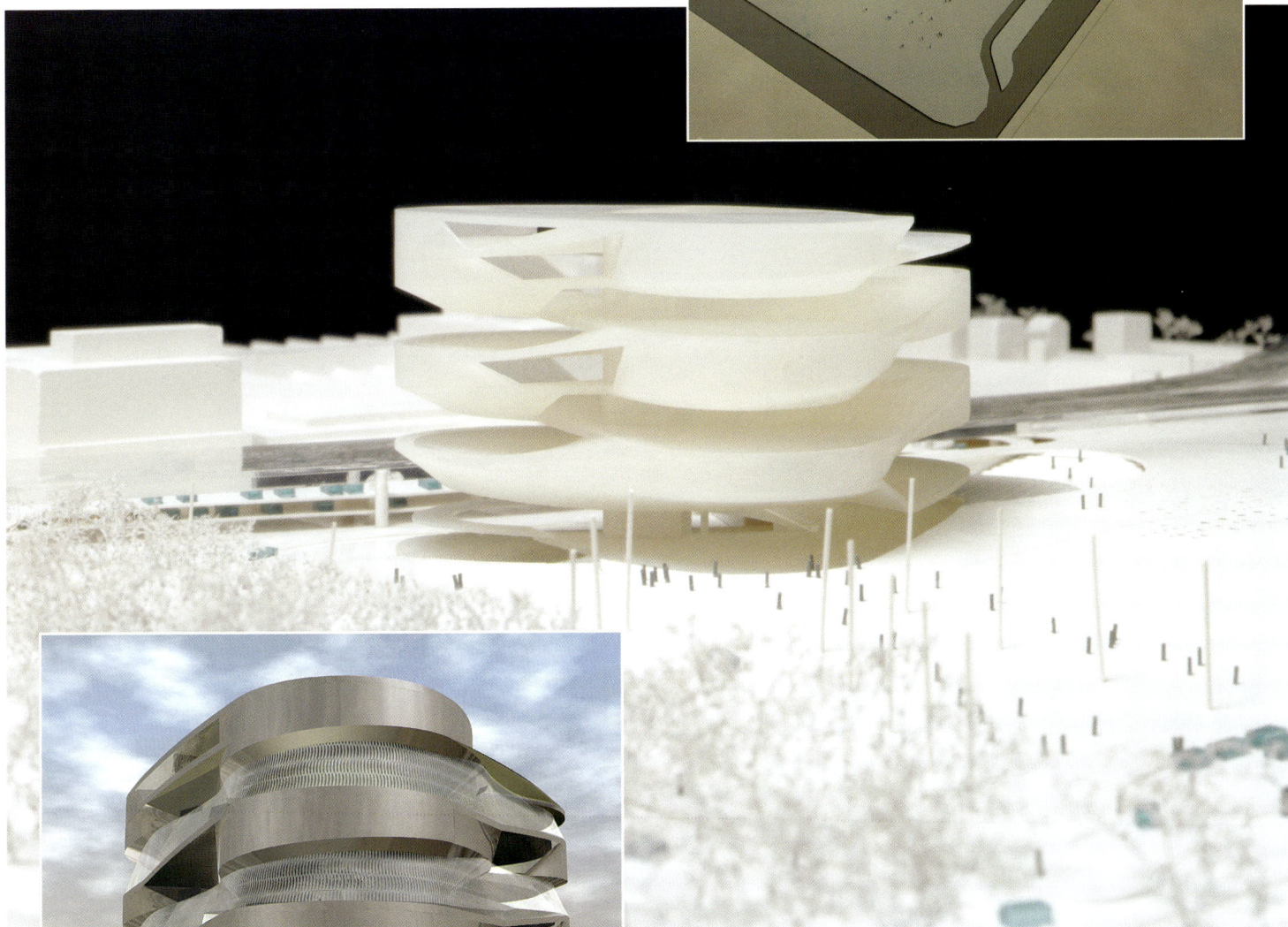

With the intention of creating a landmark, it was decided to propose a vertical structure of some 47 meters in height that would stand out among the freeways and rolling hills that surround the site. Its geometric forms respond to the rounded forms of the industrial buildings of the zone such as the Mercedes Benz test

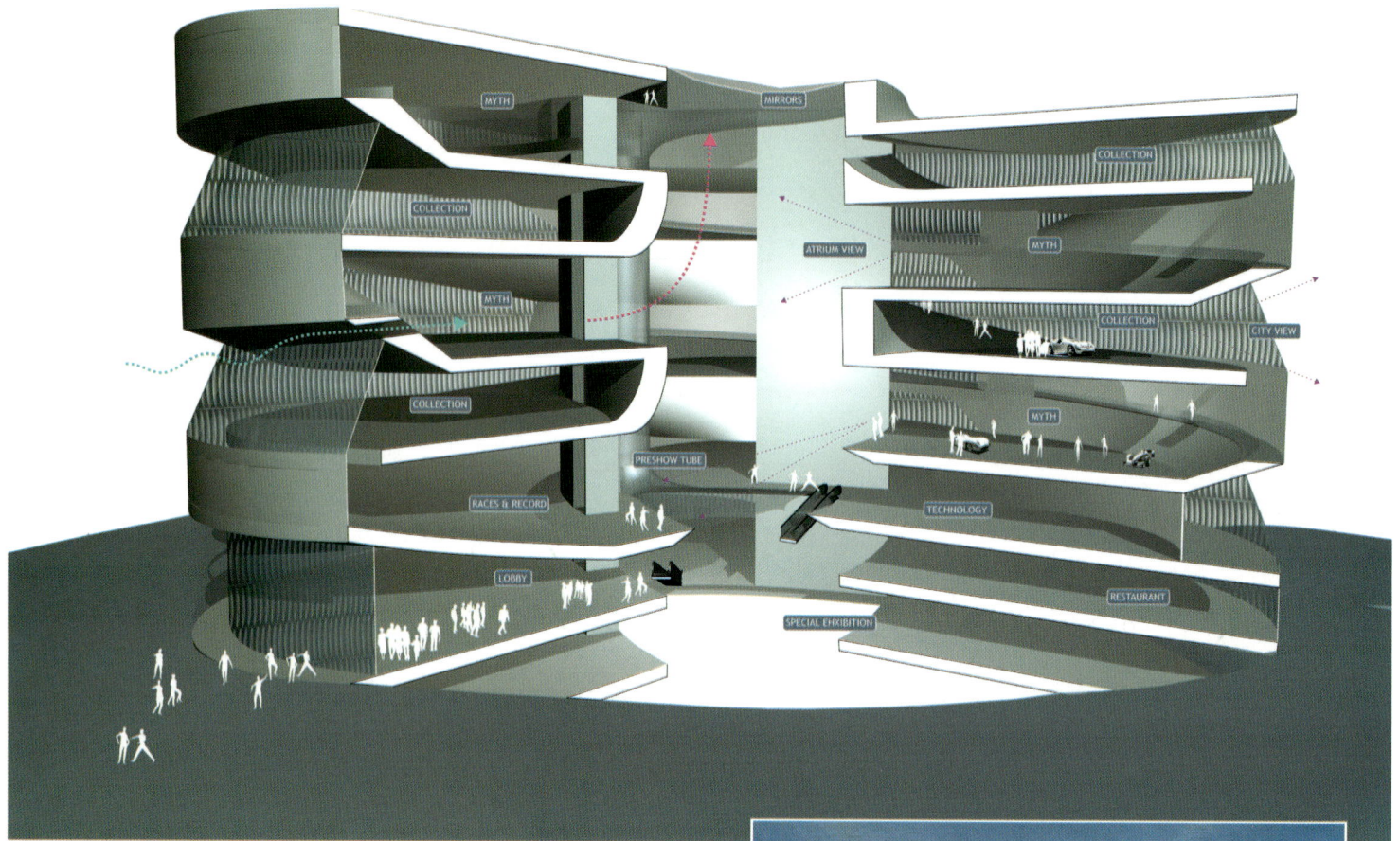

circuits, the gas and gasoline deposits or the football stadium. The proposal consists of creating a plaza elevated 5.60 meters above the lay of the land to form the base in which the museum will be situated and a variety of activities can be carried out. The concept of this project, which offers some 20,000 m² of exhibition space for the different models of automobiles, is a trefoil, a double helix that can be explored in any direction. The "trefoil" has been made up of six platforms at different levels which rotate around a central void that is triangular in form. As a result, the

museum is visited from top to bottom. Firstly, the visitors take an elevator to the top floor and carry out their visit by descending various ramps that connect the different levels. On the entrance floor, on the same level as the plaza, the entrance hall, the restaurant and the stores have been situated. Below this level the children's museum, a flexible exhibition space and the administrative offices are found. The exterior aspect of the museum reflects the technological intelligence that the make intends to transmit. It consists of an outer casing of smooth sculptural forms which change in appearance according to the meteorological conditions and the time of day. An innovative facade in glass and carbon fiber reinforced plastics intensify the effects.

# National Museum of Twenthe

Enschede, Holland, 1995

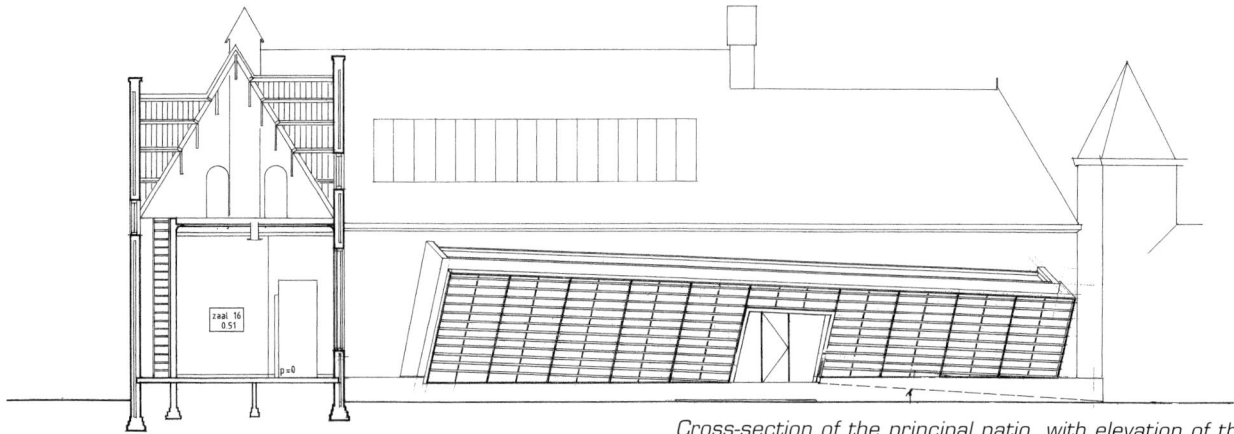

*Cross-section of the principal patio, with elevation of the pavilion.*

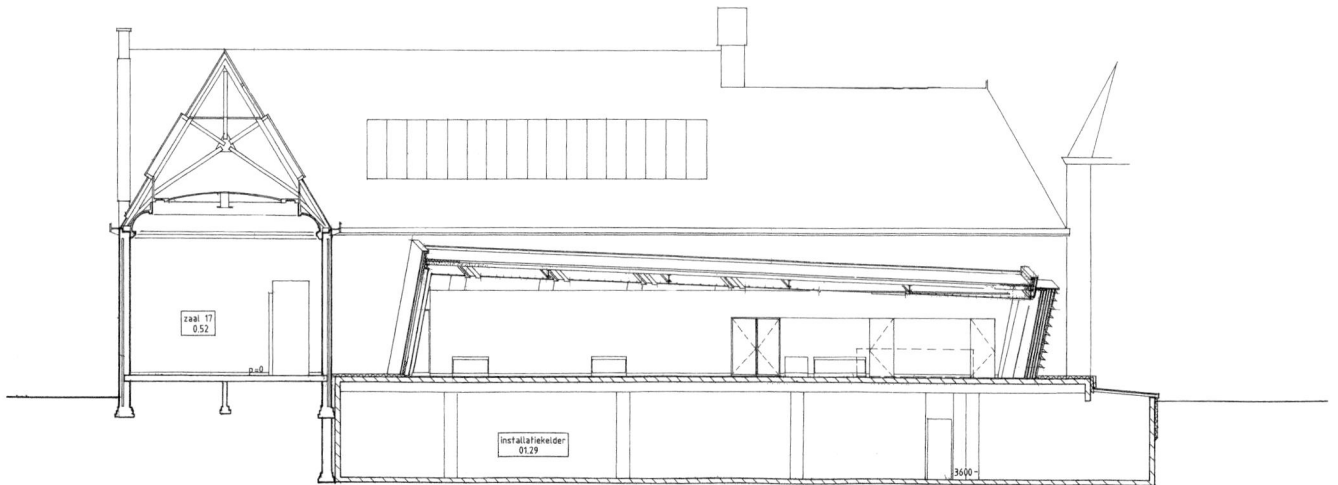

*Longitudinal section of the pavilion.*

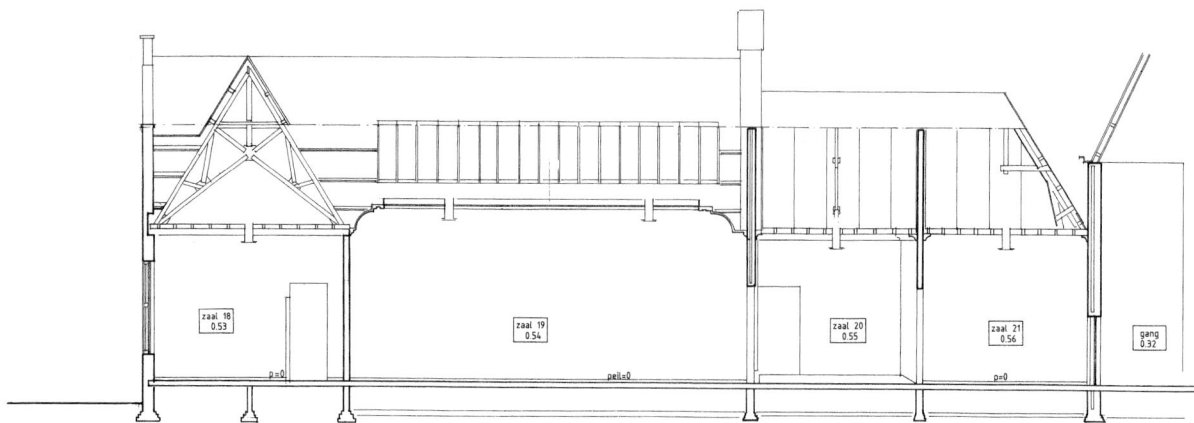

*Longitudinal section of one of the wings of the museum.*

The first stage was started in November 1995, the second in March 1996. Client: Rijksgebouwendienst, Project Direction (The Hague).
Constructor: Bouwbedrijf Punte bv, Enschede. Collaborators: Harrie Pappot (project coordinator), Oost Hovenier (in charge of the project). Landscape Architect: Lodewijk Baljon.

The old building that houses the National Museum of Twenthe is found in a large block in the capital of the region, Enschede. It has a reasonably symmetrical form with two large sides and two smaller sides. The original building was constructed in 1928 and, making the most of the site's geometry, it was planned as a group of bodies set in parallel to the adjoining streets which en-

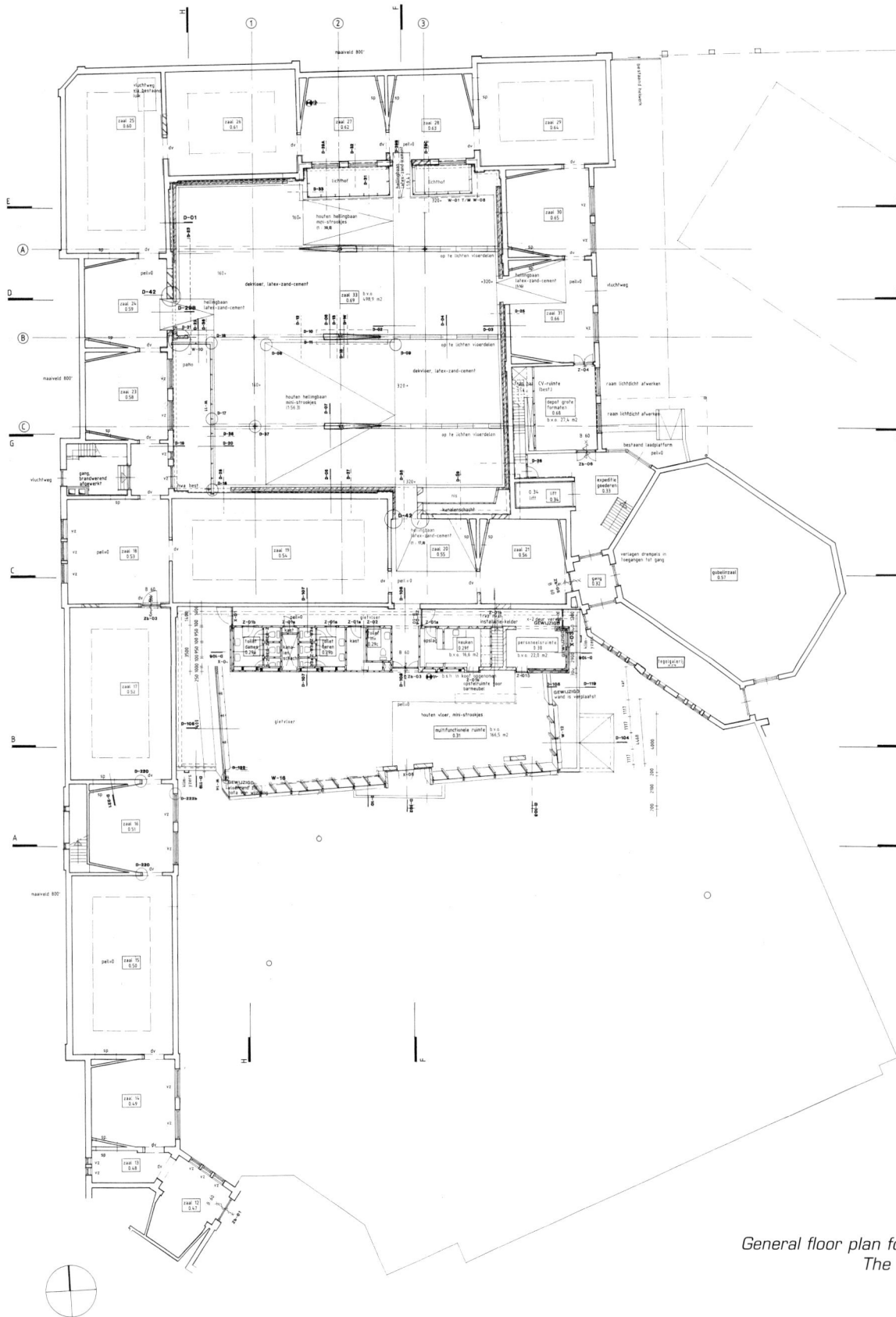

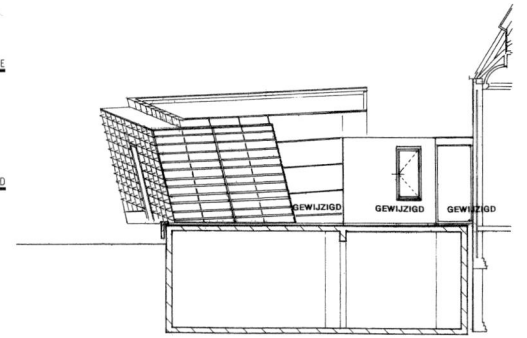

Side elevation of the multi-purpose pavilion.

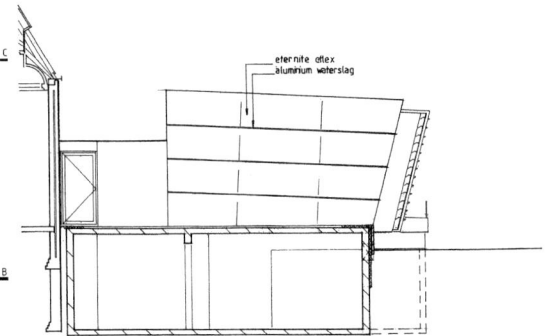

Side elevation of the pavilion, including old adjoining building.

General floor plan for the Museum of Modern Art after the intervention. The old patio has been converted into the new main hall.

close a large central courtyard. Later enlargement led to the addition of a second rectangular body in the rear of the block which creates a second smaller courtyard. The entire building has been treated in a late Neo-Romantic style based on a brick walling system and pointed roofs but with a planimetry reminiscent of municipal urban schemes of the 18th century.

The intervention was centered on the roofing of the rear courtyard, with a view to this area being used as the Museum of Mod-

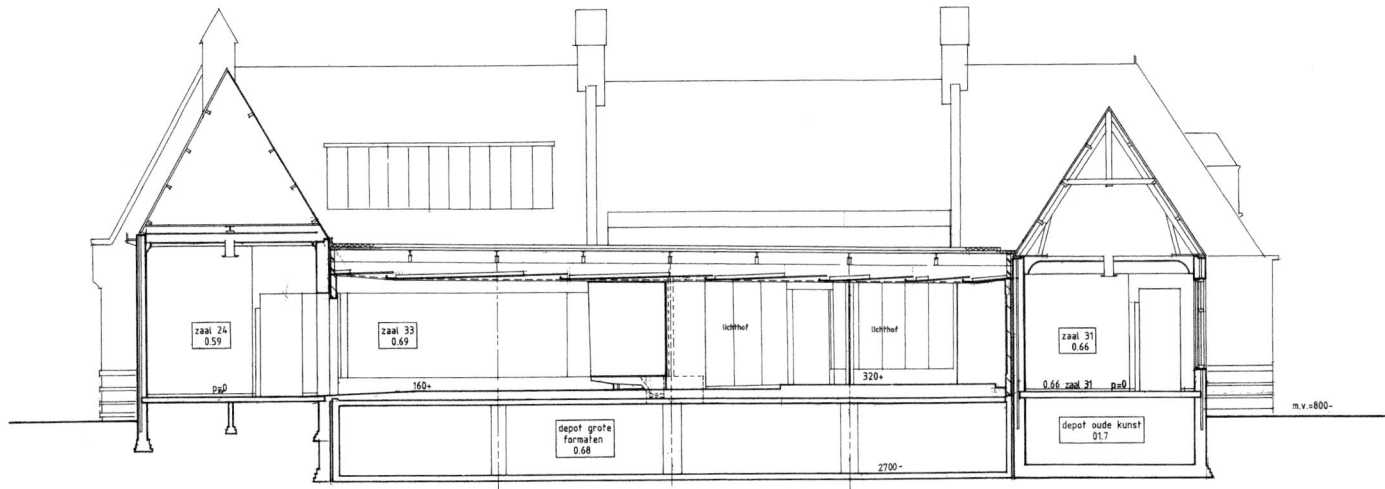

*Cross-section of the rear patio, converted into the main hall of the new museum.*

*Longitudinal section of the rear rectangular body, with the pavilion to the extreme right.*

ern Art, along with the construction of an element to connect this to the main courtyard. A number of smaller interventions, such as new access ramps and steps in the main entrance, have also been undertaken. All of this implied the refurbishing of the interiors. In this work, important aspects such as the illumination, air-conditioning and heating systems had to be taken into account.

The small glass and aluminum volume situated in the main courtyard connects this area to the new museologic itinerary. In

his proposal to abandon any intent upon synthesis or dialogue with the architecture of the old construction, Van Berkel presents this element at an angle with respect to the overall gravitational axis and superimposes it over the old building to which he shows complete indifference. In reality, this body, the presence of which is so important, accommodates no more than an elongated piece of the installations and the multi-purpose hall. His proposal is, however, much more intentional than initially demanded by the program: the interior body in aluminum is completely closed. To

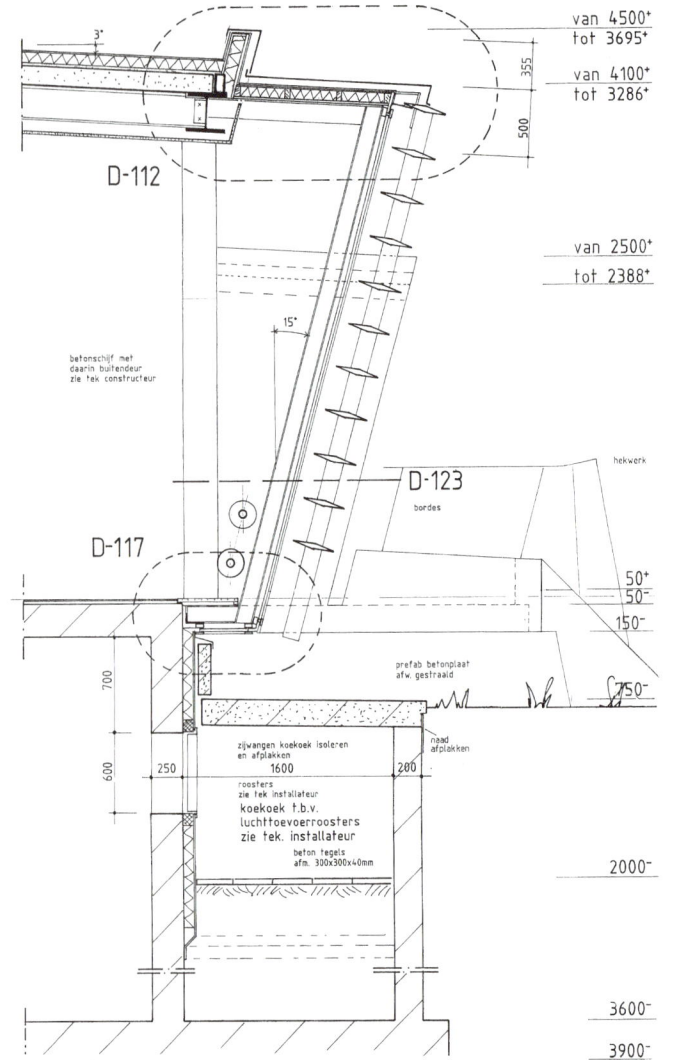

*Detail of the outer cladding of the multi-purpose pavilion. Section.*

minum slats of the cladding are parallel to the roof. In addition, this small pavilion overlaps in cantilever a small pond that occupies part of the courtyard. In other points, it also escapes from being completely level: the other extreme of the body rests elevated on a plinth various centimeters higher than the courtyard. The museum is entered through a door situated at an intermediate height which is accessed by means of a small ramp.

This small pavilion should fulfill the function of a lookout point over the large courtyard from the new museum. However, curiously, the views of the courtyard from the interior are limited by its very own architecture: the large inclined plinths that support the roof impede a clear vision of the exterior. The inclined alu-

this, a long narrow exterior body has been added that shuns from any form of parallelism with the outline of its outer cladding. The roof is inclined towards one of the sides and the horizontal alu-

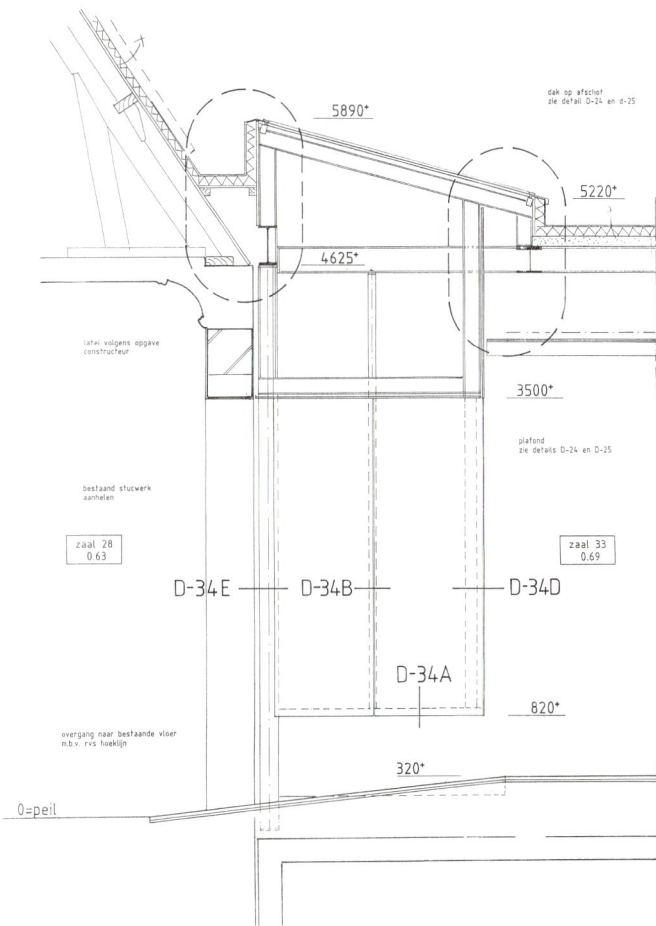

Detail of one of the glass patios below the skylight. The partition walls do not reach the floor.

In the foreground, the piece of concrete in cantilever that supports the partition walls of the exhibitions.

minum slats or the 'twisted' position of the system of reference coordinates also create visual barriers.

**Ben van Berkel** opted to construct a completely new atmosphere in the areas where modern art is exhibited by means of an exhaustive treatment of its six interior faces. The first criteria of the intervention was concerned with the entrance of natural light: the space delimited by the old skylights were converted into light wells closed off by translucent glass partitioning walls which, in some cases, do not reach the floor and allow some of the old bricks on to be seen. The translucent glass possesses the virtue of being able to orient the light that arrives towards the rooms vertically and diffuse it in a homogenous way.

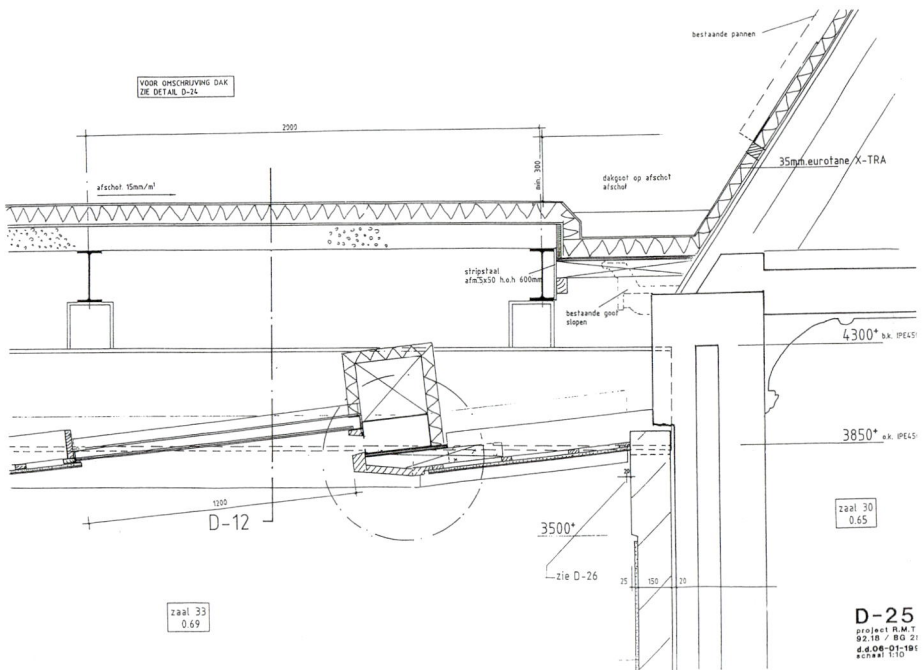

*Detail of the false ceiling with its anchoring system.*

A new false ceiling has been installed in all of the rooms. This combines opaque trimmings, in which the technical services have been installed, with trimmings of artificial light which also filteres through the translucent glass and which, in turn, adds to the light that comes in through the small light wells. Van Berkel creates an atmosphere in which gravity or the sense of verticality is diluted in a series of planes. The collocation of the elements that make up the false ceiling in inclined series adds a certain

dynamism to this weightlessness which combines with the gentle inclinations of the ramps that compensate for the differing floor heights in the different exhibition rooms.

The perimeter walls have been doubled up with concrete and support the large white partitions that form the exhibition spaces.

In addition, new screens have been created in the central part of these spaces supported by means of a heavy piece of reinforced concrete in cantilever that seems to challenge the forces of gravity. Not a single reminder of the old construction appears in these areas.

# Steven Holl

**W**as born in Brementon, Washington in 1947. There, his artistic tendencies started especially with drawing and painting: "I started to paint spontaneously, in 1959, before thinking about studying architecture. In the small town where I grew up, the only place a kid, 12 years old, could hope to exhibit a painting was in the county fair in Kitsap". It was there, along with the most select hogs and prized cattle, that I participated in the county's painting exhibitions and won various first prizes over a period of years.

He studied architecture at the University of Washington where he was influenced by some of his teachers such as Astra Zarina and Herman Pundt. Pundt taught him the history of architecture based on no more than four architects: Brunelleschi, Schinkel, Sullivan and Wright and fomented individualism and hope in his students. He won a grant to study in Rome for six months. There,

Loisium Visitors' Center

Simmons Hall

Musee des confluences

he was very impressed by the Pantheon: "Every day I went through the same ritual, I would leave my windowless apartment early in the morning and walk to the Pantheon of Rome." In 1970, he followed a postgraduate course at the Architectural Association in London.

After his first professional experiences in California, he established his own studio, *Steven Holl Architects*, in New York, city in which his painter brother was living. There, he met other artists such as Donald Judd, Dennis Oppenheim and James Turrell who helped him develop in his work as an architect.

Holl has been a teacher at the Columbia University of New York since 1981. He has also taught at the University of Washington, in the Pratt Institute in New York and at the University of Pennsylvania. With reference to teaching architecture, he states: "It is not so much information that is needed, but solid knowledge that allows intuitive skills to be cultivated and developed."

Steven Holl has also participated in a number of exhibitions, both one-man and mixed, such as those at the MOMA (1989), in the Walker Center in Minneapolis, 'Architecture Tomorrow' (1991), 'Parallax' (2000) which was shown in New York and Rome, 'Architecture+Water' (2001) or 'A New World Trade Center' (2002) in which he displayed his proposal (developed in collaboration with Richard Meyers) for the devastated Ground Zero in New York.

He has received many prizes among which six National Prizes form the AIA and seven Progressive Architecture Prizes stand out. In 1997, he was awarded the Medal of Honor by the New York Delegation of the AIA.

The North American architect **Steven Holl** is a professional who is difficult to classify. He does not easily fit into any of the current architectural tends that have developed during the time that he has been working.

His work is centered on two factors: the 'idea', the architectural concept that gives coherence to what he is doing, and the 'phenomenon', the user's sensory perception. In his own words, "My intuition led me to adopt this hybrid that lies between a conceptual way of working and an approximation to phenomena."

Each new project becomes a search for those concepts that are suitable for the place, the scheme and the client. It is what he himself denominates as the capturing of essence of the unique architectural opportunities of each project.

**Steven Holl** describes this process:
*"We start each project with information and disorder, confusion of objectives, ambiguities in the scheme and an endless list of materials and forms (…) Architecture is the result of working within this indetermination."*

**Holl** states that he starts from zero in every project, without basing himself on prefabricated solutions or stylistic resources. In his working methodology, intuition holds a fundamental role: "The doctrines of this laboratory cannot be trusted. Intuition is our muse." In searching for the particular 'magic' of given circumstances, his pursuit for the 'decisive conceptual diagram' draws him close, in a way, to the renowned capturing of the 'decisive moment' by the photographer Henri Cartier-Bresson, in which deductive thought is suspended so as to understand the authentic possibilities of the site. Rather than leading to a unique idea, this process often ends up with a number of alternatives.

As stated by Rudolf Steiner, **Holl** also believes that "the history of a physical place has meaning and influences the architectural work." Before these facts, says Holl, it is possible to recognize them or to ignore them: "An architect should be as prepared to confront the responsibility of challenging the plot as to harmonizing with it."

In 1987, he wrote his book-manifesto Anchoring. This deals with what he considers to be the connections of architecture with its site, history, phenomena, idea… the adaptation of his projects to their sites does not imitate the traditional architecture of the zone, but makes them subtle and sophisticated. For example, in his project for residences in Fukuoka, the concept 'empty space, articulated space' is an interpretation by the architect of the qualities of the traditional Japanese domestic space as well as about Zen gardens. In this project, residential blocks prefabricated in concrete are intermixed with various inaccessible empty spaces in which ponds have been installed. Steven Holl explains how having had the idea clear as of the beginning helped convince the developers of the necessity of leaving these spaces out of use and without being landscaped. The second idea that he incorporated into the project, which has led to the individualization of all of the homes, is the transformation of the residence thanks to the possibility of rotating some of the partition walls. In a traditional Japanese home, there is a differentiated use of some of the spaces depending on whether it is day or night (tatami room). The fact that all of the apartments in the development are different has had human and social repercussions. Neighbors have started visiting one another with the excuse of seeing the differences between their respective flats. This, in turn, has led to the creation of a greater cohesion among the members of the community.

**Holl** is, in many ways, in debt to the maestros of the Modern Movement. However, he is critical of them for their failed proposals for collective housing which entailed excessive repetition and standardization and which by no means came to satisfy the users. With reference to their residences in Makuhari in Japan, Steven Holl states: "We are not creating homes for a mass of thousands of people, but for thousands of individuals". This exaltation of individualism from Steven Holl is reminiscent of some of the North American maestro Frank Lloyd Wright's values. He is also doubtful about the possibility of universal cultural values, an international style that could work in all places of the world, existing.

**Steven Holl** has at times defined his view as being that of a 'position of resistance', in the sense that he tries to maintain a line of investigation and creativity as opposed to simply accepting already assumed solutions. What motivates him is not the possibility of accumulating commissions, but the internal possibilities of the projects that allow architecture to take place. In his own words: "The resistance is being able to confront the situations with an idea in your head: this is the key. I am always receptive because I believe if you really are creative you can find a way of making architecture come out of almost any circumstance". To sum up, for him, the resistance is the subtle art of knowing when to maintain a position and when to give way.

His architecture hinges on the knowledge that the real meaning of a building lies in the phenomenon of the experience of walking through it, in the perception of its physical characteristics, of the tactile qualities of its materials, of its light, its sounds and silences. Steven Holl recognizes that he has been strongly influenced by phenomenological philosophy and by the authors Merleau-Ponty and Ricoeur:

"I have always thought that the light, textures, details and spaces constitute a form of silent meaning but of greater intensity than any textural manipulation."

Maybe, it is because of this interest in the effect of the light in the spaces that Holl produces many of his initial sketches in watercolors. This technique allows a greater facility for toning down the light. His interest in materials becomes an interest in construction. An example of this is his imaginative use of prefabricated concrete panels in the Chapel of St. Ignatius. In his career, he has used a great variety of materials for casing that range from wood (as in the house for Martha's Vineyard or in the House Y) to double skins of laminated perforated oxidized copper (as in the Sarphatistraat Offices in Amsterdam). Although his work takes in a great variety of ideas, materials and spaces, it can be said that on many occasions a building by Holl can be identified as being such. However, he himself denies wishing to possess his own style, on the contrary, he says he tries to avoid developing easily recognized aesthetics: "It would be nonsense to say that I have no inclination towards certain things. But I fight and make an effort so as to overcome these tendencies."

In short, Holl's work unites conceptual strength and tactile intimacy. It represents the search of an architect "with as much physical as conceptual intensity, with the strength to move the eye, mind and soul."

**Loisium Visitors' Center**
Langenlois, Austria

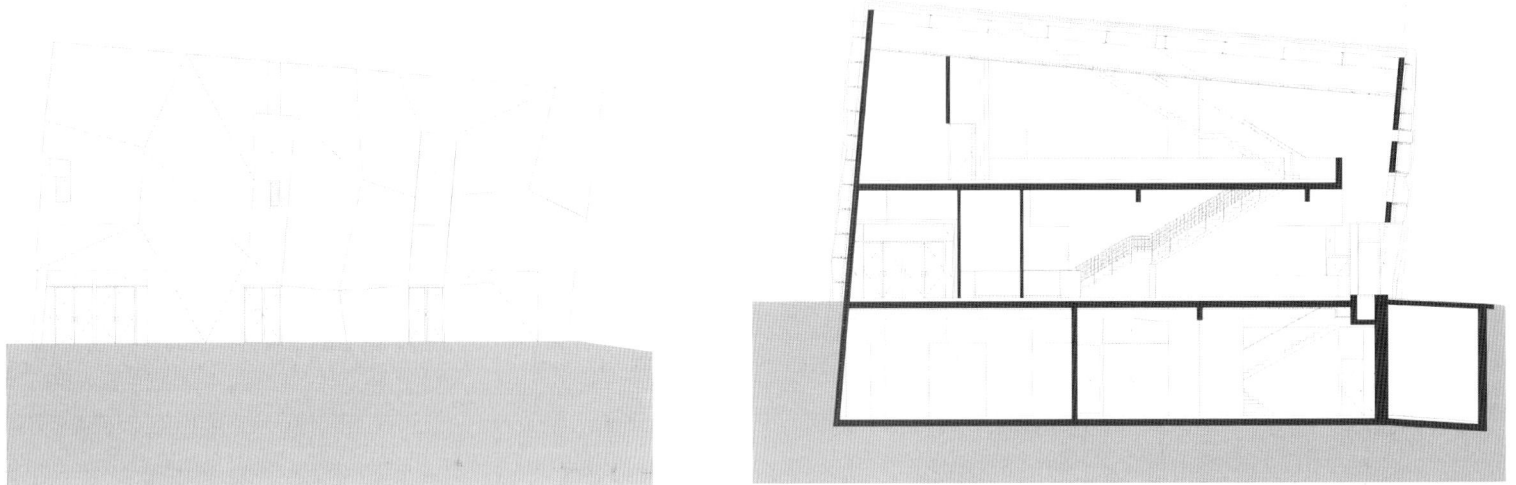

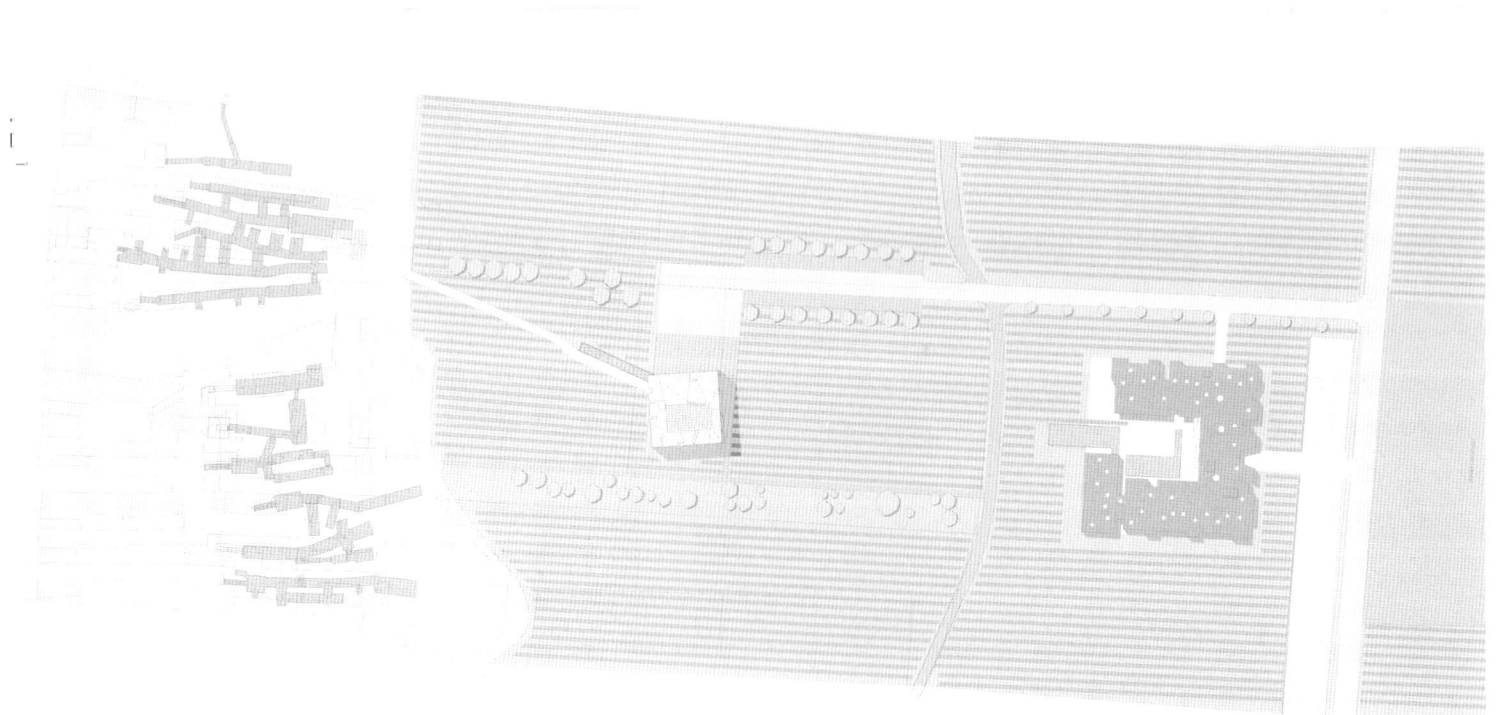

## Loisium Visitors' Center

Langenlois, Austria 2001-2003

Outside Langenlois, 60 minutes west of Vienna, among rolling vineyard-covered hills a new Wine Center has been raised. For the production of wine, these premises possess a system of underground canals built in stone with vaulted ceilings that are some 900 years old.

The project comprised three parts: the vaulted passages, which provide access to the visitors, the wine center, a hotel with restaurant, conference rooms and wine spa.

SOUTH ELEVATION

EAST ELEVATION

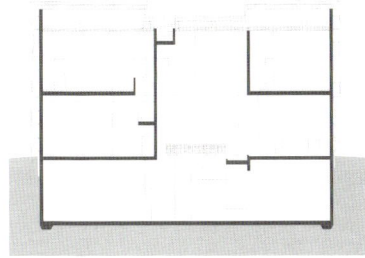

EAST- WEST SECTION

NORTH ELEVATION

WEST ELEVATION

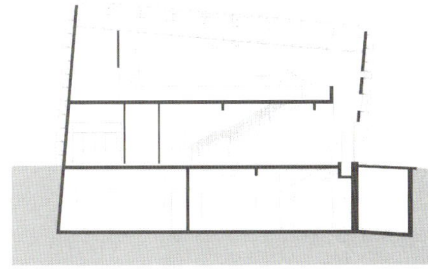

NORTH- SOUTH SECTION

MECHANICAL

SOUVENIR SHOP

STORAGE

EVENT

LOB

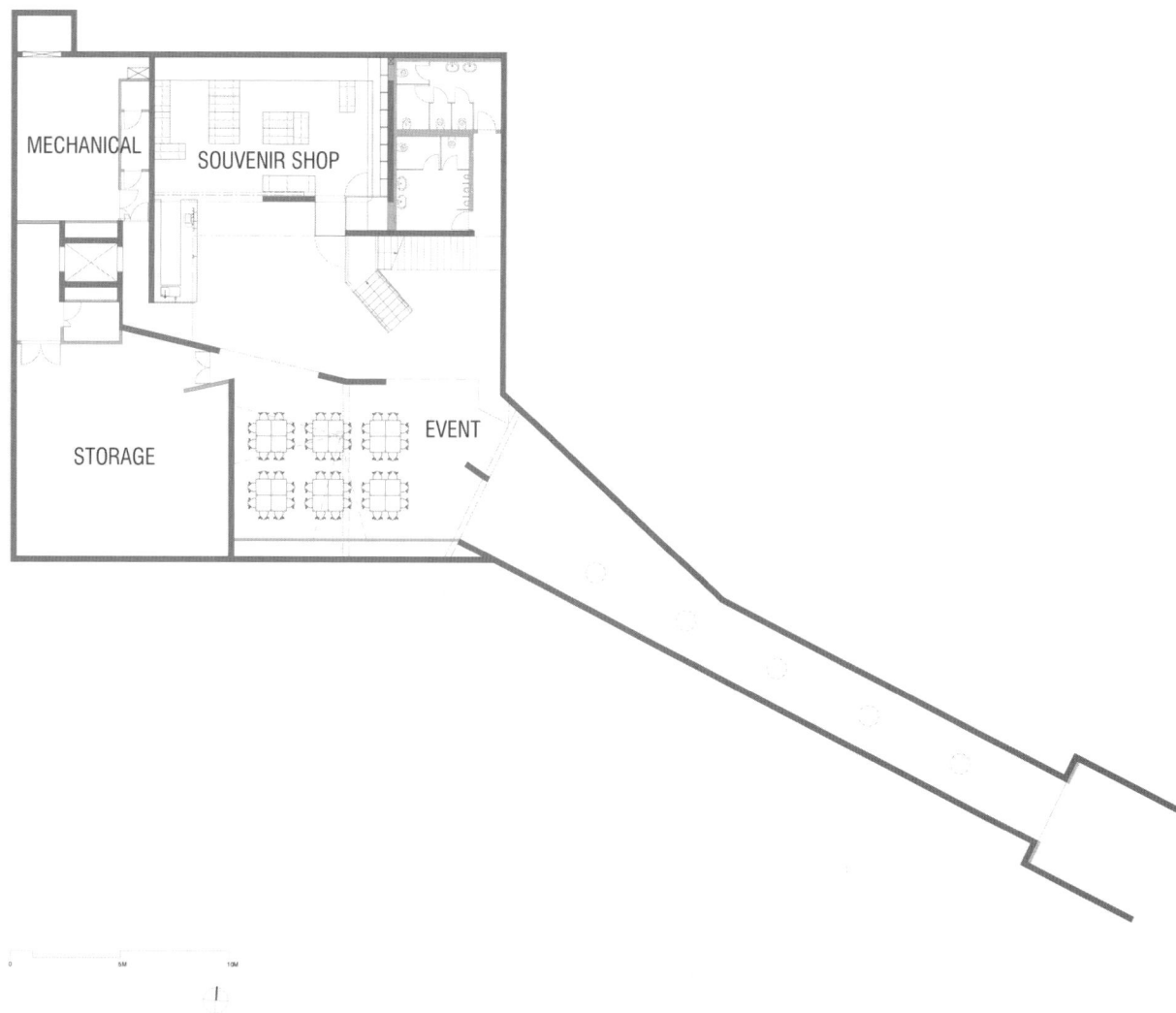

The geometry of the old vaults intersects with the cube formed by the pavilion of the wine center and provokes openings through which the space is illuminated. From the pavilion, which is on a gentle slope, the old vaults are accessed by means of a ramp with a 5° gradient. On entering, the visitor perceives an extraordinary space in which the café is found. The return trip is undertaken through another passage with a ramp that is illuminated by light reflected off a swimming pool. On the lower level of the building, we find a wine bar, a multifunctional area and a store with local products and books. Steps and ramps connect this to the ground floor, where there is a well-stocked wine store, and also to the upper floors on which there are seminary rooms and

the offices. On special occasions, the terrace, from where spectacular views of the landscape can be enjoyed, is open to the public.

The three parts of the project, the vaults, the wine center and the hotel-conference center, relate to one another in section in three different ways: on top of the land, in the land and below the land. As in the layout of a city, the distance between the files of vineyards is continual in all of the landscape and connects the three elements. The square floor plan, 57 m x 57 m, has been placed in line with the strict geometry of the vines. As if it were a part of a city, the variety of spaces and activities offer a great variety of experiences to the visitors.

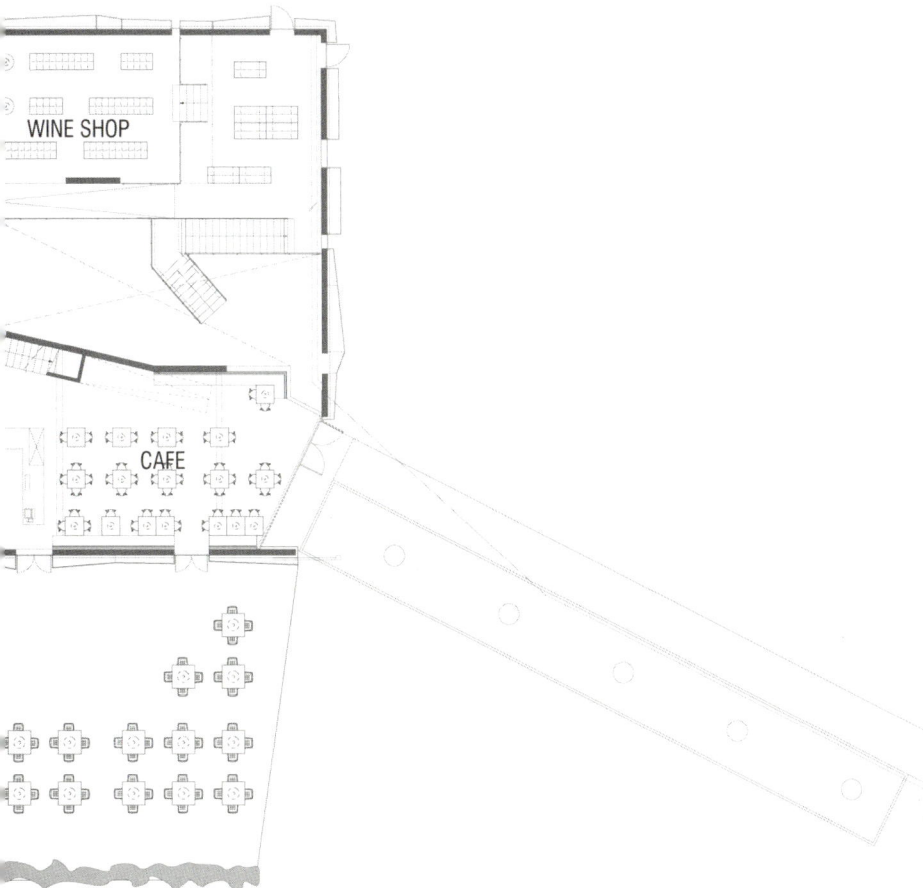

WINE SHOP

CAFE

OFFICE

SEMINAR

## Simmons Hall
Cambridge, MA

## Simmons Hall

Cambridge, MA 2000-2002

This residence for 350 students, conceived as part of the campus, is based on the idea of porosity, on a bath sponge. The building is a vertical section of a ten-story city 84 meters long. The urban concept offers a diversity of activities and services

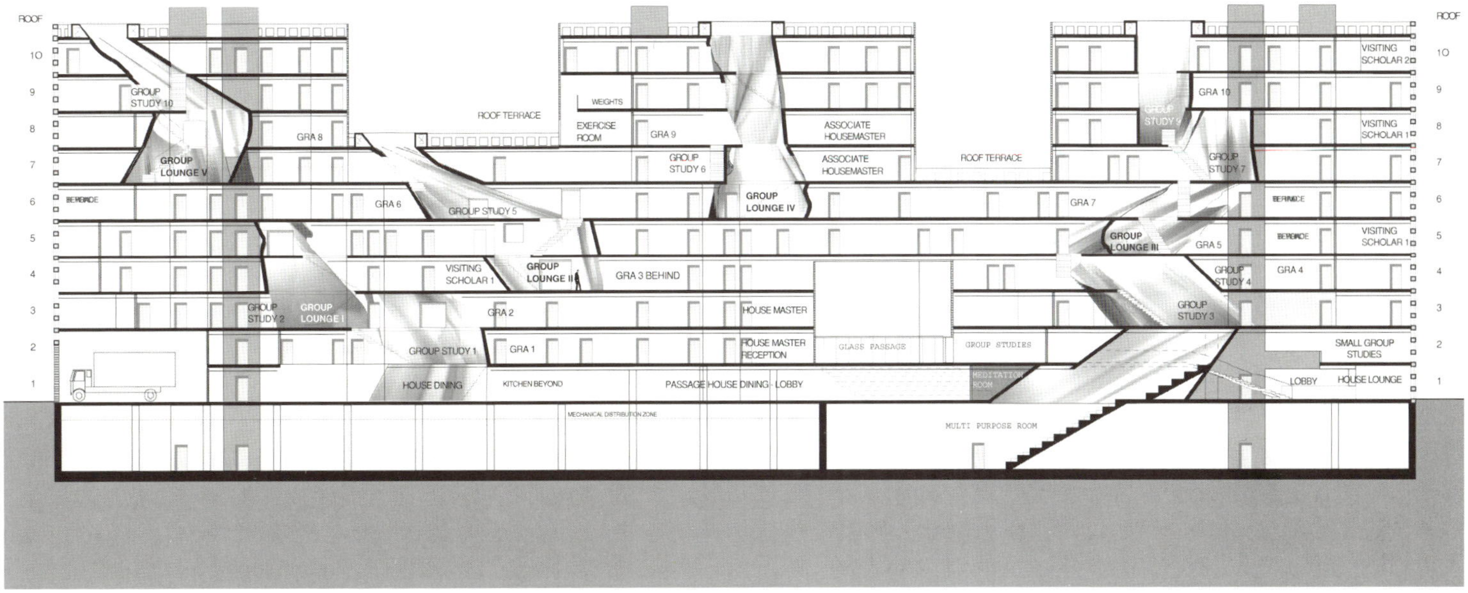

ROOF
10
9
8
7
6
5
4
3
2
1
GROUP STUDY 10
GRA 8
GROUP LOUNGE V
ROOF TERRACE
WEIGHTS
EXERCISE ROOM
GRA 9
GROUP STUDY 6
GRA 6
GROUP STUDY 5
VISITING SCHOLAR 1
GROUP LOUNGE II
GRA 3 BEHIND
GROUP STUDY 2
GROUP LOUNGE I
GRA 2
GROUP STUDY 1
GRA 1
HOUSE DINING
KITCHEN BEYOND
PASSAGE HOUSE DINING - LOBBY
MECHANICAL DISTRIBUTION ZONE
ASSOCIATE HOUSEMASTER
ASSOCIATE HOUSEMASTER
GROUP LOUNGE IV
HOUSE MASTER
HOUSE MASTER RECEPTION
GLASS PASSAGE
GROUP STUDIES
MEDITATION ROOM
MULTI PURPOSE ROOM
ROOF TERRACE
GRA 10
GROUP STUDY 9
GROUP STUDY 7
GRA 7
GROUP LOUNGE III
GRA 5
GROUP STUDY 4
GRA 4
GROUP STUDY 3
VISITING SCHOLAR 2
VISITING SCHOLAR 1
VISITING SCHOLAR 1
SMALL GROUP STUDIES
LOBBY
HOUSE LOUNGE

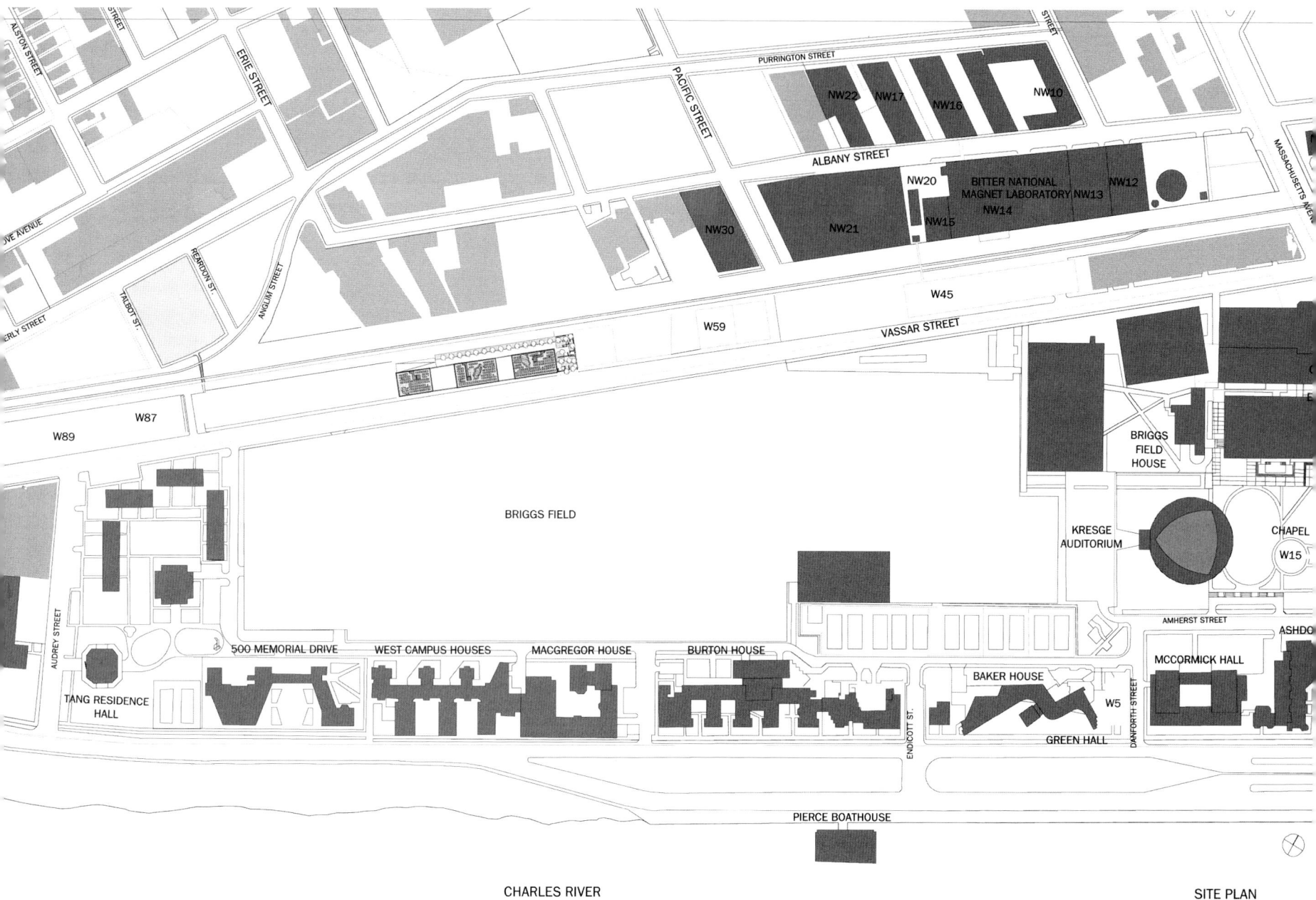

ALSTON STREET

ERIE STREET

PURRINGTON STREET

PACIFIC STREET

NW22  NW17  NW16  NW10

ALBANY STREET

NW20  BITTER NATIONAL  
MAGNET LABORATORY  NW13  
NW30  NW21  NW15  NW14  NW12

W45

W59  VASSAR STREET

REARDON ST.

ANGLUM STREET

TALBOT ST.

OVE AVENUE

ERLY STREET

MASSACHUSETTS AVENUE

W87

W89

W5

BRIGGS  
FIELD  
HOUSE

BRIGGS FIELD

KRESGE  
AUDITORIUM

CHAPEL  
W15

AMHERST STREET

ASHDO

AUDREY STREET

500 MEMORIAL DRIVE  WEST CAMPUS HOUSES  MACGREGOR HOUSE  BURTON HOUSE

MCCORMICK HALL

TANG RESIDENCE  
HALL

BAKER HOUSE  W5

ENDICOTT ST.

DANFORTH STREET

GREEN HALL

PIERCE BOATHOUSE

CHARLES RIVER

SITE PLAN

within the residence, such as a theater with 125 seats and a café. The restaurant is at street level with an outdoor terrace with tables. The passages that connect the rooms (approx. 280 cm wide) act as if they were streets open to a diversity of experiences. They are public spaces to be in. They are not only there to access the rooms. The residence develops a porous morphology

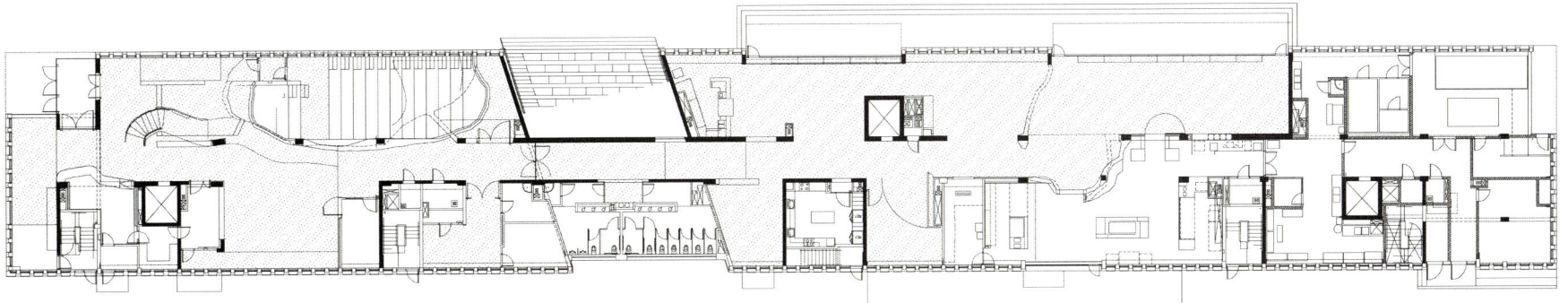

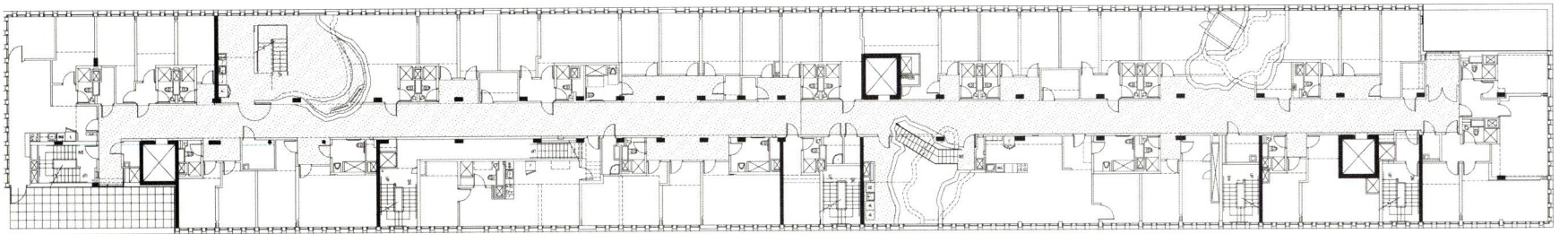

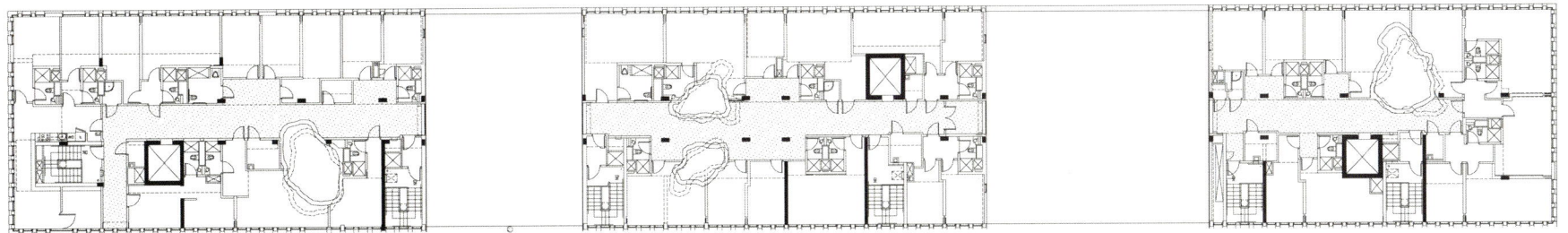

via a series of programmatic and bio-technical functions. There are five large hollows that correspond to the entrances, a look-out area and the terraces related to open-air activities such as the gymnasium. To these hollows, new cavities have been added. These are large holes that run lengthways through the building and act as lungs that bring in light and air to the sections.

The foundations of the building consist of a continuous slab of steel reinforced concrete over the sandy ground; the building 'floats' over the terrain like a boat on water.

The structure 'PerfCon', which is integrated as a facade, is a unique structure that permits maximum flexibility and interaction.

TOP ARCHITECTS OF THE WORLD

Each individual room possesses nine square windows that can be opened and regulated for ventilation, views and privacy. The wall, which is 46 cm thick, acts as a sunscreen.

The heads and jambs, reinforced with steel, have been painted in different colors according to the structural functions they fulfil.

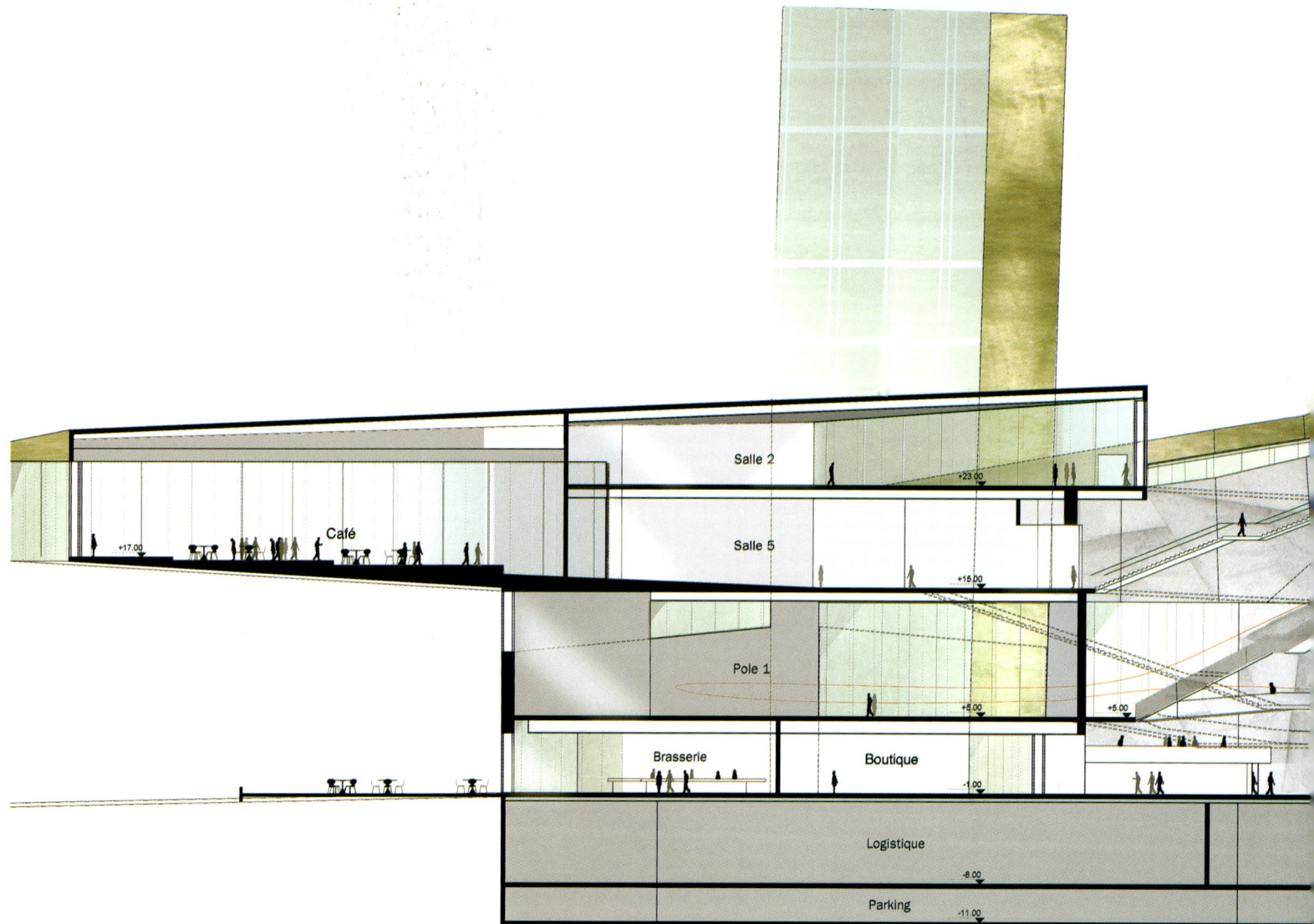

Musee des confluences
Lyon, France

**Musee des confluences**

Lyon, France 2001

The building responds to the unique characteristics of the site: the pointed and narrow form, its location between the rivers Ródano and Saone… The horizontality and the turbulence of the site are aspects that have influenced in the section of the new museum. The central concept seeks a convergence of four geophysical aspects: Material: the coming and going of elements

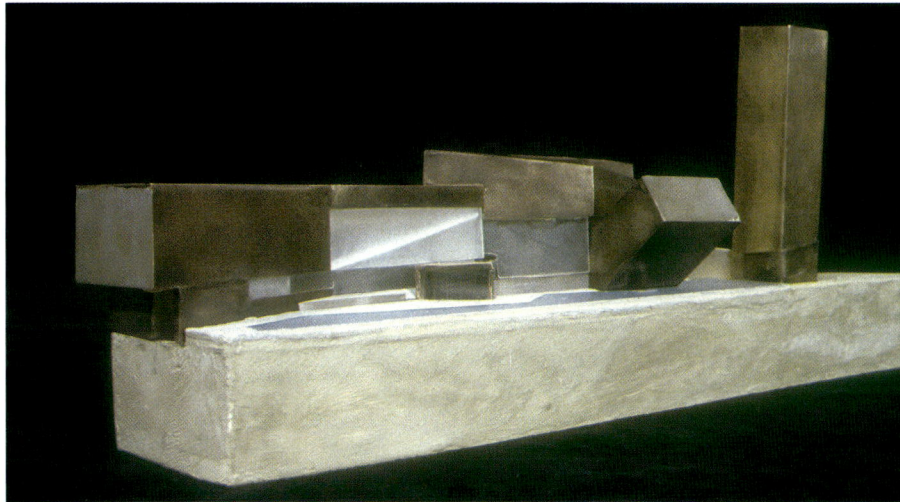

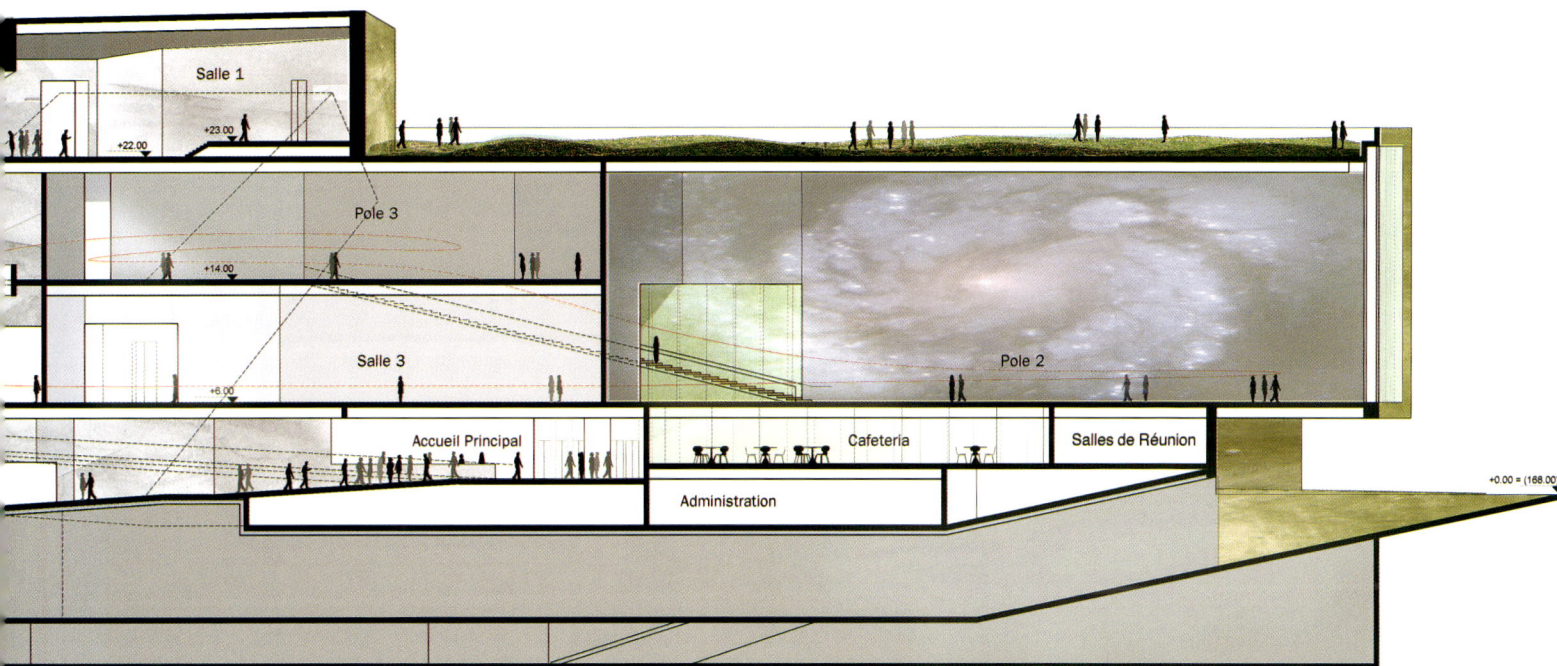

for exhibition; Energy: the great hall with its human flow; Configuration: the auditorium and the principal orientation; Correlation: the tower-classrooms in which to study and deepen knowledge.

These four vectors have been unified in a flowing form of architecture in which the transference from one space to another is extremely fluid. The intersection of the itineraries is but another

Salle 1
+23.00

Pole 3
+14.00

-2.00

-1.00

Logistique
-8.00

Parking
-11.00

Grand Auditorium

+22.00

+15.00

+1.00

potential of the proposal. From the central room, a large cantilevered prism emerges which dominates the view of the confluence of the two rivers.

The structure of the building is in steel which, thanks to the structural calculations carried out by computer, maintains sections of a standard thickness. The skin of the building corresponds to a copper alloy with a golden patina which responds well to the atmospheric contamination of the area.

# Eduardo Souto de Moura

as born in Oporto in 1952. He studied architecture in the Escuela de Arquitectura de Oporto (ETSAP) where Fernando Távora was his teacher during his fourth year. In those years, the 1970's, when what was really in fashion was discourse on semiotics, history or sociopolitical themes, Souto de Moura remembers Távora as "one of the few (teachers) who made us draw". During this period (1974), he joined Alvaro Siza's office as a draftsman. With reference to his old collaborator Siza remembers: "I soon realized, with certain displeasure but greater joy, that I would not have a collaborator for long".

Souto de Moura worked for Siza until 1979 when, according to Eduardo Souto de Moura himself, Siza

Casa do Cinema

fired him: "it was not I who left. One day he said, 'You cannot continue here, you have got to think about your professional life, and not work for another architect'".

In 1989, he obtained his title as an architect and opened his own office. The Braga Market, which had a many repercussions, was one of his first projects. He has won competitions from the beginning such as the first prize for the Centro Cultural del SEC in Oporto, or the competition for the remodeling of the Plaza Mayor in Évora. In 1987, he also won the first prize in a competition for a hotel in Salzburg. He has been named for the Mies van der Rohe Prize on seven occasions and awarded with the Stone in Architecture Prize along with many others which include the FAD 1999 Prize and the Heinrich-Tessenow Prize.

Souto de Moura has also developed a theoretical and teaching side. He was assisant teacher in the Facultad de Arquitectura de Oporto from 1981 to 1991 and he has been a visiting teacher in many universities: París-Belleville, Harvard, Dublín, the ETH in Zurich, and Lausana. He has also given seminars in Europe and the United States and he presented numerous exhibitions.

Since 1997, Souto de Moura has had his architect's office in the same building as Alvaro Siza and Fernando Távora. In words of the latter: "This 'house' became necessary because it existed before it was built, due to our friendships, familiarity and teachings (...) I am sure that it is an unusual situation among architects'".

In his latest works and in his search for greater liberty, **Eduardo Souto de Moura** has brought into question the labels attached to him by the critics with reference to his former undertakings. Neither the Braga Stadium nor the Casa do Cinema "Manoel de Oliveira", or even the two houses in Ponte de Lima are works that can be immediately identified with their author.

This Portuguese architect, who studied under Fernando Távora and collaborated with Siza for a number of years, has often been described as a contemporary version of Mies from the south. He is a disciple of the Modern Movement's aesthetics, but sufficiently down to earth to understand where he is and the times in which he is building: "I was a postmodern architect producing modern works". In his architecture, there is a search for adaptation, for example, in the relationship between the materials used and the constructions of his country: "I do not think it correct to construct in wood in Portugal because no building tradition in this material exists. What does exist in my country is a long tradition in constructing in stone". It is not really a question of wanting to modernize traditional Portuguese architecture, a regionalist criticism along the lines of those made by Kenneth Frampton, but of making the most of the circumstances: "I am thinking of the house in Alcanena that has a large patio and a large brick wall. This material came from the demolition of a factory and it was only necessary to pay for the transportation". Certain circumstances, those of the real world, in which the control of time and of the agents implicated in a venture take over and occupy the greater part of the development of the project: "Civil construction in Portugal is an underworld of clandestine species (…) Today, we have to confront the misbalance between those who wish to construct, what we want to build and the time imposed upon us". An important part of being an architect is achieving a positive syntony with others participating on the project, from the client to the bricklayers. As far as the time necessary to complete a project is concerned: "The time is discounted as of the end".

One of the most outstanding characteristics of his architecture is its precision. The construction details defined in his office have always attracted attention from other architects for their fineness and apparent simplicity, at times paradoxical: "The problem consists in that the simpler the image seems, the more torturous its construction has been". In his first works, a loosiana obsession to show the qualities of each material in an independent way is observed. A good example of this is can be found in some walls of the Cultural Center S.E.C. in Oporto in which all of the successive layers of materials that they have been made up of are displayed in the lateral parts as if the wall had been finished with a clean cut. In his writings, **Souto de Moura** also seeks precision and at times has been known to quote from Eugenio de Andrade: "Only the exact word is of use to the public". With reference to this rigorous tendency Eduardo Souto de Moura comments: "Precisely for having established this rigor or this uncompromising attitude in the scheme of any house, it becomes a question of making a certain elegance stand out, a finished result, a rigorous manifestation that accepts no intermediary situations. This prejudiced me, or I could begin to do it".

Maybe in this line, we can come to a better understanding of the changes in his latest works. In these, we continue to find the radical aspects of his first works, as much in the material as in the concept (in the play on opposing intentions in the two houses in Ponte de Lima, to give an example). In these works, the elegance is not the principal objective (although for this reason, they do not cease to be elegant). It could be said that there has been a distancing from the Modern Movement's classical language, of any 'tic' in style, to experiment with the possibilities offered by each project one by one. It is possible that his travels in Mexico and Peru have had something to do with this. In the Casa en la Serra da Arrábida, influences from the architecture of Barragán or even from the paintings of Georgia O'Keefe can be felt. In the Braga Stadium, Eduardo Souto de Moura talks of having been inspired by bridges constructed by the Incas of Peru for the roofing and by the ruins of Machu Pichu for the terraces. In the entrance areas below the terraces, we can also find echoes of Louis Kahn. It would be possible to talk about the richness of his references.

Lately, **Souto de Moura** talks of his great interest in the notion of comfort: "In Távora I was looking for, above all, an aspect that is not currently in fashion, the feeling of comfort that a work transmits, the result of a chain of qualities that are neither linked to taste nor form which architecture should have." It is not a question of trying to recreate the atmosphere of an English pub, but to give the user the power of decision within a space, of trying to find a degree of adaptability among the qualities of a space. This could be explained as a certain capacity of the users of the building to be able to experiment with different situations regarding the light, the land, the different points of view, the landscape (interior and exterior) and the changes of color. This is the architecture of Souto de Moura, architecture in times of change which, at times, stops to question itself.

## INTERVIEW

ATRIUM - Alejandro de la Sota said that an architect was someone who tries to, "Pull your eyes over the wool," instead of someone who tries to, "Pull the wool over your eyes." What can you tell me about this?
ESM- I think there is an alternation. Sometimes, we have to pull somebody's eyes over the wool and on other occasions, we have to pull the wool over somebody's eyes. It depends on the case. I understand that De la Sota's intention is always to do the best job possible. At times, it is necessary to stop, listen and talk to the client to know what it is that he wants to be able to continue doing your best.

ATRIUM - How do you approach a new project?
ESM- I always start with a sketch of a floor plan to develop the distribution and to see if it works. While drawing the plan, I'm thinking and drawing sketches of the volumes. We always make a maquette, the same day. We start the maquette of the terrain and the first

sketches at the same time. I find myself using more and more maquettes as there is always less and less time to think slowly. You've got to see things quickly and decide. It is a problem of time. Nowadays, in architecture, everything is wanted very quickly and good architecture is incompatible with speed.

ATRIUM - Are there any themes which interest you in a constant way in your projects?
ESM- At the moment, there is a theme that I'm interested in: the window. Making holes is very difficult and at the moment, I'm trying to make some. There are more abstract languages that are useful for certain types of constructions while others need doors and windows. And I, as I haven't made windows for some thirty years, I feel like a child writing with my left hand.

ATRIUM - You make it sound difficult...
ESM- When you dominate a language – it's a little like cooking sausages – everything always comes out right. And it's good to be looking for other things.

ATRIUM - Having looked at your projects and having read some of the texts that you have written, I wanted to ask you about three concepts that I feel are close to your work: Adequacy, Precision and Comfort
ESM- As far as adequacy is concerned, architecture may have many adjectives, but it can never be unnatural. It may be set against nature (this is a condition), but it can't be unnatural. It should create empathy (not necessarily sympathy) with its setting whether in a positive sense or not. It's got to be natural (not in the sense of naturalist), but in the sense of adequacy. We've got to have the feeling that the building has been there for years and that if the building wasn't there, something would be missing. For me, precision... You've got to do it well to be convincing. About comfort, although some maestros such as Távora have maintained this, it is a characteristic that has been lost to an extent. Comfort means building places in which you feel good. This aspect, something 'cozy', is coming back. It is also a little, the coherence in the drawing. For example, if it is necessary for there to be light in a space, it's got to be there although the facade may not turn out as you wanted it to. The building I live in is a cube that is closed on the two sides and open at the back and front. We've got two bathrooms in the side parts, and to be coherent, they were designed without windows. Towards the end, I thought, "Am I going to be in the bathroom without light?" So, with a lot of courage, I opened three windows. Architecture isn't a theorem, it's a living thing that can have incongruities, contradictions... All of this is also related to adequacy.

ATRIUM - So, the three things are related...
ESM- Yes. Rigor as well. Architecture should sell itself and the way of doing it is with the maximum of professionality and rigor possible. If not, we're not convincing.

ATRIUM - In the three works to be published in this book, Braga Stadium, the Cinema House "Manoel de Oliveira" and the two Houses of

Ponte Lima, it seems that there iyou have a desire not to repeat yourself, to experiment with a diversity of solutions. What place does experimentation occupy in your work?
ESM- In one of the two Houses in Ponte de Lima, I fulfilled a desire to build a house in cantilever. This allowed me to create an outside living room below it, a tidy one, a living room without walls. There is an intermediary space between the house and the territory.
To begin with, the second client wanted a house the same as the first. I said no. They were two different families. When I started, I was thinking of making a vertical house (with a room on each floor). This was also an experiment that I was interested in. The council said no, and talking to the clients I realized that they wanted a house with a tiled roof. I'd never built an inclined roof and I started thinking about what a tiled roof represented for us in the 21st century. It is a very different house from the first and it includes the decision of situating two perpendicular planes so as to give the impression that the house is the same, but that it is inclined. There is a sort of winter garden

between the facade and one of these planes. One is difficult to understand without the other. During the project, I thought of making them in different materials, but when I saw the concrete I said, "No. They've got to be the same." There is an interaction between them. They are the same family.
Their relationships with the exterior geography are very different. In the cantilevered house, the distant views are appreciated, the trees, the sierra. The other, as it is inclined, has views of a greater proximity. These are two ways of seeing the relationship with the surroundings.

ATRIUM - When I saw the project, I became very curious to know that sort of relationship there was between the two clients. How did each choose their house?
ESM- They are brothers-in-law. First, we made the cantilevered house and later the brother-in-law came and said he wanted another exactly the same. I refused because I don't think any two lives are the

same and, besides, the circumstances were different. One had more children and the section of the second house, which was higher, would allow for two more beds. The form was justifiable.

ATRIUM - I would like you to talk to me about some comments you have made: "Today we have to face up to the imbalance between those who want to build, what we want to build and the time imposed on us".
ESM- One of the principal materials of the architect today is time. All of it has to be filtered.
You can't go around with preconceived ideas. You don't need much time to copy, but if you really want to resolve a problem, first you've got to fully understand what the problem consists of. And once you understand it (you don't always come to fully understand it) an answer is materialized. All of this requires time, knowing the client, knowing the constructor, knowing oneself. It is the fixed norm of architecture, it needs time. The client worries about time because time is money. Time means paying interests.

ATRIUM - In what way do you think the new technologies, such as the CAD programs or Internet, have effected present-day architecture and more particularly your own? What do you think of computer programs as design tools?

ESM- It's very simple. I don't use computers. I have many. My collaborators use them for 3D and to make presentations. In competitions they are obligatory (there is always this obsession for the proximity to reality). They don't help me think. I draw to do this. With 3D, I find it difficult to see if the spaces work. I always have to take the image from the screen and onto paper. With maquettes, it is easier to work. I work with materials that can be cut a lot. In this way, it's easy to see and change things.
Regarding Internet, if I need something, I ask my daughters. In my opinion, in order for information to be useful, it's good that it's difficult to find. For example, the facility that my daughters now have to do their work may lead to them not fully assimilating the information.

ATRIUM - Your architecture. Do you intend it to be contemporary is the sense of following the rhythm of its time, or is it in some way timeless? I get the feeling that some architects emphasis one of these two attitudes in their work. For example, Rem Koolhaas describes the attitude of his office OMA towards urban metropolitan circumstances in this way: "We are a bit like a surfer on the waves".
ESM- It has both attitudes: we are of our time and we should understand our reality, but we should also confront what we do with esta-

blished criteria in order to know what we are doing and not to fall into the ridiculous situation of constructing buildings that have no meaning. For example, what meaning does it have now to construct a tiled roof or a window? Understanding contemporary methods (we can't build in the same way as they did in the Old World because we have different technologies), but learning from previous experiences. Architecture can't be new because it would be stupid not to use past information. We can't start from zero. In one way or another, all drawings are a redrawing of something. Neither can we repeat it in the same way given that we have other technologies and other methods. In fact, surfing isn't my specialty.

ATRIUM - How do you relate architecture to other arts? I've read about your interest in Donald Judd and Joseph Beuys…
ESM- Among the arts, there are connections, but each one has its specific characteristics: painting has its characteristics, the cinema others… Analogies can be made between the framing of photographs, the cinema and opening windows in a wall for example. Each art is different, but it is also true that one can make use of other languages. The forms are available to be used.

ATRIUM - From your answers, I feel that you try to accumulate knowledge so you can select something from it that may be useful later on.
ESM- You've got to create a visual dictionary; also travel and read. After a series of analogies, you may find this useful.

ATRIUM - What do you most like about being an architect? What do you least like about being one?
ESM- What I like most is the process. Once a building has been finished, I forget about it. What I like is seeing it grow and thinking that it all started with a blank piece of paper. What I like least is the bureaucracy. It's horrible. And, now, you can't do anything. Rules and regulations have got into everything. You have to go into loads of details. Things have also been complicated by legislation. I'm just starting a project in l'Empordà. You're obliged to construct as if you were building an old house: inclined roof, walls finished in stone. The realities of today aren't the same: you're obliged to build a 'fetish'.

ATRIUM - You have your professional office in the same building as Álvaro Siza and Fernando Távora. You were a student of Távora's and you worked with Álvaro Siza for a number of years. It would seem that you have close relationships. Does it help you in some way to work so close to one another?
ESM- We've worked together a lot although, now, maybe we do so a little less. We bump into each other when we enter and, sometimes, when we leave as well. The three of us worked on a job for Italy together. I've also done some projects with Siza. When I have doubts, I sometimes go and compare Távora's opinions with Siza's. I listen and then do what I think best. Siza has said this, Távora the other… it helps me think.

ATRIUM - Do you consider that there has been an evolution in your projects and in your architectural ideas over the last few years?

ESM- The difference is that I'm getting more interested in what we were talking about before, the adequacy of a project. I'm interested in things becoming more and more real, more adequate and more natural, all of this without ceasing to be beautiful. It's got to be pretty although it's not so elegant. The drawing being elegant at the planning stage doesn't interest me so much now. I'm more interested in what exists once it's been built, the people, the light…

ATRIUM - How do you go about getting your client's confidence?
ESM- I work a lot so the clients think: "For the same money, this guys works twice as much as any other." When it comes to making a decision with the client, by not saying this has to be like this simply because it has to be like this if we haven't made ten maquettes and explained why it is the best decision. This firstly helps you convince yourself and, later, convince others about the decisions you make.

ATRIUM - What do you think is the present-day role of the architect in the development of our cities?
ESM- He's had more, but now it's the political and economic factors that carry much more weight. The architect now comes in fourth place. Firstly, the politicians decide, then the real estate agents and developers, next the client and later the architect. And he does what he can.

ATRIUM - And how do you see the present tendency to privatize public spaces? I see that there are big differences in how this tendency is seen in Europe and the United States.
ESM- In the United States, the cities grow due to private initiatives; the city is a void between things. In Europe, public spaces have traditionally been subjected to urban planning… Here, the first directive is the plan that tells you what you can do, then comes what the developer wants to invest, the materials that you can use… then the direct client, and the architect is the last in line of the decision makers.

ATRIUM - And how do you see the present situation in Oporto?
ESM- Bad. I see things very abandoned.

ATRIUM - Lisbon seems to be more looked after, perhaps.
ESM- Yes. Portugal is in extreme economic crisis. The economy is concentrated in Lisbon, and I see Porto becoming more and more marginal and this is reflected in the city. The center of Porto is empty and abandoned, degenerated.

ATRIUM - What is your opinion about the existence of a star system of architects? Cities such as Barcelona, Madrid or Florence presently seem to be more interested in acquiring 'brand name' buildings than in planning their urban spaces in general. What do you think about this situation?
ESM- This is a question that comes from Barcelona because Barcelona is a city with a tradition of urban planning. Sometimes the public spaces are planned first and later the buildings are built. I believe that now things are being done the other way round, Mr A, B, or C is asked to build a building-object. It is a result of globalization. Thinking and building the city – this characteristic of the school of Oporto and of Barcelona, with Bohigas, Martorell, from my generation, Eduard Bru, Pep Llinàs, Josep Lluís Mateo…-- that debate doesn't seem to be continuing. There isn't a global idea of the city; each architect carries out his projects. For example, Koolhaas, Foster, R. Rodgers, J. Nouvel, F. Gehry and others are in Lisbon and Oporto. In Barcelona, several of these architects are also working. They are the ones who are everywhere. It's what's bought: projects that may become icons. The fact that these architects are invited to participate in competitions here should make it easier for those from here to work in other places. The idea is that there should be an exchange. It's not a question of only the Dutch working in Holland or only those from Barcelona working in Barcelona… It's the communications that make this possible. In principle, it is easier to build far away than it was before. The means are easy, but the content isn't so easy.

ATRIUM - What changes do you see, or would you like to see in the present panorama of architecture?
ESM- More than changes, it's a question of understanding the problems. I can't say that I want to change this, that or the other. Each problem has to be understood in it's own terms. The major problem of contemporary architecture, in my opinion, is time. It's got to be understood that with time the necessary investigation to lead us to the most adequate solution can be carried out. Images are sold like flashes because there isn't enough time… you've got to convince the politician, the client and so on quickly. There are so many things that could be achieved such as constructing a building in such a way that it isn't necessary to install air conditioning, for example. Everything can be done if they give you time. I think things are being done badly.

ATRIUM - And there aren't always reasons to be in such a hurry…
ESM- Yes. Sometimes, they are in such a hurry for the architect to finish the basic project, then they take three months to make decisions and, then, ask for the executive in 15 days. It's something I don't understand. This also happens in competitions.

ATRIUM - Does travelling help you in your work? Can you tell me something about your journeys in Mexico and Peru?
ESM- I think that to understand architecture, you have to see it, so you have to travel. I usually have a reason for travelling. In fact, I've been to Mexico several times to see the architecture of Luis Barragán. The idea I had previously acquired of Barragán from books was that of painteresque architecture. When I was there, I saw that I was wrong. The scale of his houses and buildings impressed me. They are so much larger than I had thought, but everything is so well proportioned… For me it has been a great inspiration. The windows also interest me a lot. In Guadalajara, I saw the first of Barragán's houses which are more painteresque. As far as Peru is concerned, I'm interested in the relationship the architecture has with nature. For example, how there are places where natural and artificial elements can be confused such as in the stone steps at Machu Pichu. In Greece, I went to see Epidauros in order to see how the ancient Greeks managed to close an open space, and without a roof ■

# Casa do Cinema
"Manoel de Oliveira"

The building is in the form of a cube, similar to the surrounding houses, which suffers some inflexions in response to its overall dimensions: an inclined trapeziform roof for the Auditorium.

In fact, two 15-story towers are planned at a distance of approximately 35 meters away which will fragment the space of the library in two and orient us towards the river and the sea.

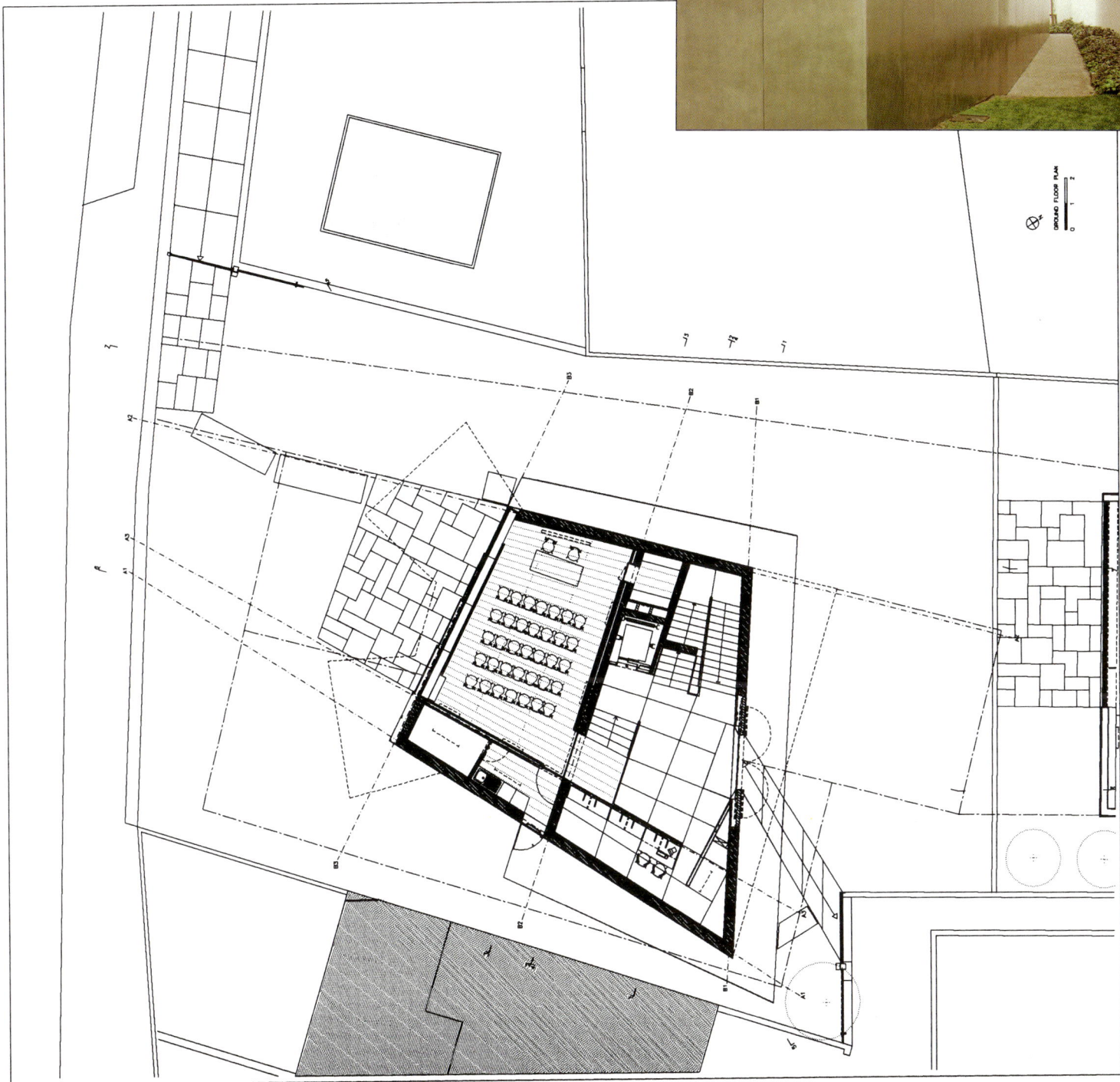

GROUND FLOOR PLAN

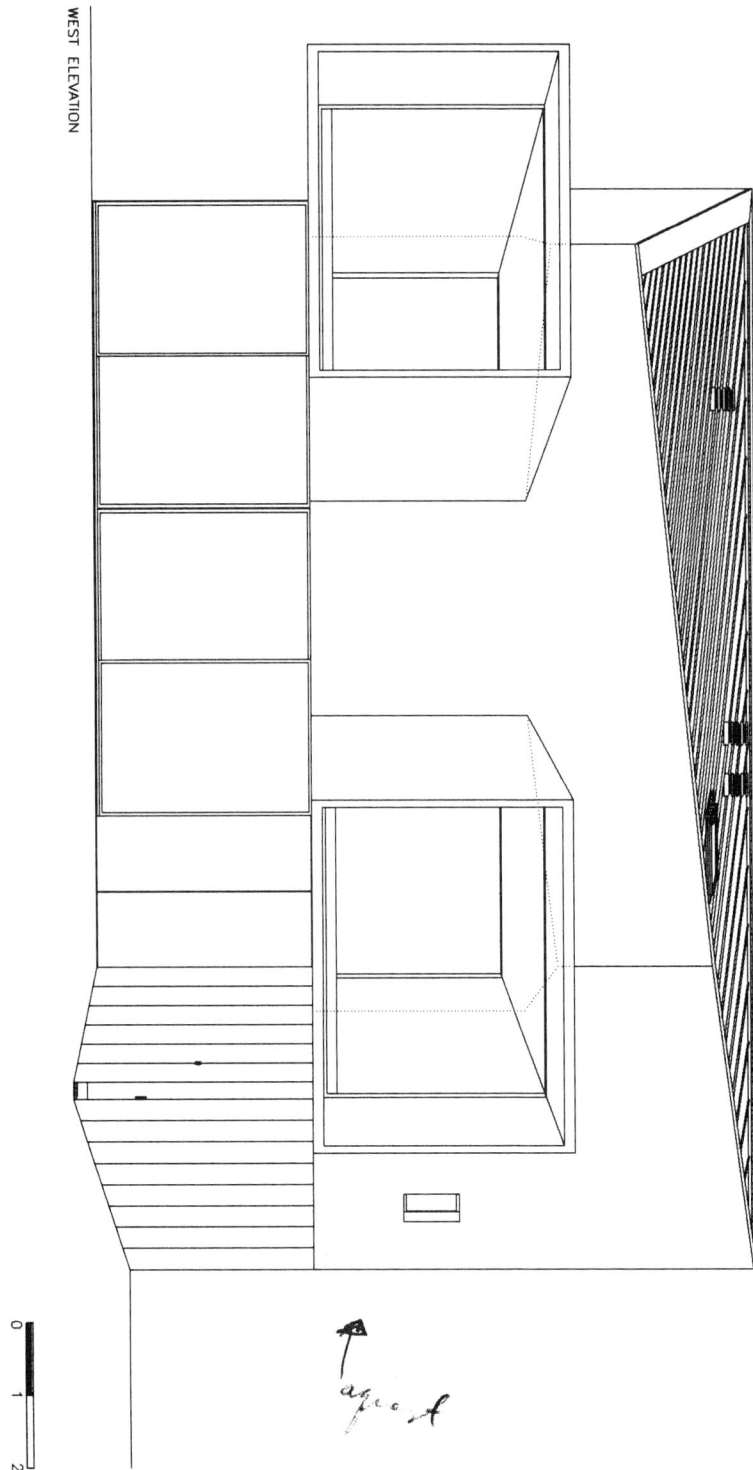

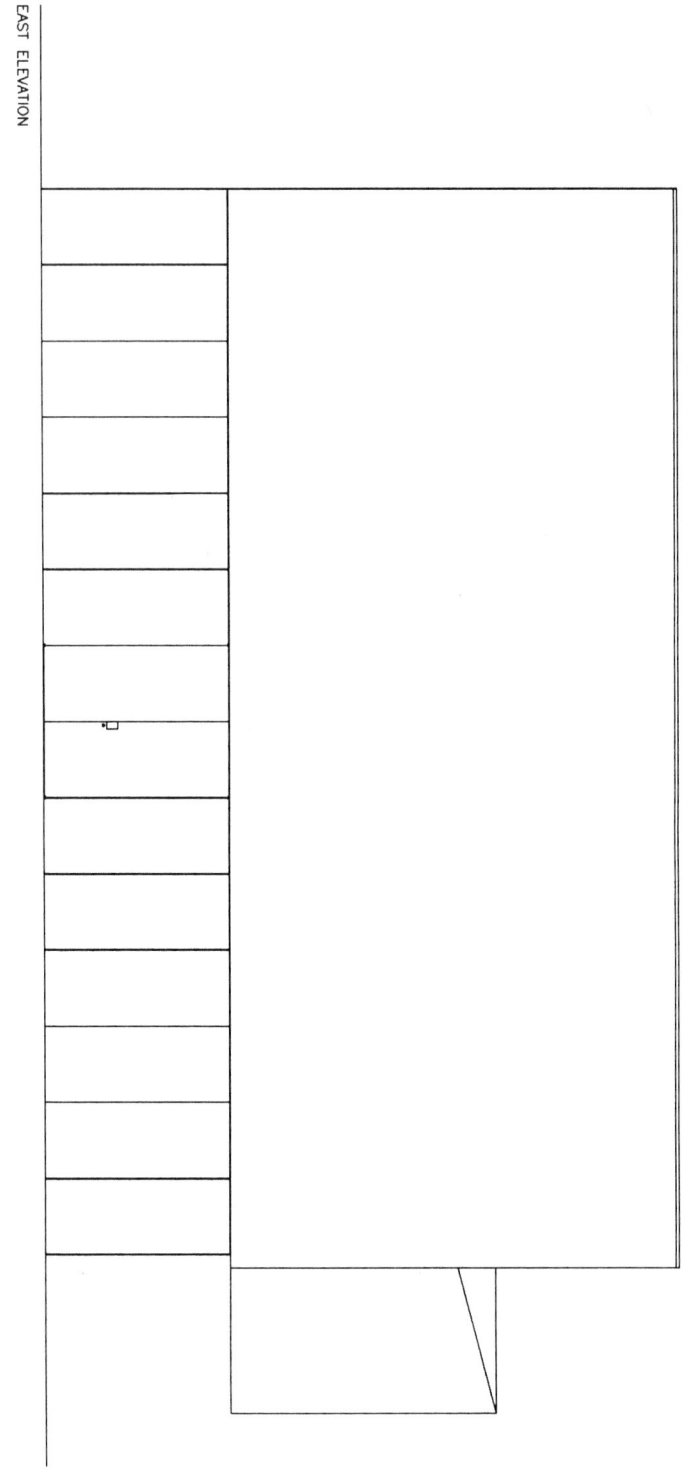

In the exterior, the roof is covered with zinc, over the first floor with a single layer in dark gray and over the ground floor it is covered with sheet aluminum fixed with fiberglass.

In the interior, there are acoustic ceilings, plastered walls and dark-wooden floors in the rooms while the hall and staircase are paved in matt gray marble.

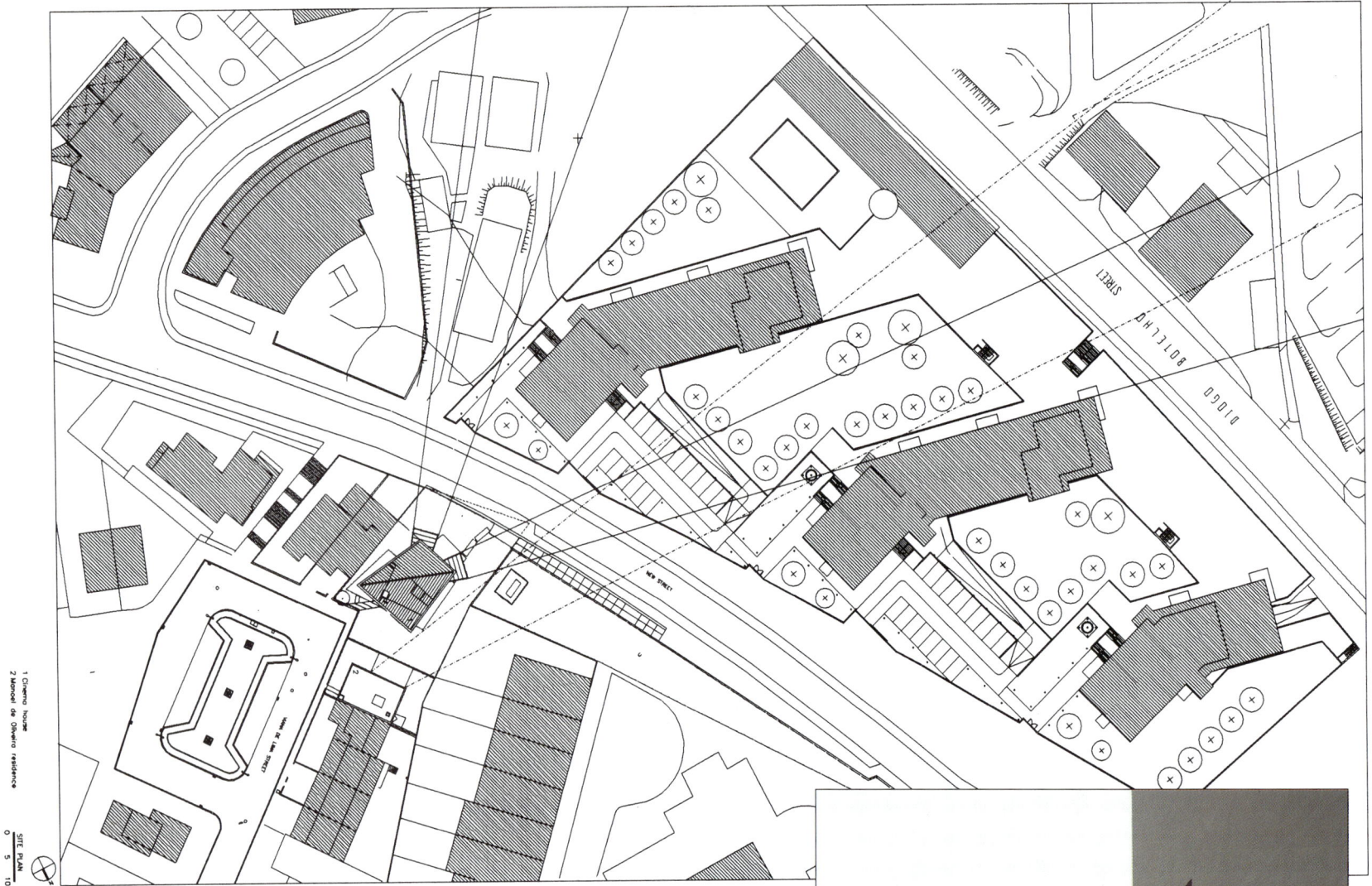

The project also included an access and some exterior spatial arrangements in the area of the new street to the south of the construction. The addition of this 'tail' considerably modifies the shape of the building.

# Residential Building in Oporto

Rua do Teatro, Oporto, (Portugal), 1992-1995

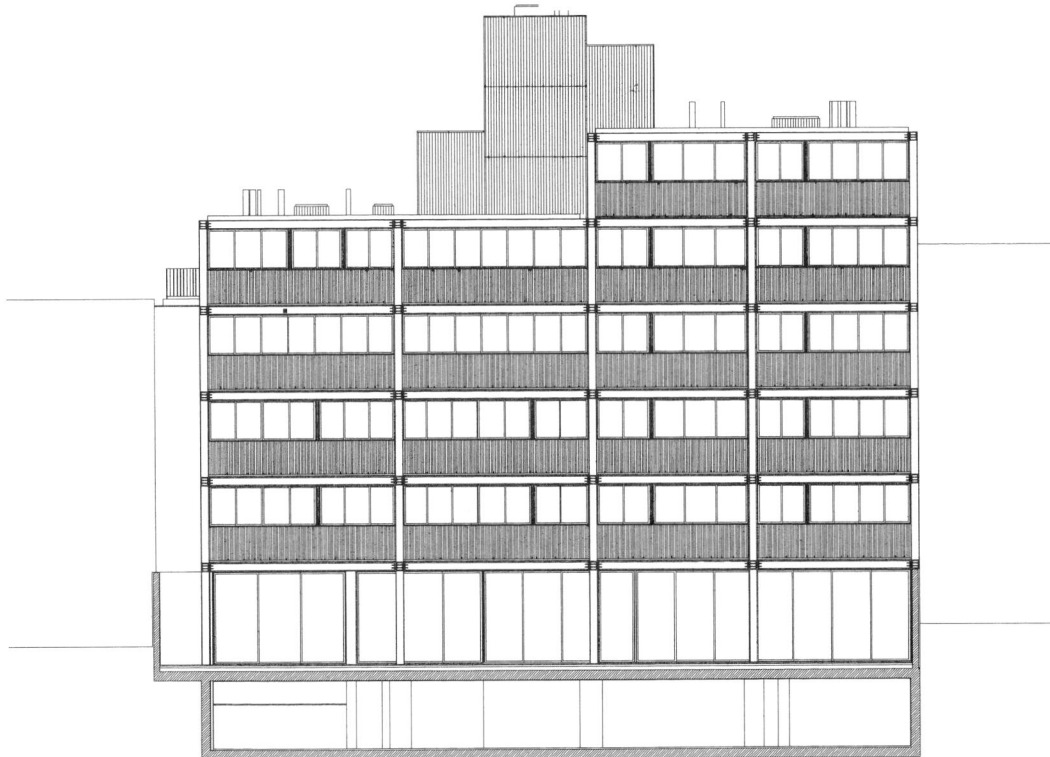

La Rua do Teatro is found outside the medieval walls of Oporto in the urban sprawl that came about due to the city's growth during the 18th century. Being situated on plots of similar dimensions and proportions, all long and narrow, its construction follows quite strict model types, even in the construction solutions. The new residential building designed by **Souto de Mou-**

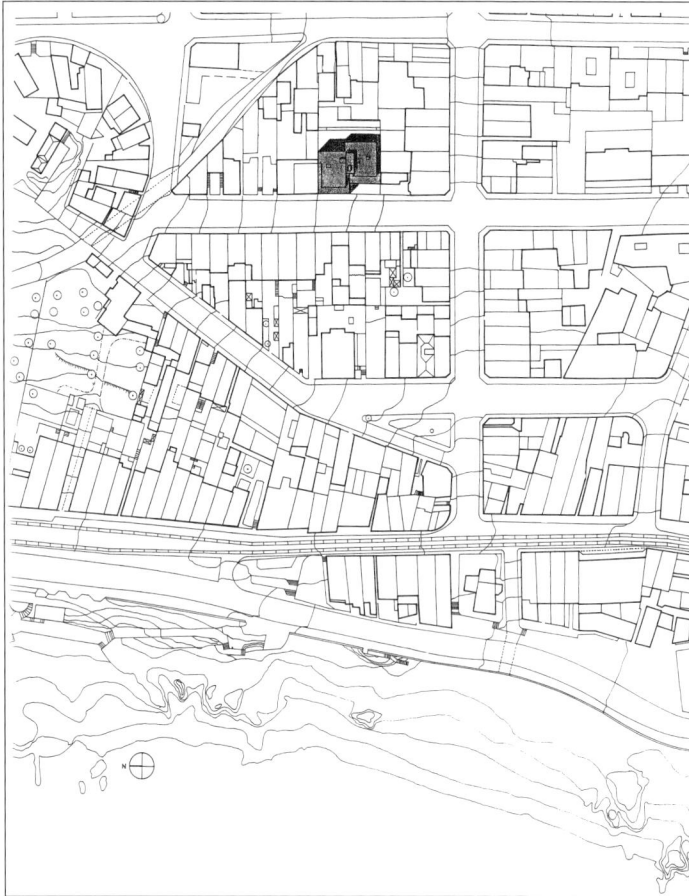

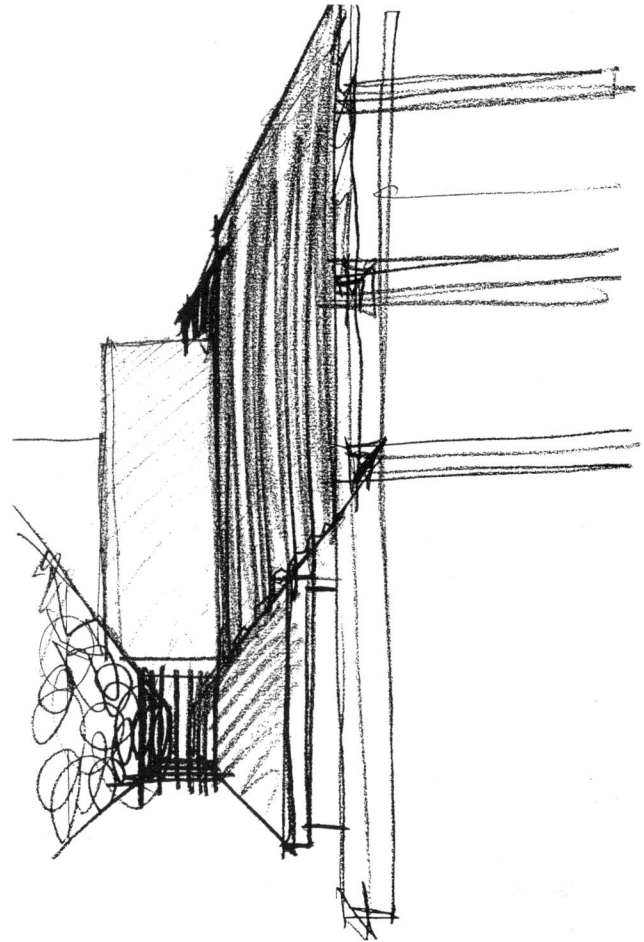

*A view of the access to the interior courtyard.*

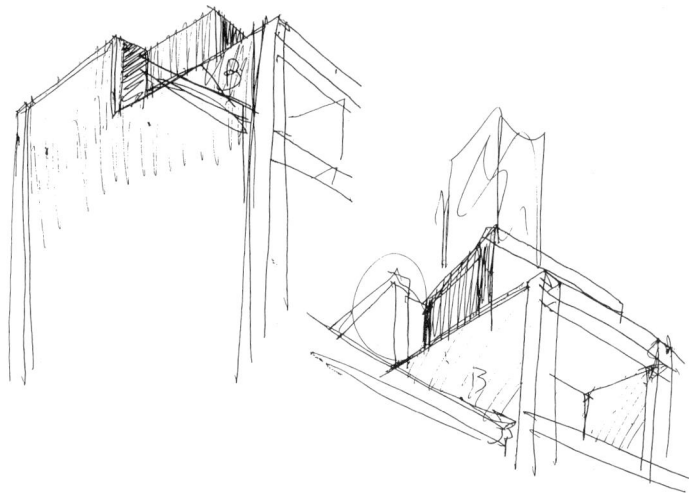

*A sketch of the project. A study of volumes.*

*A view from the street.*

ra is situated on a plot that is exceptionally wider that others in the surroundings. This is probably the result of the annexation of two old adjoining plots. In as much as that the neighboring buildings are of a considerably reduced scale and possess some

common characteristics which can clearly be typified, in his project Souto de Moura proposed to maintain a continuity of criteria with these buildings although he opted for particular solutions in its execution.

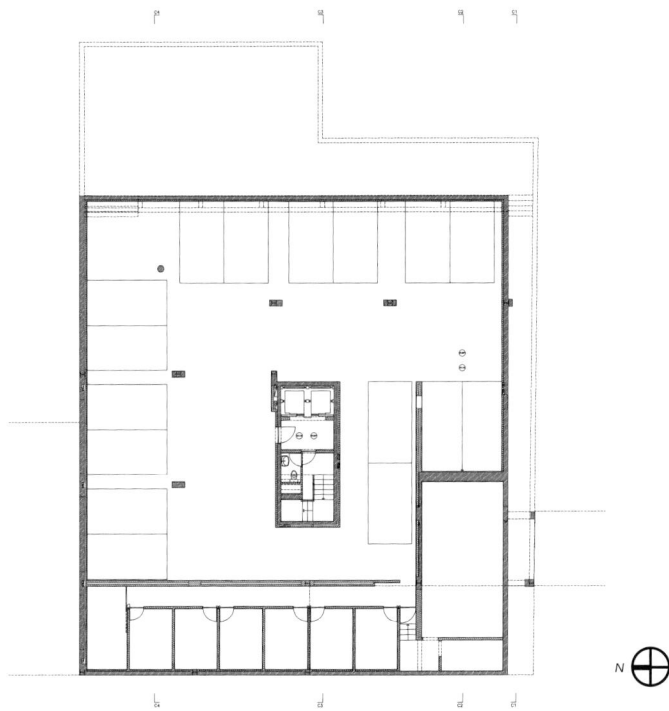

*Floor plan of the basement. Parking and storage.*

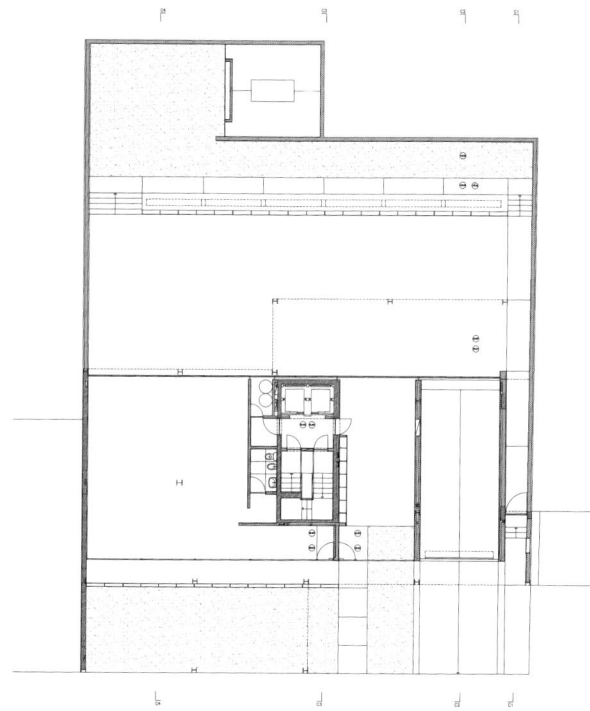

*Floor plan of the ground floor. Access to the residences and to the parking facilities.*

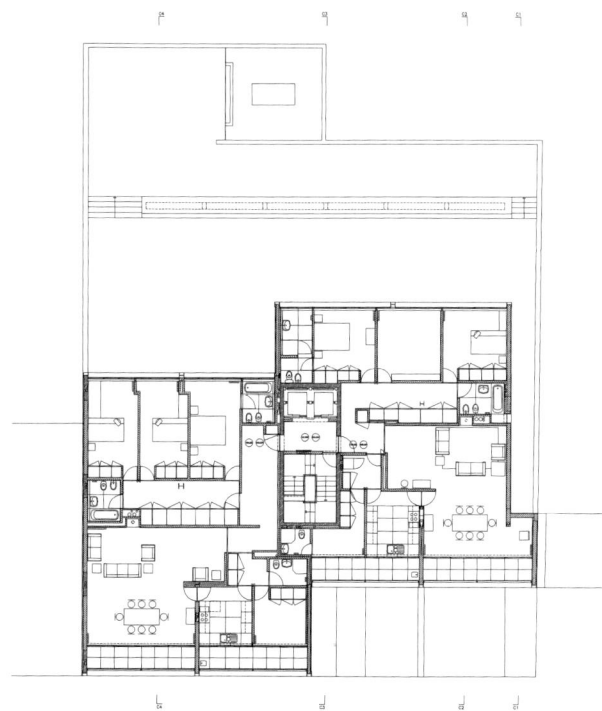

*Floor plan of the first and second levels. Standard residences.*

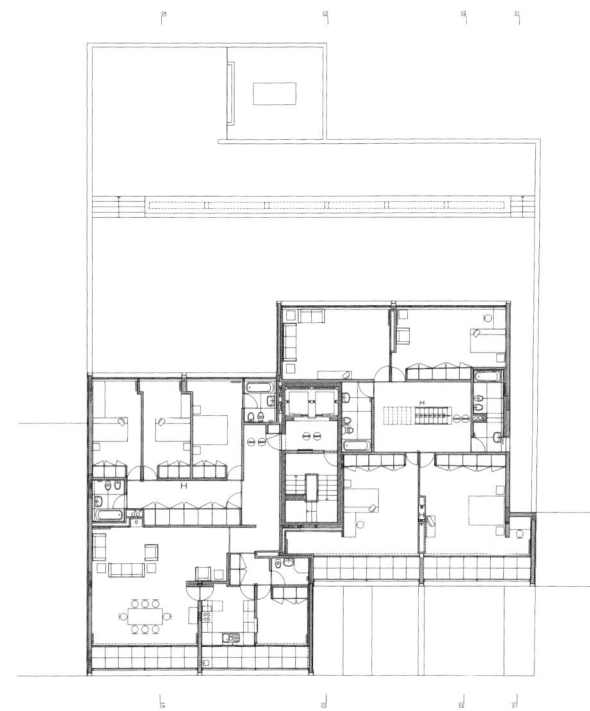

*Floor plan of the third level. Standard residence and duplex type A.*

The street runs past the plot with an accentuated gradient which, when taking into account the width of the terrain, leads to a noticeable difference in height of its extremes. In addition, a particular circumstance exists: the two immediately neighboring buildings are aligned in different ways: the one on the left is further forward and the one on the right is some meters further back. The building on the left is higher and deeper while that on the right is lower and of a lesser depth. Souto de Moura

*Floor plan of the fourth level. Entrance to the duplex type A and duplex type B.*

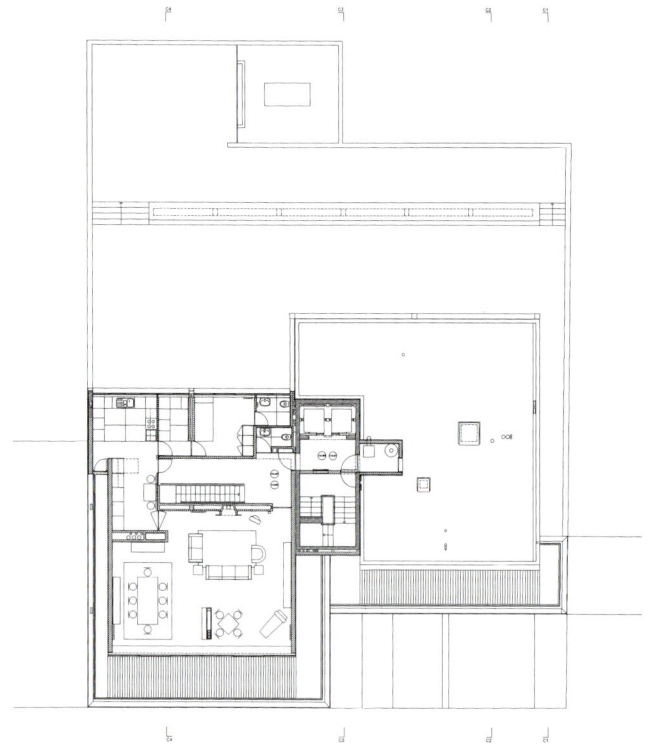

*Floor plan of the fifth level. Entrance to the duplex type B.*

has proposed a play on volumes within his own building that strictly obeys the alignment of the neighboring houses. As a result, two clearly differentiated bodies reproduce the reduced scale of the surrounding buildings. Souto de Moura gives special

emphasis to the differentiation of both blocks and elevates the body of the higher part of the plot with an extra floor. The upper level of the two blocks is set back in such a way that the two bodies, in reality, become four. The last decision made in this pro-

*Cross-section 1.*

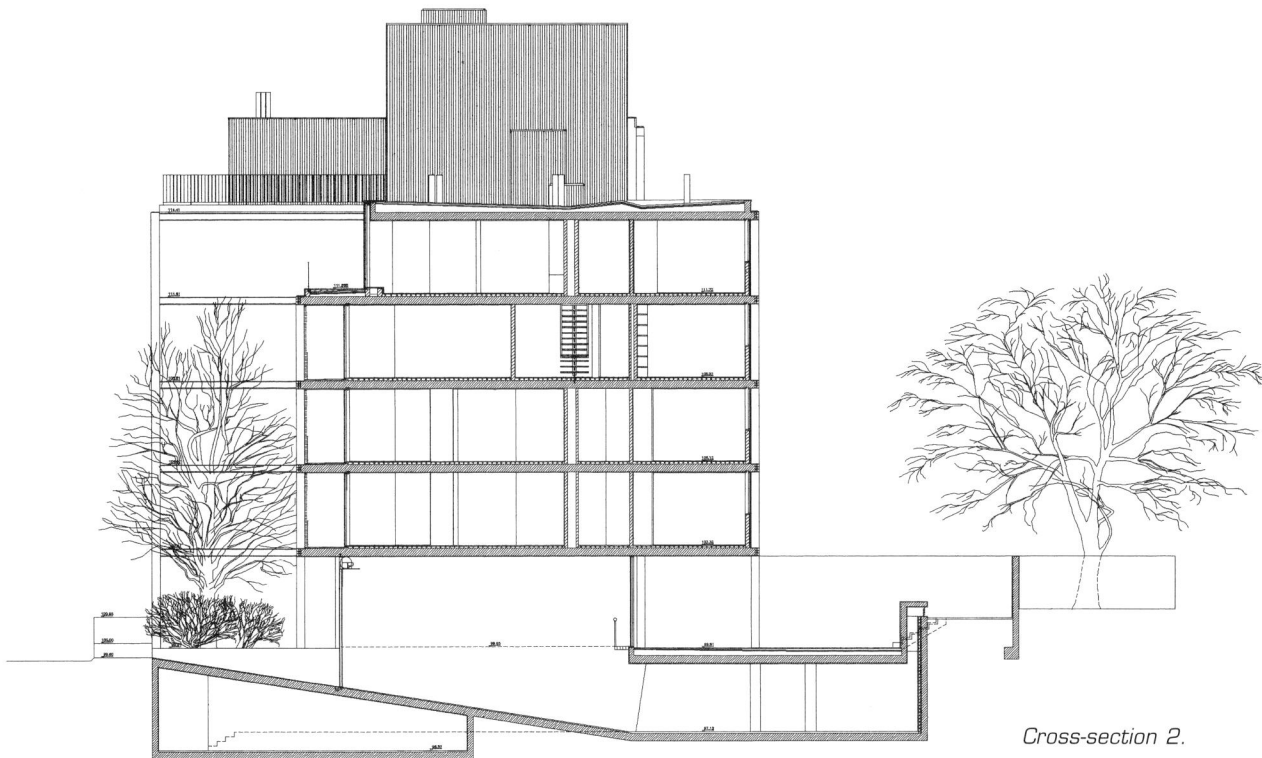

*Cross-section 2.*

cess of volumetric decomposition consisted in placing the stair-well on the axis of both bodies and, in this way, forming a fifth volume, which is somewhat higher, to complete the group. With this handful of basic operations, an important continuity with the urban morphology of the zone has been achieved which Souto de Moura refers to as, "the achievement of the banality through a construction project." The desire to adapt to the neighboring houses is crowned with a small magisterial gesture: the lo-

Cross-section 4.

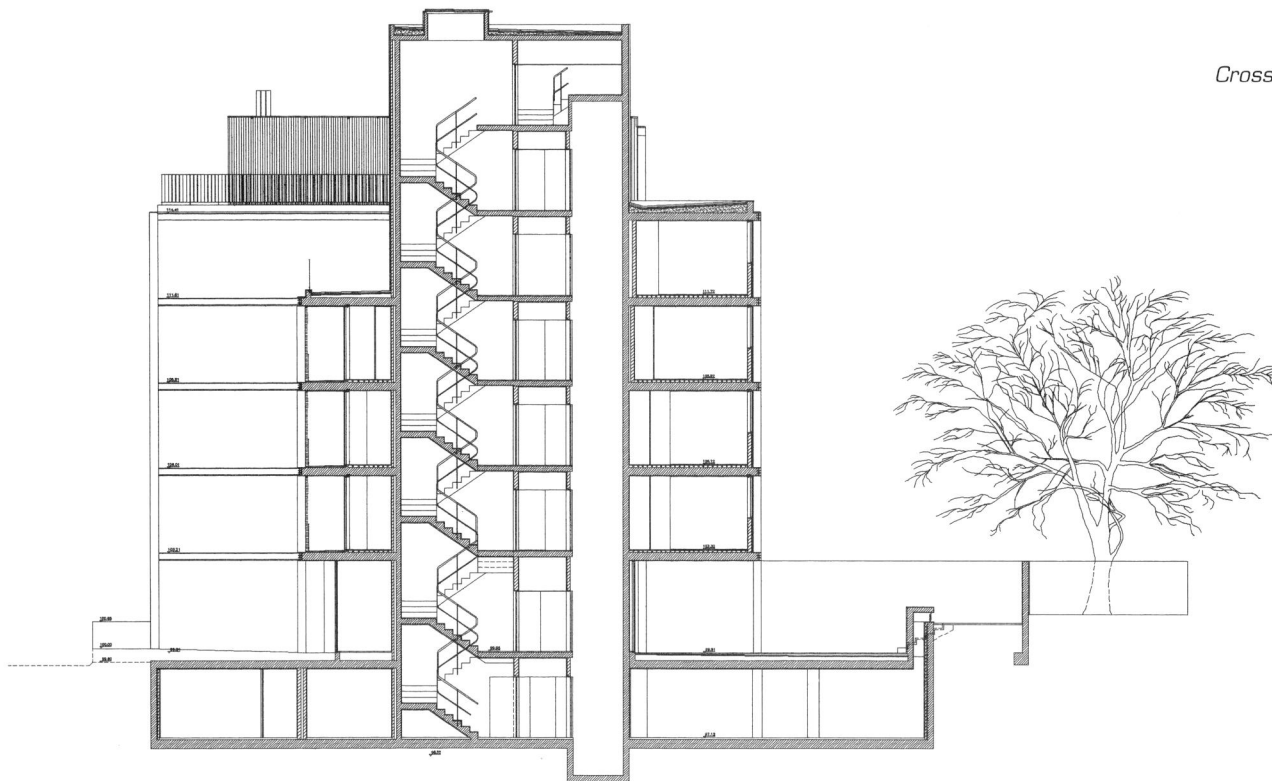

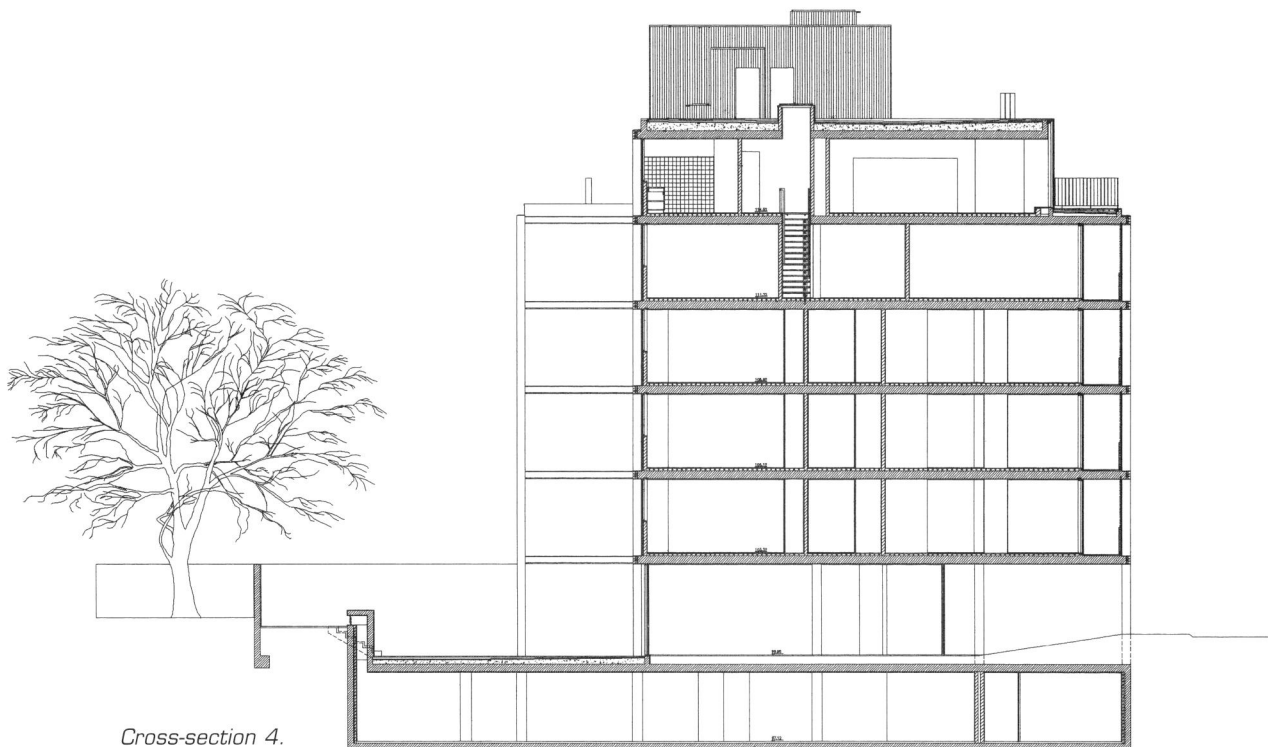

wer body is only supported by the neighboring building in the distance marked by it depth and it slightly steps back with respect to the boundaries at the rear. The measuring of this system of volumes is far from arbitrary: both bodies present two gauges in their floor plans of the same surface area and of practically the same dimensions which each correspond to a unit of distribution which allows the residences to be typified. The entire complex has been constructed over a framework of steel beams in the

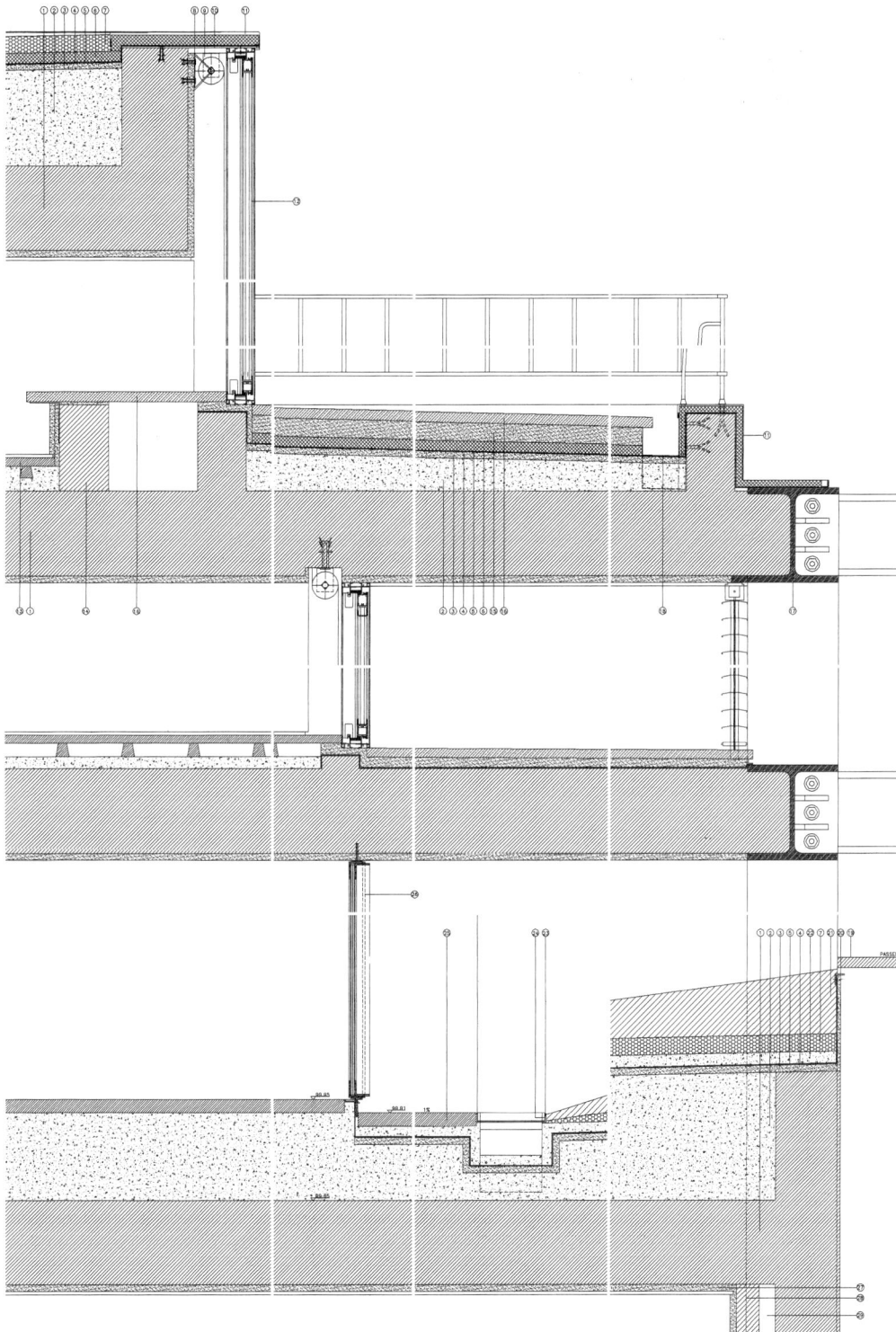

1. Concrete.
2. Lightweight concrete.
3. Regularization.
4. Geotextile.
5. Waterproofing.
6. Roof-mate 30 mm.
7. Conglomerate.
8. Frame in which to fix blind.
9. Blind.
10. Metal bar.
11. Zinc sheeting.
12. Sliding frame G.K. (technal).
13. Flooring.
14. Bricks.
15. Morter.
16. Slate.
17. Steel profile.
18. Zinc guttering.
19. Mortar.
20. L-shaped profile 30x3 mm (cut) in stainless steel.
21. Earth.
22. Protective layer of mortar.
23. L-shaped profile 25x3 mm (cut) in stainless steel.
24. 25x8 mm stainless steel bar.
25. 30x30x4 cm tile.
26. Stainless steel frame.
27. Plastering.
28. Hollow 7-cm brick.
a29. 5-cm air chamber.

form of an H and follows a regular network which only alters when it reaches the facade at the back. Here, the residences in the lower body are mounted over the stairwell and obtain more facade surface than in the lower part.

The result allows for the higher body to have five floors while the lower one has four. The layout of the residences is quite simple: the three first floors accommodate two abodes per landing, one in each body. These residences are basically symmetrical in their

conception although with important variants in their particular design. Souto de Moura opts for an unusual distribution, such as positioning the bathrooms in the facades or the magnificent way of relating the two parts of each flat by means of an ample cen-tral space. By means of the continual presence of the structure, it is possible to appreciate the mark of Mies's distributive proce-dures in a number of details, although never executed in exactly the same way, but reproduced in their essence. If the pillars in

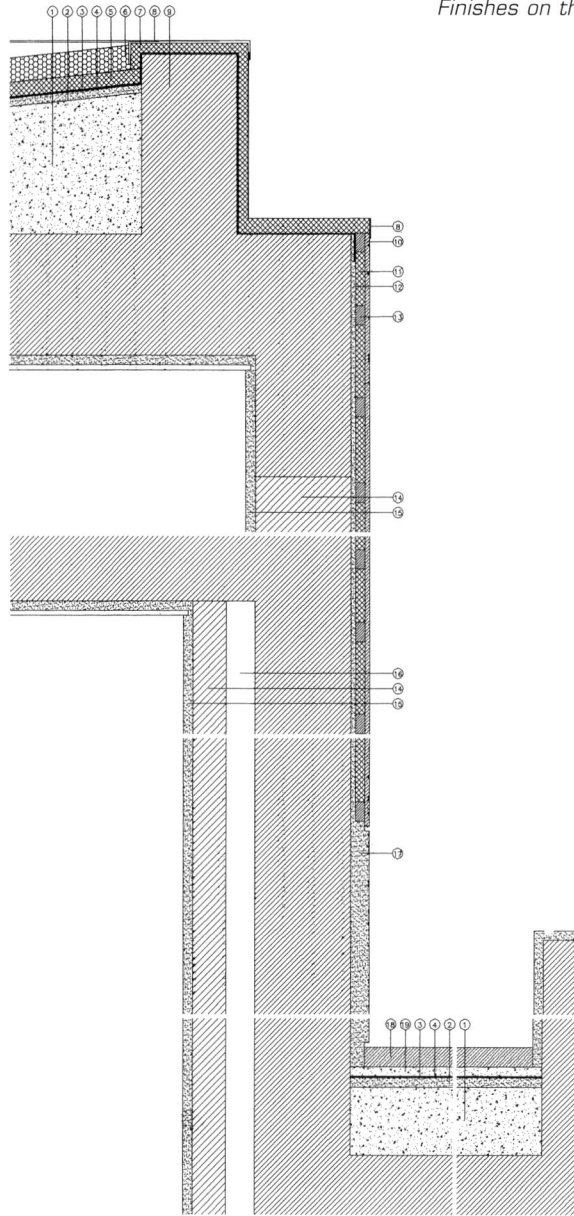

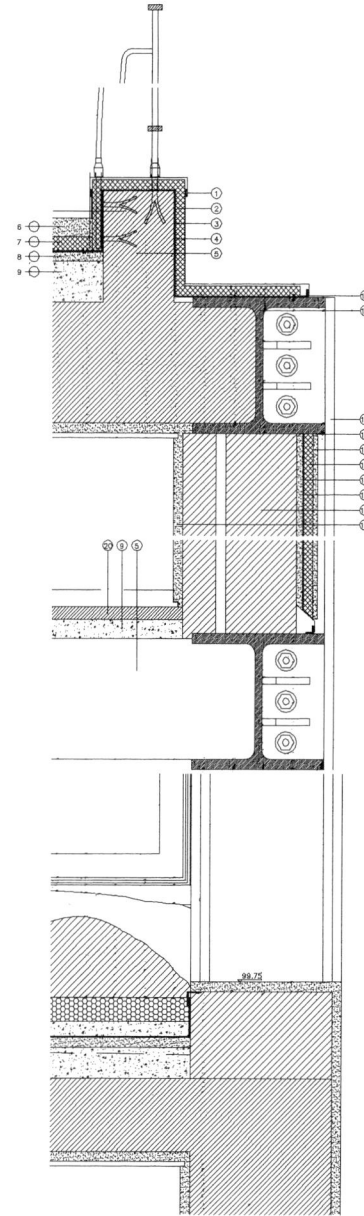

1 - Lightweight concrete.
2 - Regularization.
3 - Geotextile.
4 - Waterproofing.
5 - Roof-mate 30 mm.
6 - Conglomerate.
7 - Roof-mate 20 mm.
8 - Zinc sheet.
9 - Concrete.
10 - Slate tiles.
11 - Wall-mate 20 mm.
12 - Regularization.
13 - Wooden fillet.
14 - Brick.
15 - Tinted plastering.
16 - Air chamber.
17 - Plaster and rendering sand.
18 - Mortar.
19 - Protective layer of mortar.

1 - Zinc sheet.
2 - Roof-mate 20 mm.
3 - Waterproofing.
4 - Geotextile.
5 - Concrete.
6 - Mortar.
7 - Roof-mate 30 mm.
8 - Regularization.
9 - Lightweight concrete.
10 - L-shaped profile in steel 16x6x3.
11 - Steel profile.
12 - Side flap of steel profile.
13 - Cordon putty.
14 - Projected plastering.
15 - Wall-mate 20 mm.
16 - Cerezite.
17 - Regularization.
18 - Brick.
19 - Tinted plastering.
20 - Flooring.

the H form are almost always integrated into the decoration, their previous condition to the operations of distribution are evident. And the liberty with which Souto de Moura breaks the regularity of the network, accepting small distortions, seems to be a da-

ring reference to Mies's approach. The two upper floors are occupied by two large duplexes, organized in a very peculiar way: the entrance from the lift leads on to the last floor which contains a large living room, the kitchen and the dining room, at the back,

and an area for the services. A single flight of stairs leads down to the lower floor where there are three spacious bedrooms and a day room for the children. The space that receives the aforementioned flight of stairs provides access to the services, but does not communicate with the building's communal staircase. **Souto de Moura**'s project is, in syntony with other con-

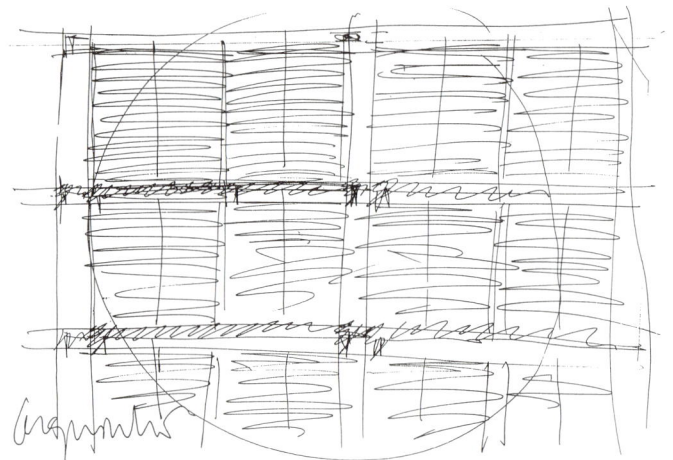

temporary residences, a good example of how the nonexistence of previously conceived ideas is the best way to carry out authentic investigation and arrive at a result based on reflection and observation rather than on an intent to impose a series of images that existed before the project and its circumstances came into being  The two principal driving forces behind the residential building in Oporto (the urban morphology and experimentation with domestic spaces) lead to a result that gives priority to its adaptation to its surroundings and to the necessities of the occupiers over the seduction of an image.